Shades from the Sky

North Wales

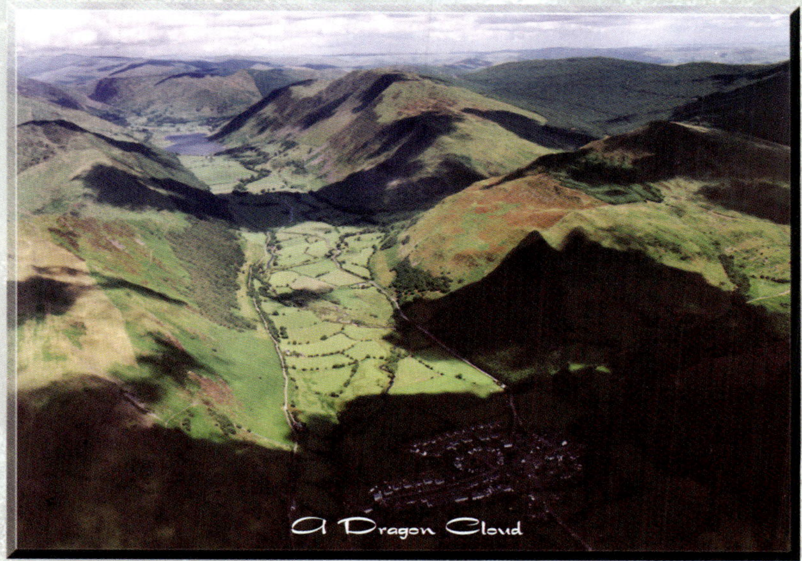

'Their Lord they shall praise,
Their language they shall keep,
Their land they shall lose
Except Wild Wales'

TALIESIN: Destiny of the Britons

Volume One

A ValleyStream Publication

Published by

ValleyStream Publications

Conwy, North Wales, LL32 8UX

www.valleystream.co.uk

Publication Producer & Digital Imaging - Stef Bate

Graphics Production Assistant - Ange Davies

Production Assistant - MiMi

Script Researcher - Gill Clarke

Graphics/Research Assistant - Robin Evans

Aerial Photographer - Gwilym Davies

Pilot - Arfon Evans

Background Images - SGB - A Davies - Derek HT Jones - Bridie Page - Library

ISBN: 0-9546413-0-2

Printed and bound by Cambrian Printers, Aberystwyth, Ceredigion

(Special thanks to Dean - Lois - Heather)

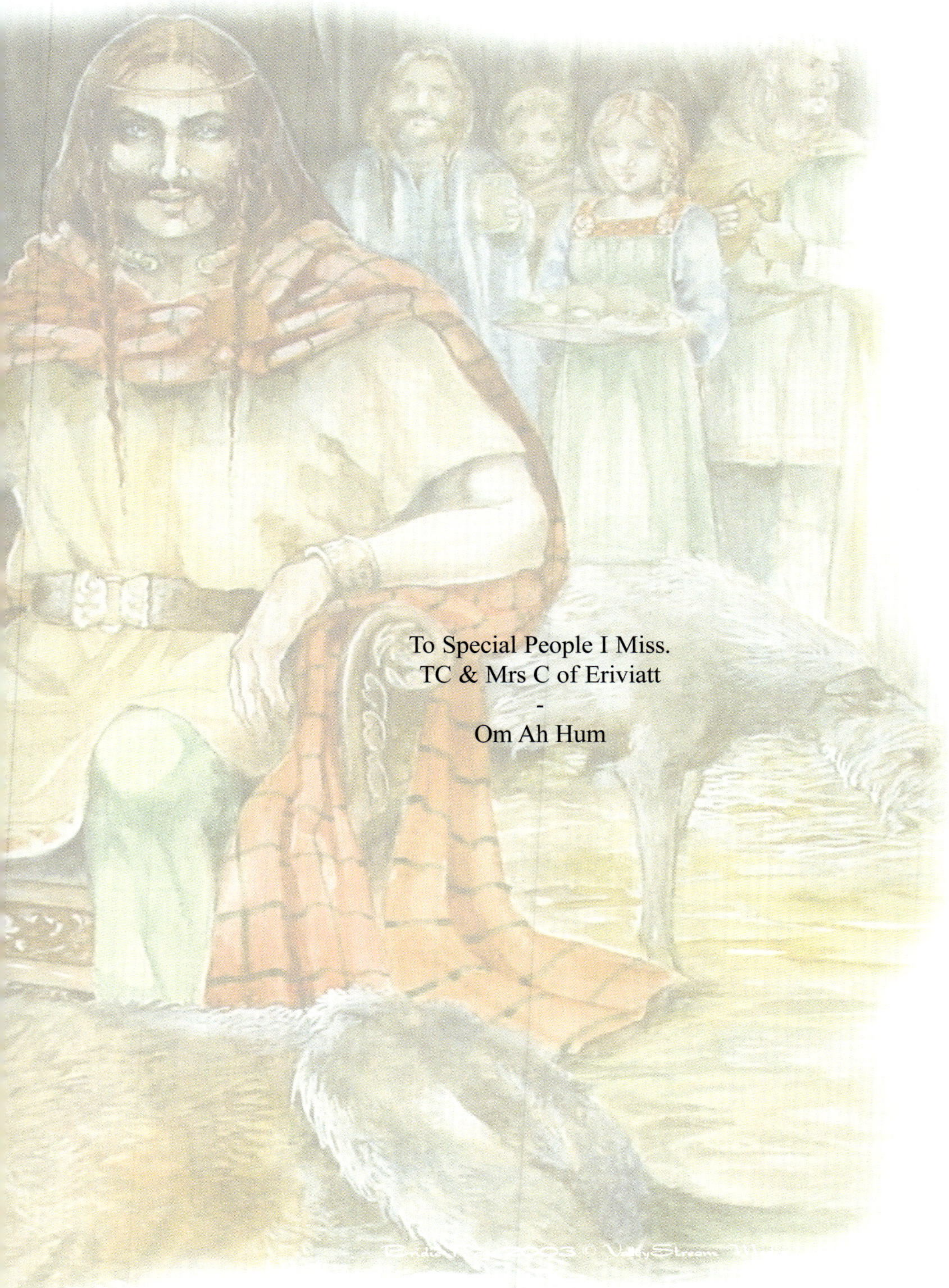

To Special People I Miss.
TC & Mrs C of Eriviatt
-
Om Ah Hum

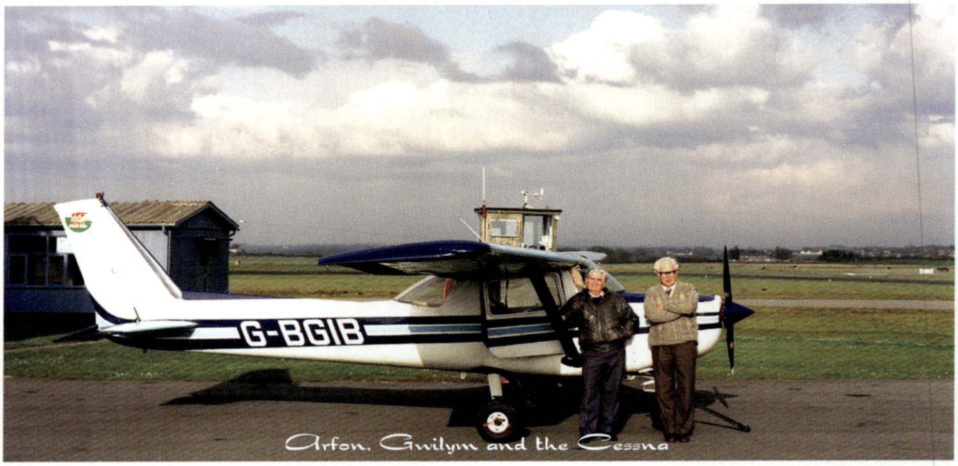

Arfon, Gwilym and the Cessna

Introduction

At weekends local farmer Arfon Evans leaves his life on the land and heads for the sky. In the 1950s Arfon flew Meteor jet fighters with the RAF. These days he's a member of the Mona Flying Club on Anglesey, and his aircraft is a small, two-seater Cessna.

For many years Arfon's been accompanied on his flights of fancy by amateur photographer Gwilym Davies. Gwilym juggles up to four Mamiya cameras, using fast colour film which he develops himself at home. Once in the air they're coasting the currents and circling Wales at heights up to 5,000 feet (1,525 metres) and reaching speeds of around 100 miles per hour.

Even so, Gwilym pokes his head out of the open window, aiming for his best shots of the countryside below. Climbing above the mountains and the clouds, he's built up an intriguing portfolio of photographs with an extraterrestrial quality.

Over the last few years Gwilym, now aged 85, has been working closely with Producer Stef Bate and ValleyStream's production team after Stef had been approached in 1996 by a good friend of Gwil's, film consultant Frank Bailey, to see if he could do something to help Gwilym with his photographs. ValleyStream began the lengthy compilation and development of his unique aerial photographic collection of more than 32,000 images of North Wales, taken over the last 25 years, into a library. It was a challenge sifting through so many albums of transparencies to form the 2 databases, creating "The Gwilym Davies Collection".

Gwilym was once asked: does he find it difficult taking photographs from a plane. He replied in his usual humorous way: "No, it's pretty simple really. All you do is put the penny in the slot and the aircraft will go for you". Of his cameras, he describes one as "being born in a cradle, having a quality like a docile lamb". Just like a true poet!

We really hope you enjoy this "cherry-picked" selection of some of Gwil's breathtaking photographs, which we would like to share with you.

Welcome to his world of **Shades from the Sky.**

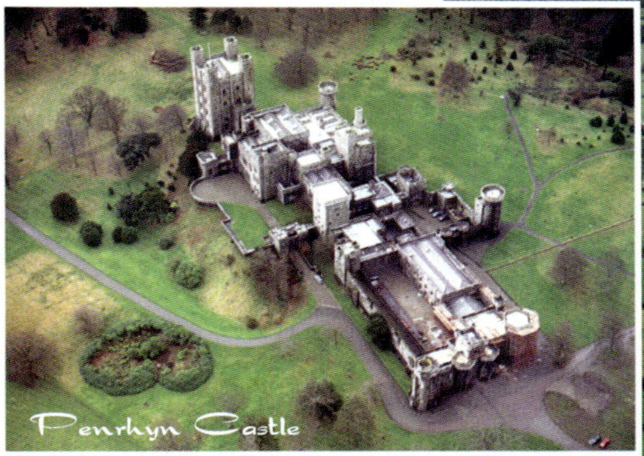

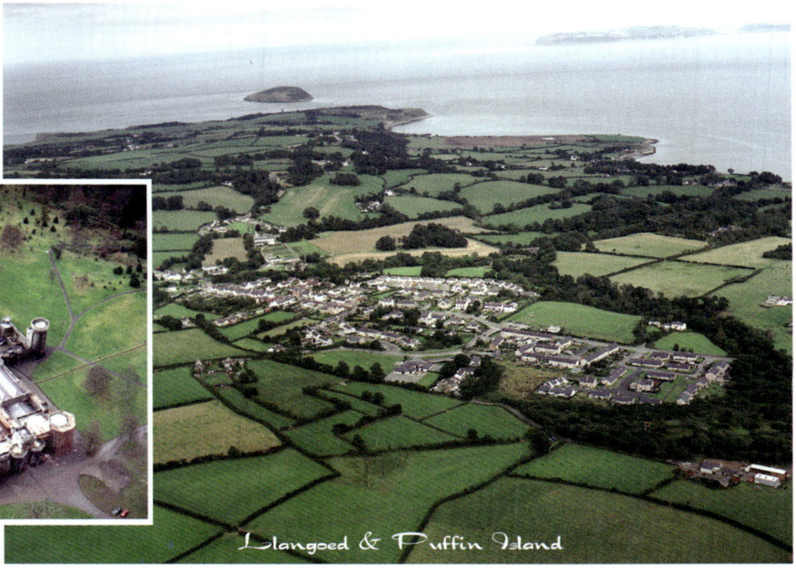

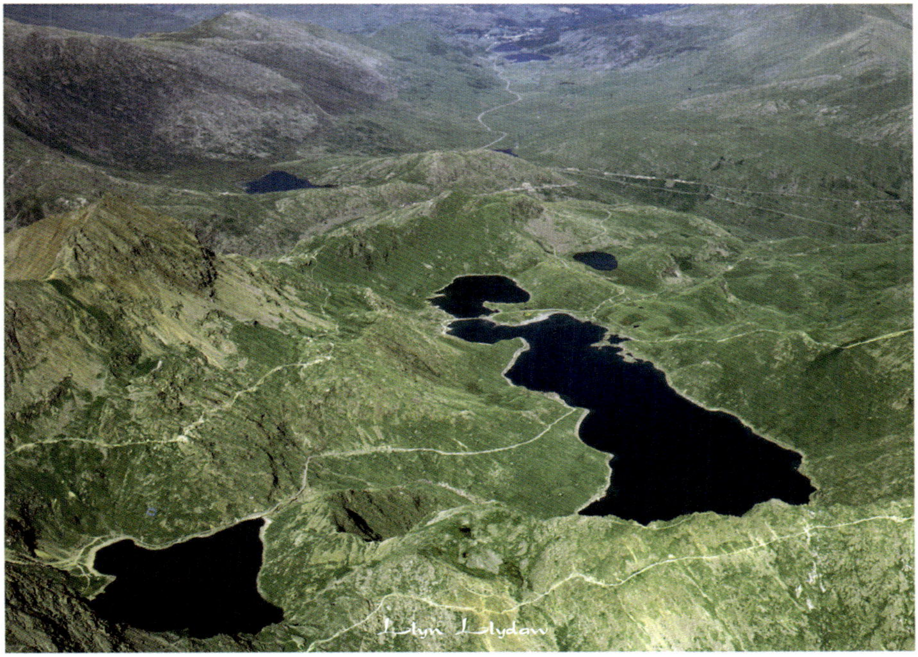

From the Eye of an Eagle

Sleep overnight on top of Cader Idris and in the morning (legend tells us) you'll be either a corpse, a madman or a poet. But perhaps the mountains bless all who just *see* them with the gifts of madness or magic, because from the Stone Age to the New Age the rugged beauty of Wales has inspired numerous painters, musicians, poets and dreamers.

We have all seen the magnificent scenery of the mountains, wooded valleys and coastlines from the ground, steeped in traditional Welsh culture and enriched in Celtic history. But to view the landscapes of North Wales from the air on a crystal clear day would be a rare, once in a lifetime occasion for most of us, even if given the opportunity.

At cloud-level the waters of the Conwy and Mawddach estuaries and the sandy beaches of the Llyn Peninsula make fantastic patterns. Above the mountains the structures of the stone castles, Portmeirion, and Telford's Bridge over the Menai Strait can be relished. Flint Castle stands in awe amongst galvanised tin buildings. No competition. The Snowdon peaks, Bala, Harlech, Trawsfynydd, Bardsey Island, Ysbyty Ifan, Amlwch Port, Rhuddlan Castle and an endless collection of many other fascinating views. From the sky, the land and the sea below tirelessly weave a timeless tapestry of stunning colours and beautiful shapes, creating this spectacular corner of Britain.

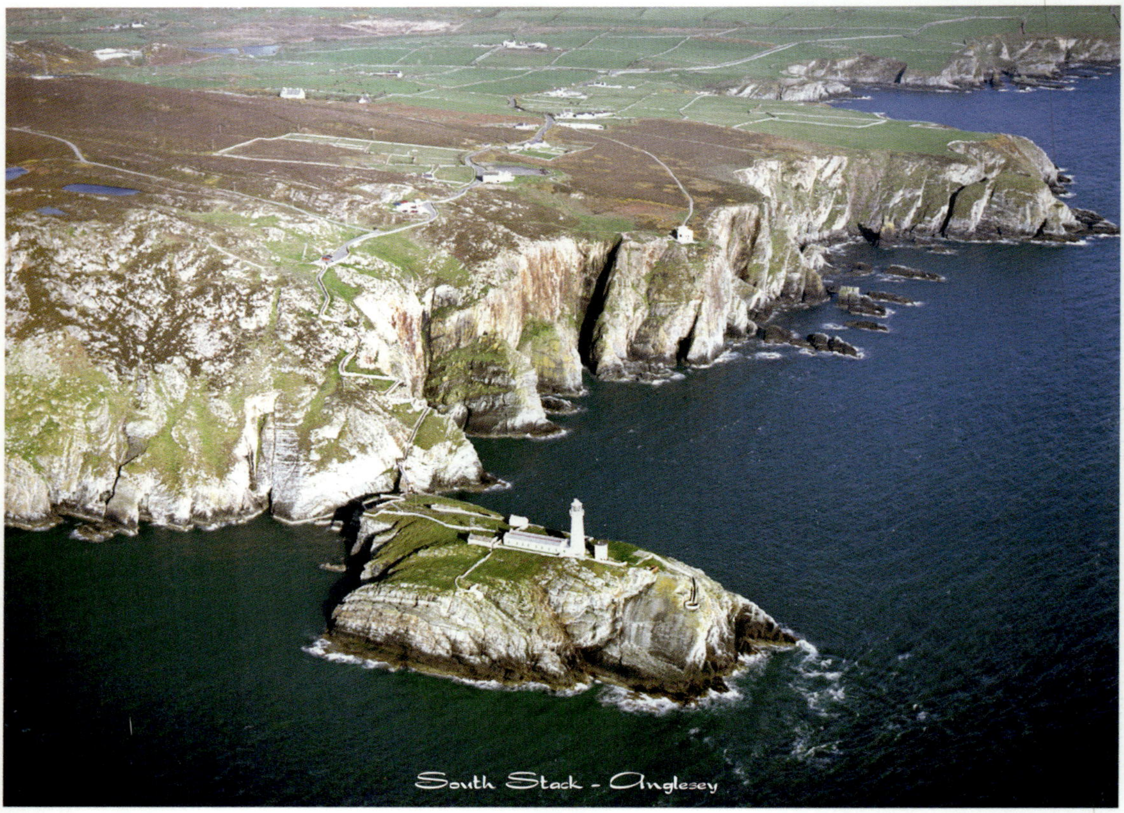

South Stack - Anglesey

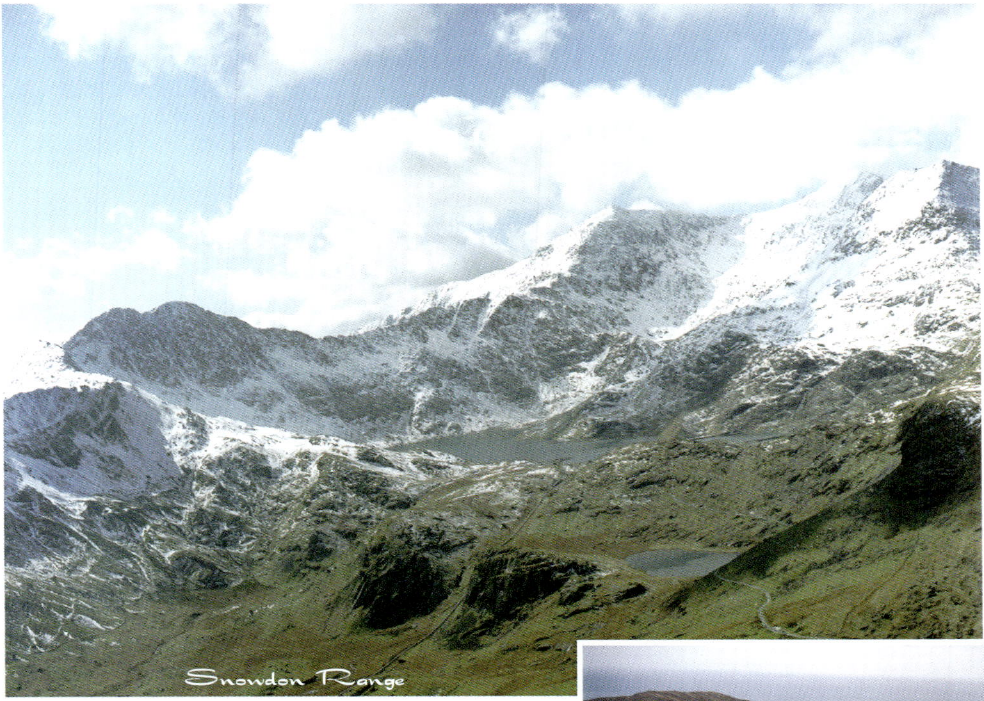

Snowdon Range

● The lofty peak of Mount Snowdon offers a Golden Eagle's eye view over the mountains, valleys and silvery coastline of Wales. On a clear day you can see past Anglesey to Ireland, down the Llyn Peninsula to South Wales, and north to the Isle of Man.

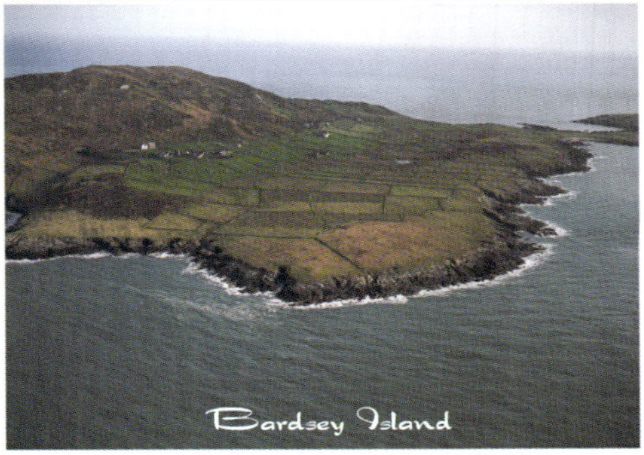

Bardsey Island

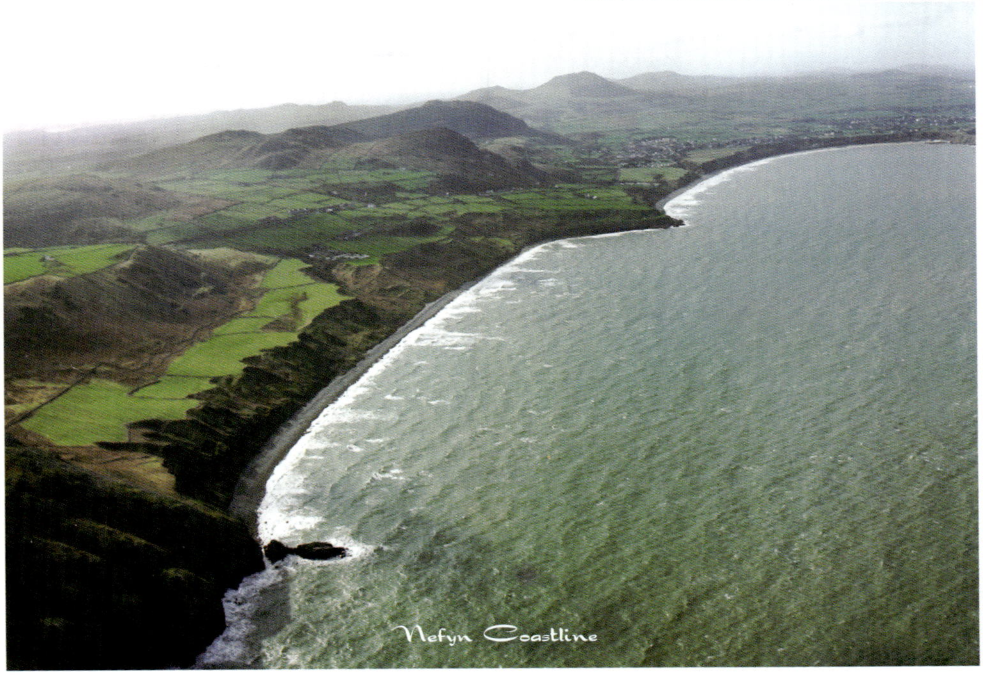

Nefyn Coastline

Creations by the Sea

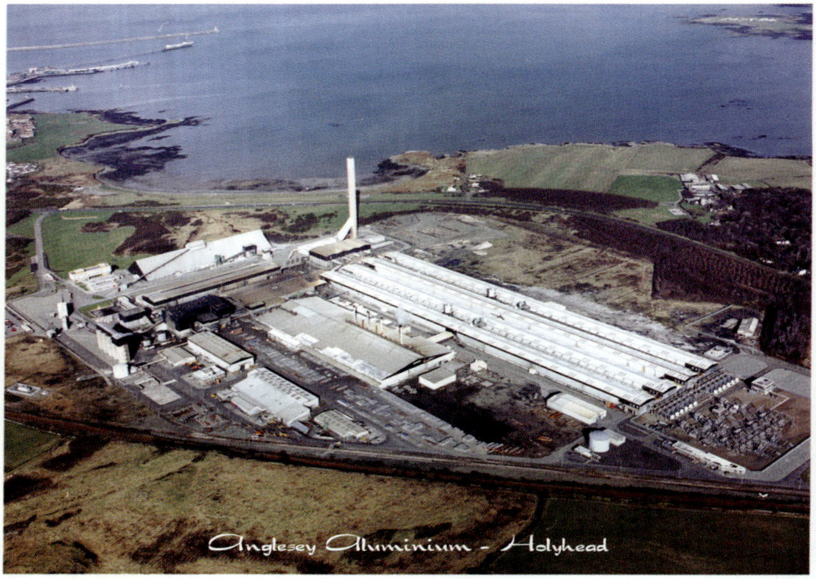

Anglesey Aluminium - Holyhead

• The smelter at Anglesey Aluminium has produced aluminium since 1971. The raw alumina and coke arrive in ships from Humberside to the jetty at Holyhead, then travel by conveyor belts in discrete underground tunnels to the works. The company is jointly owned by Kaiser Aluminium and Rio Tinto Zinc. RTZ also owns the second largest copper mine in the world. The copper mine at Amlwch was once the largest.

• Based at Amlwch, the Octel works took bromine from seawater to produce an anti-knocking agent for use in motor engines. The hazardous chemicals involved were taken daily by rail to Ellesmere Port, liquid chlorine in white tanks and DBE in grey ones. With the onset of unleaded petrol, Octel closed down in 1983. The next company, Great Lakes Chemicals, used six large seawater pumps to produce bromine for dynamic dyes and pharmaceuticals.

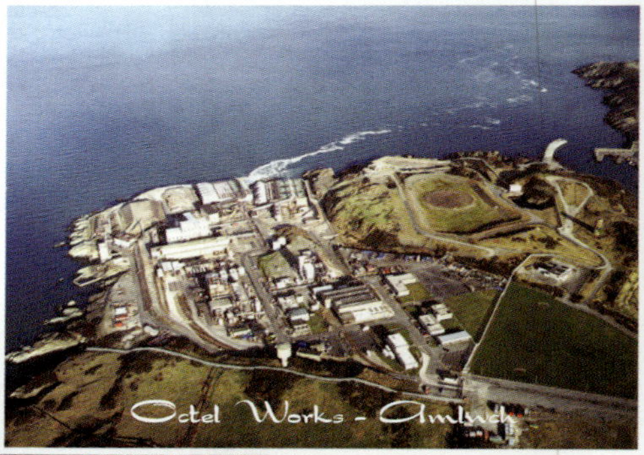

Octel Works - Amlwch

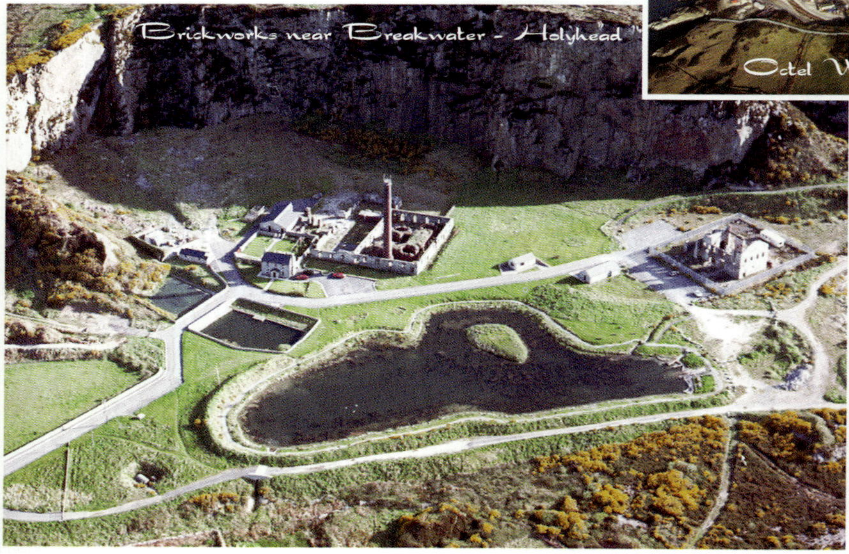

Brickworks near Breakwater - Holyhead

• The Breakwater Country Park at Holyhead is built on the remains of a former quarry which supplied chunks of quartz for the wave-lashed breakwater. When the breakwater was finished, the site became a brickworks.

• Isolated at Cemaes Bay on the northern tip of Anglesey is Wylfa Nuclear Power Station. It was opened in 1971 and is expected to give up its white ghost soon. Wylfa's two gas-cooled reactors produce electricity and are closed down every two years for major overhauls. The type of Magnox reactor involved was originally designed to run for only twenty years and to produce plutonium for heart-stopping nuclear weapons.

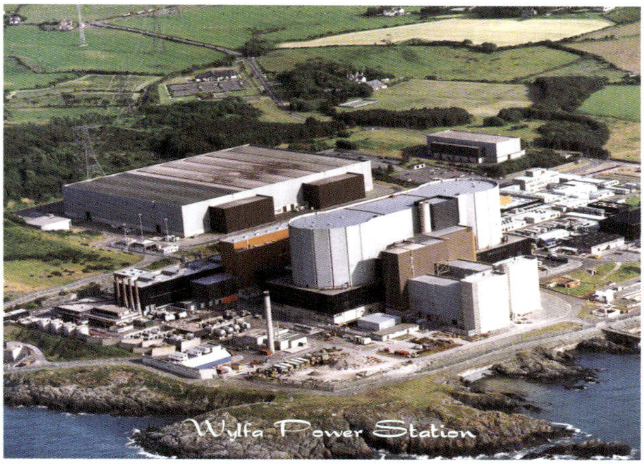

Wylfa Power Station

• West of Amlwch a brickworks was established at Porth Wen Bay in Victorian Times. All the raw materials were transported here by ship, and the rough waters churning around the quay damaged many vessels against the rocky shore. The bricks were made of locally found yellow clay and were used to line kilns or furnaces because they withstood high temperatures.

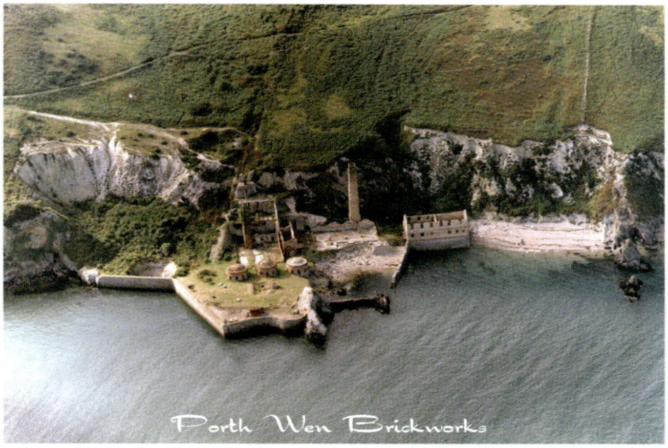

Porth Wen Brickworks

• One method of making the custard-coloured bricks was to cut them out with a wire before baking. Another involved simply pressing the clay into shape, thereby creating a shallow "frog" in the centre. High-quality tiles were also produced, under the watchful eye of a masterful Japanese glacier.

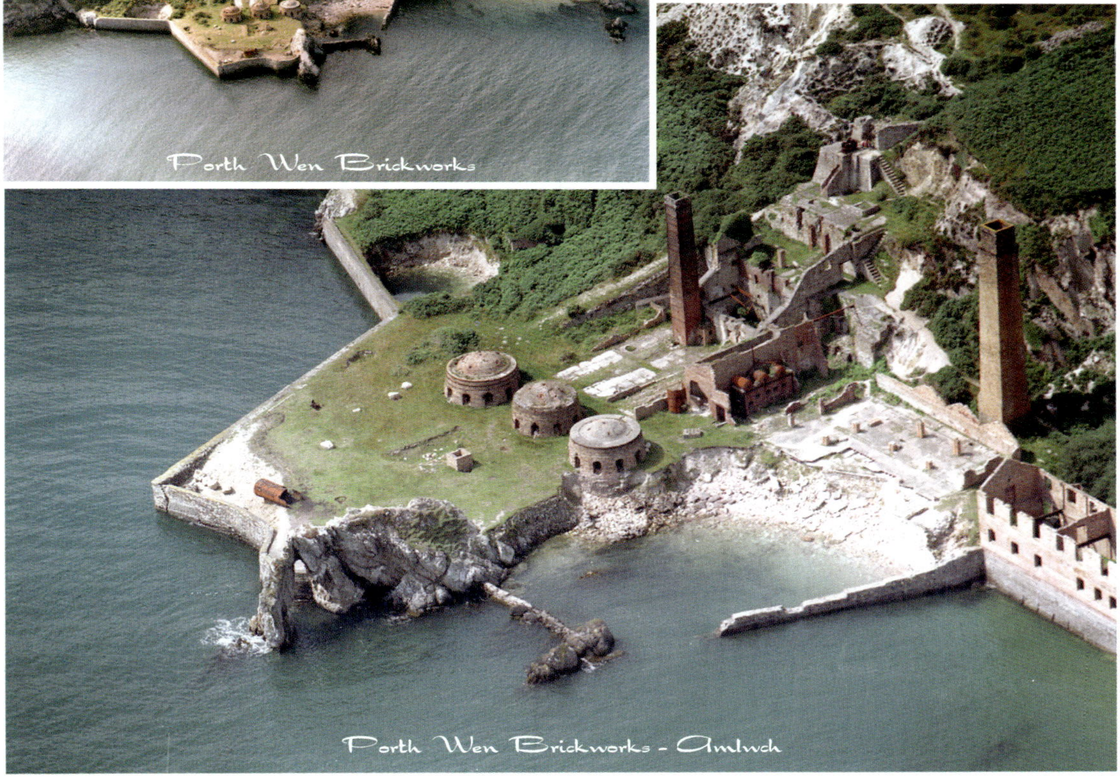

Porth Wen Brickworks - Amlwch

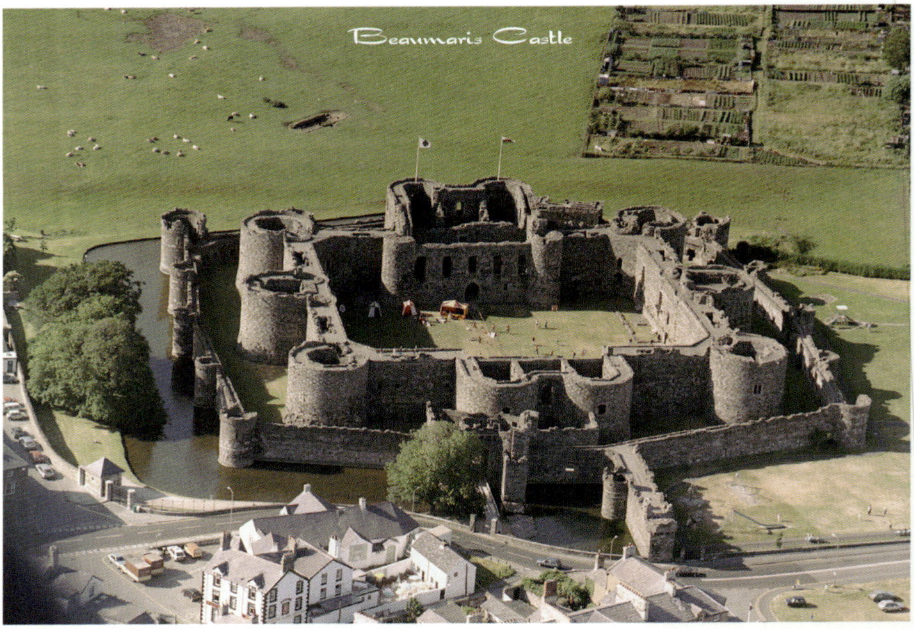

- Beaumaris takes its French name (Bellus Mariscu) from the "beautiful marshes" on which the Castle was built. It cost £7,000 to build, and the design was an unfinished masterpiece of perfect symmetry.
- The last man to be hanged by the shaded walls of Beaumaris Gaol, Richard Rowlands, died protesting his innocence of the dark crime of murder. Before Richard died he cursed the smiling church clock facing the waiting scaffold, and it has never told the right time since.

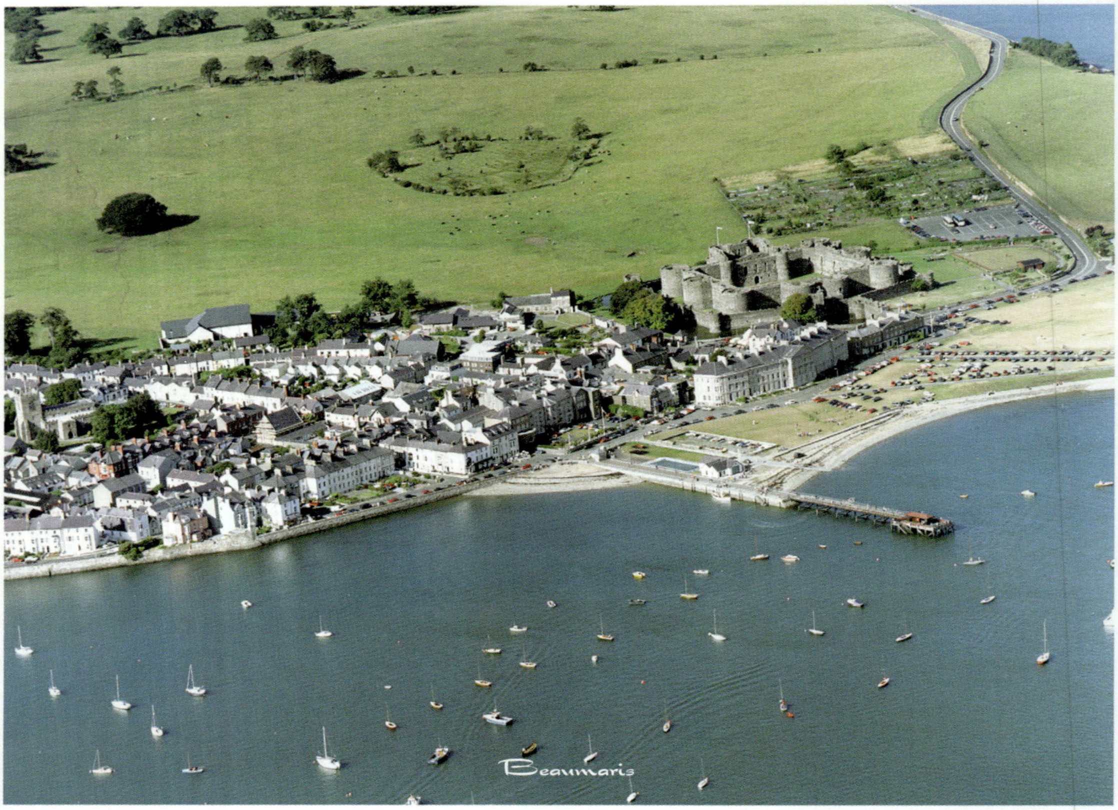

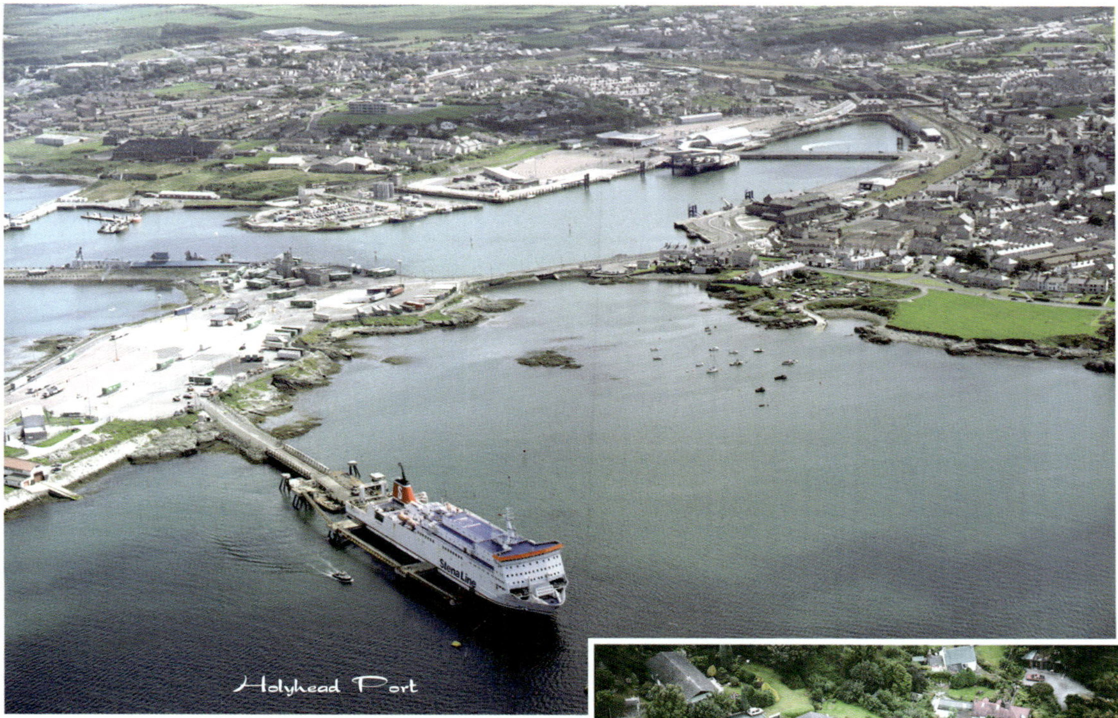

Holyhead Port

- Caergybi (Holyhead) takes its name from its origins as the site of Cybi's humble Celtic church.
- Plas Newydd was the home of the Marquess of Anglesey who lost a leg at the Battle of Waterloo. His column overtops the waving trees by the Menai Strait.

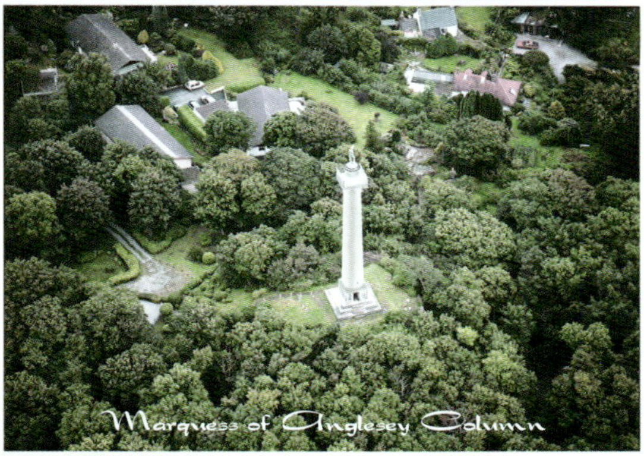

Marquess of Anglesey Column

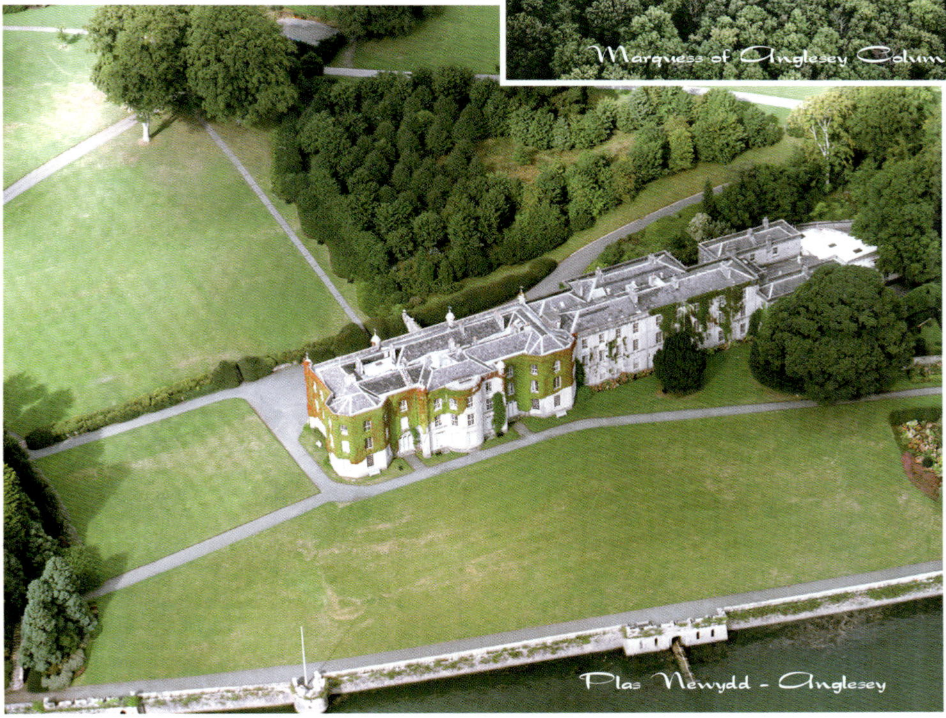

Plas Newydd - Anglesey

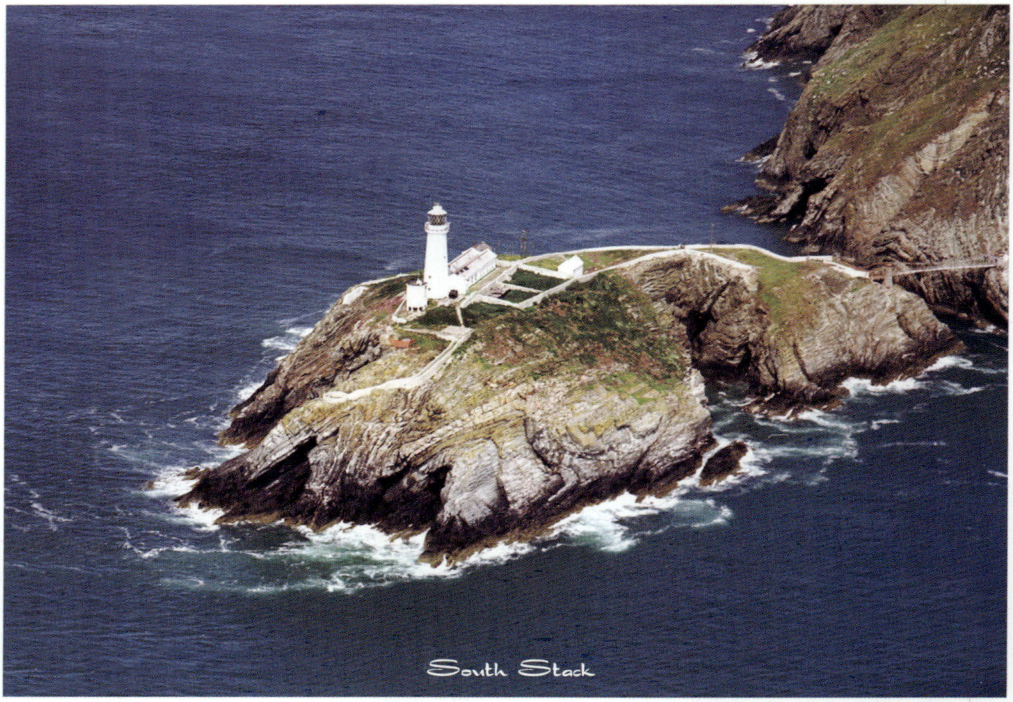

South Stack

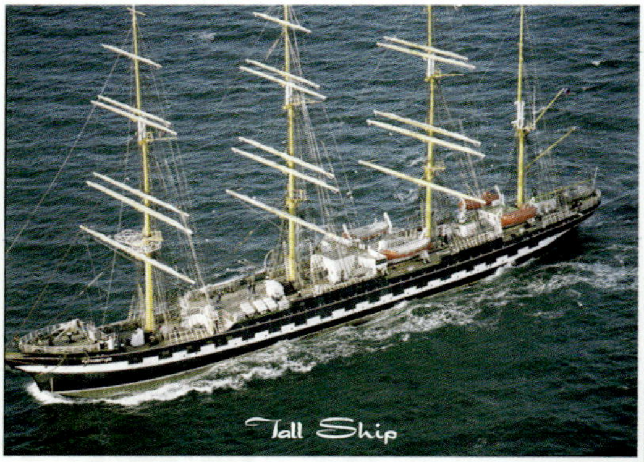

Tall Ship

● The furrowed cliffs of South Stack are haunted by hundreds of black and white razorbill, chocolatey guillemot and comical orange-beaked puffin. The Victorians encouraged them since their raucous cries gave sailors warning of land during foggy weather. The first lighthousemen reached South Stack over the crashing waves in a basket slung on a rope. Today a suspension bridge takes you across.

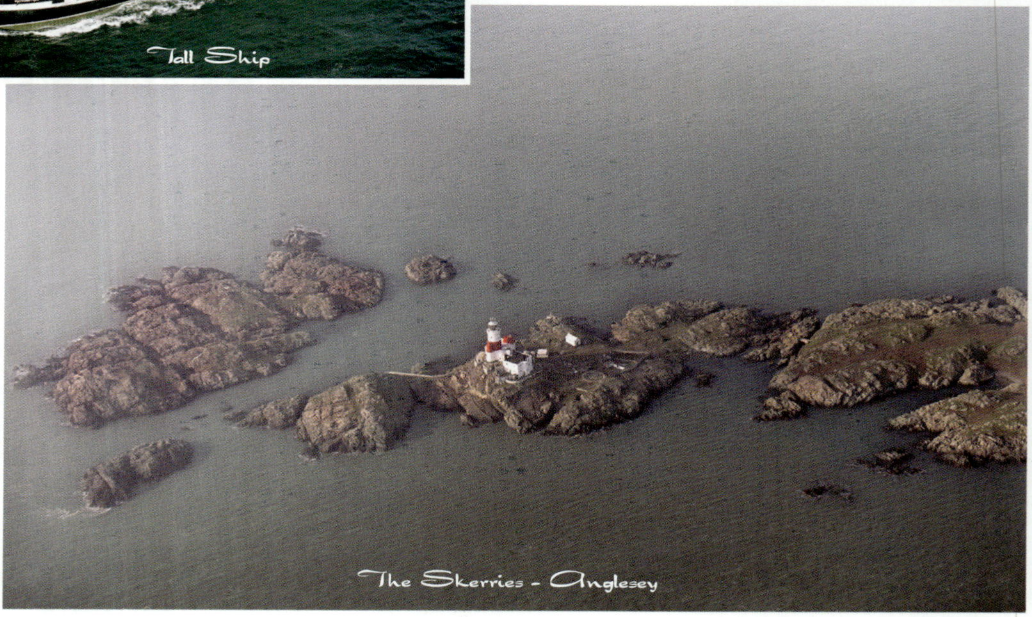

The Skerries - Anglesey

Lonely Rocks and Wreckers

The sea around Anglesey is a minefield of shipwrecks. Off the north-east coast the Skerries have a reputation for luring ships to their doom. The very first royal yacht was an elegant 50' sloop from Amsterdam called the Mary. She had been presented to Charles II but went down off the Skerries in 1675. She was found as a shivering wreck on the gloomy seabed three hundred years later.

Another ship, the Royal Charter, was returning from Australia when she foundered. As she neared the Skerries a hurricane overtook her, and she broke her back on the rocks. The Royal Charter's 450 passengers were drowned, together with her cargo of £400,000 in gold.

Some ships crashed on to East and Middle Mouse near Bull Bay on the north coast. When a lifeboat station was established at Bull Bay a cannon was fired at Holyhead in celebration. The first lifeboat to dare the storm-tossed sea was named Eleanor.

At Traeth Dulas ghost ships patrol the north coast along with grey seals. On a small island nearby, a Victorian lady stored provisions for shipwrecked mariners. Optimistically, therefore, during World War Two a grand flotilla congregated offshore, preparing for D-Day.

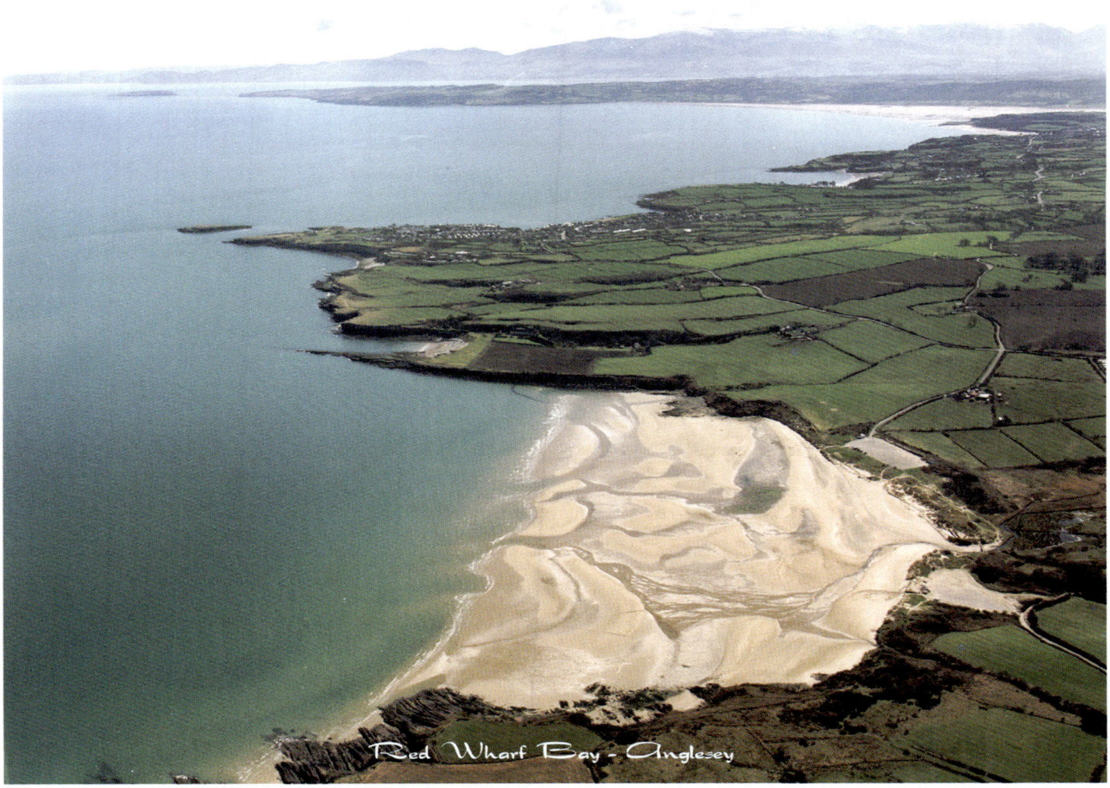

Red Wharf Bay - Anglesey

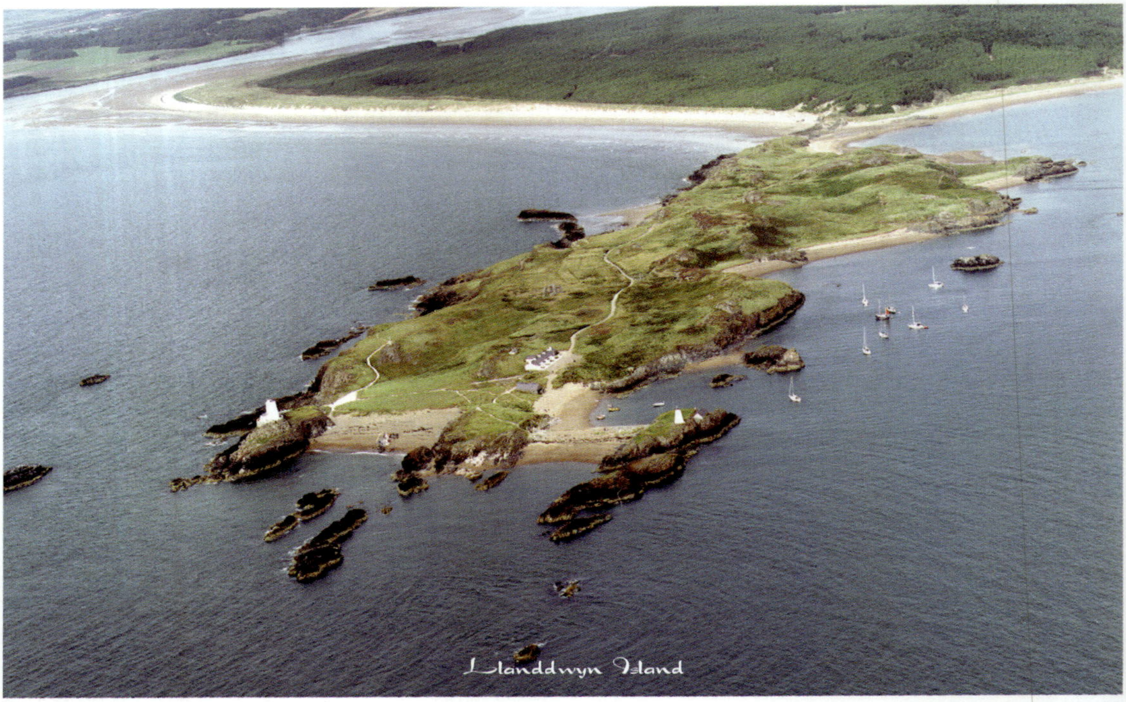

Llanddwyn Island

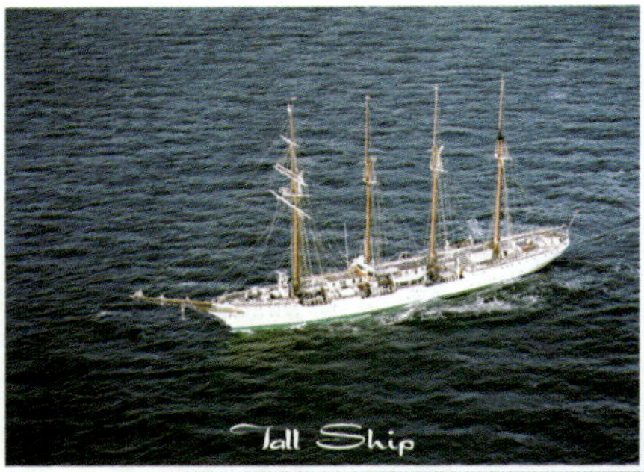

Tall Ship

- St Dwynwyn settled on a rocky spit near Newborough. Over the centuries her secluded church on Llanddwyn Island became a pilgrimage site for lovers, but the lighthouse, built like a windmill, warned of turbulent seas.
- A rich discovery of copper on Parys Mountain rewarded the lucky miner with a bottle of whiskey and a rent-free cottage. The small cove of Amlwch port was blasted out in order to cope with sea-going ships.

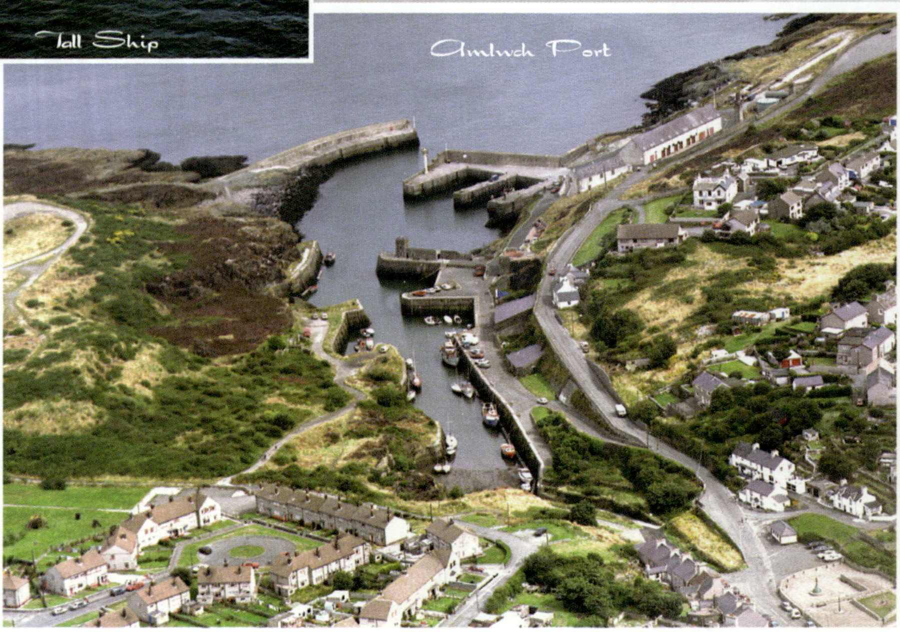

Amlwch Port

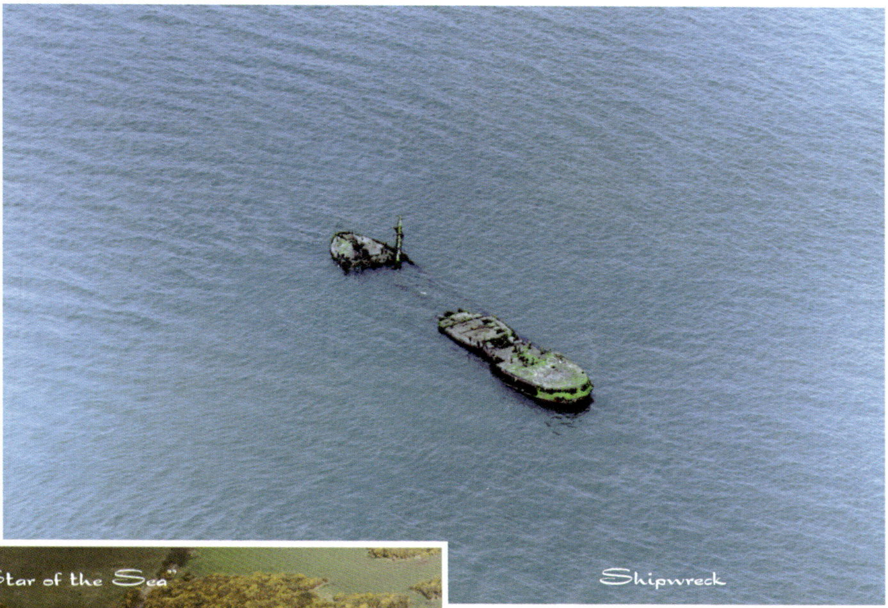

Shipwreck

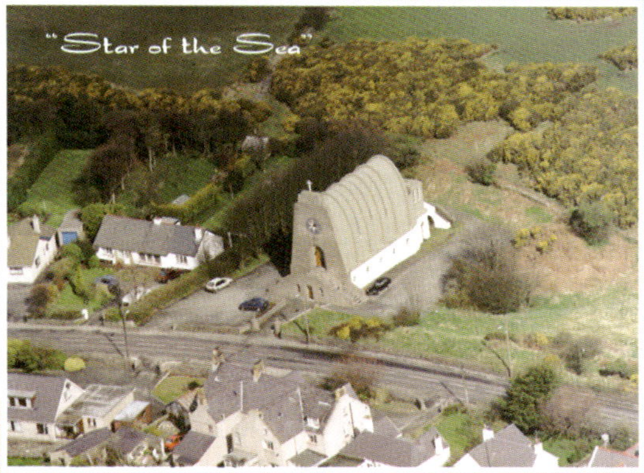

"Star of the Sea"

- The humpbacked "Star of the Sea" church at Amlwch is shaped like an upturned ship and was designed by an Italian architect.
- Out-on-a-limb North Stack is a mecca for climbers and divers, but a B17 crashed into its cliffs during WW2 and lies beneath the waves.

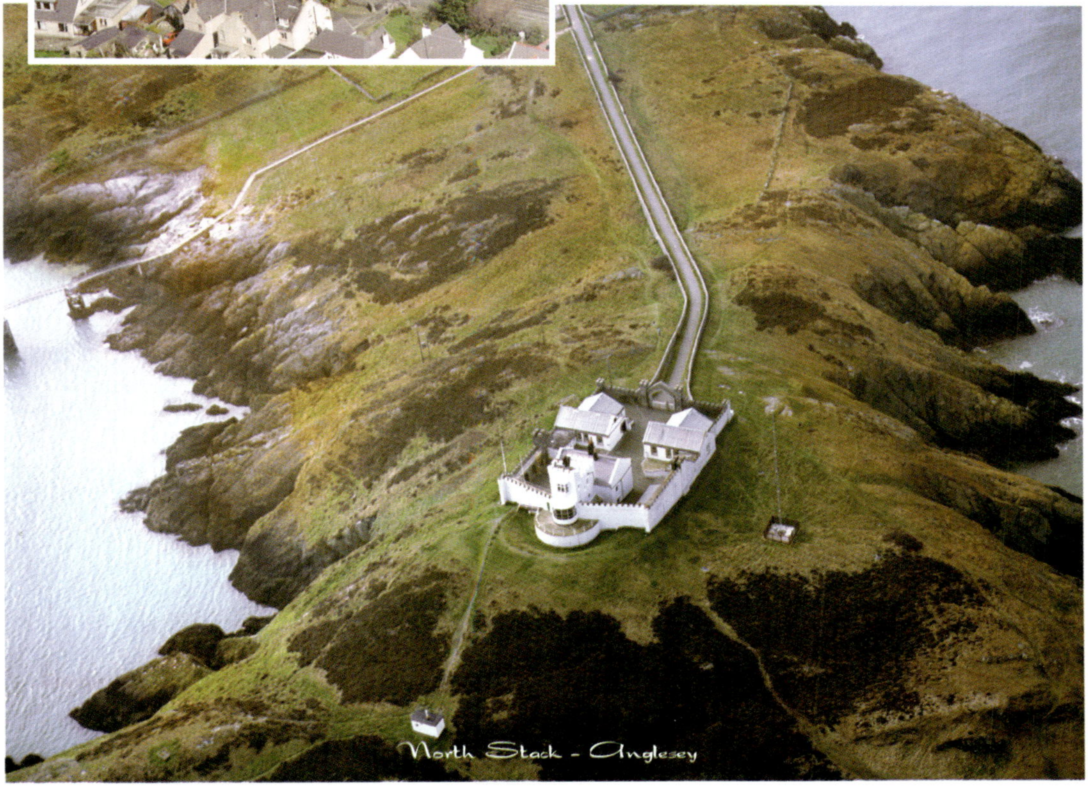

North Stack - Anglesey

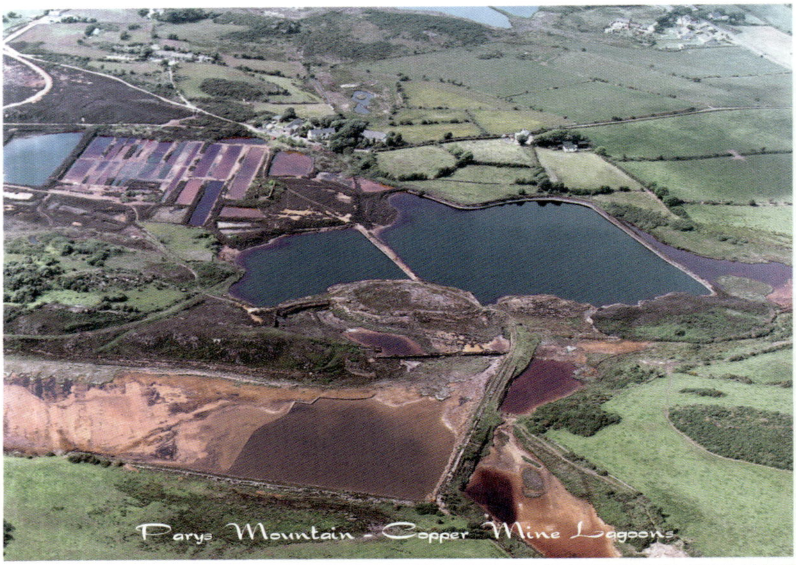

Parys Mountain - Copper Mine Lagoons

Shades of Fortune

The metallic shades of Parys Mountain are a kaleidoscope of colours disgorged from out of the earth. Poisonous but beautiful. Three hundred years ago this was farmland on a hillside of tangled trees. Although a rich copper vein was found here in 1768 which gave rise to the present heaps and flooded lakes, it was first discovered in the Bronze Age 3,000 years before. In those early times the metalworkers lit fires against the rock and hit it with stone hammers. Then they smelted the copper with tin to make their tools. Where Bronze Age men went, the canny Romans followed on, and they too mined Parys Mountain.

True success came in the 18th century. The two mines employed 1,200 people busily burrowing into the ground. Tom "Fair Play" was the designated Copper King who had a touch of gold. To pay the miners, a shiny copper Parys Mountain Penny was cut, with a druid's head wreathed with oak leaves on the back. Artists visited the Great Open Cast to paint the gleaming earths and psychedelic mineral ores.

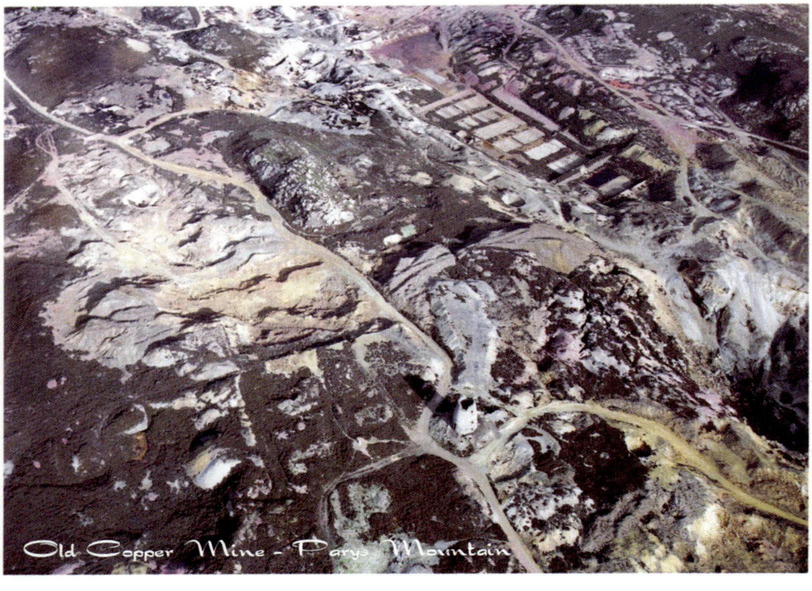

Old Copper Mine - Parys Mountain

Amlwch Port was blasted out of rock so that ships could take away the precious cargo, and Amlwch's six lonely houses increased to over 1,000. But within 40 years of finding the rich copper vein the bonanza was over. Shafts were sunk, and dusky miners arrived from Cornwall to work underground in the traditional manner, but the glittering heyday of Parys Mountain was passed.

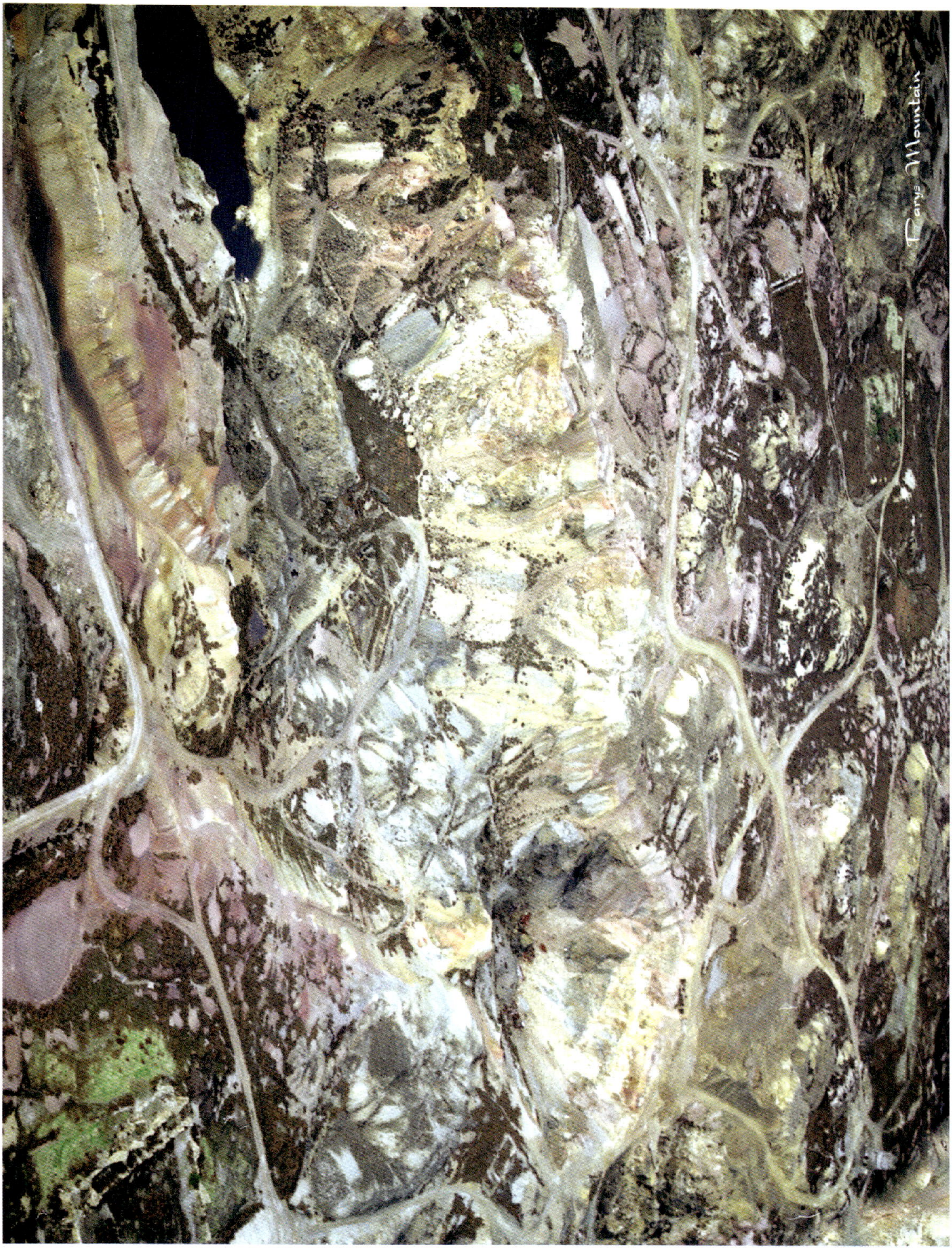
Parys Mountain

Timeless Impressions

By 600 BC the Bronze Age had yielded to the Iron Age with the arrival of the Celts. These highly cultured people introduced to Britain the Brythonic language (which developed into Welsh), together with a love of music, spoken poetry and storytelling, and of battle. They made strong iron weapons, as well as beautiful objects from bronze, silver and gold. Some war trophies they cast into lakes as offerings: the mischievous water-spirits at Llyn Cerrig Bach on Anglesey received swords, chariots, horse harnesses and slave gang chains.

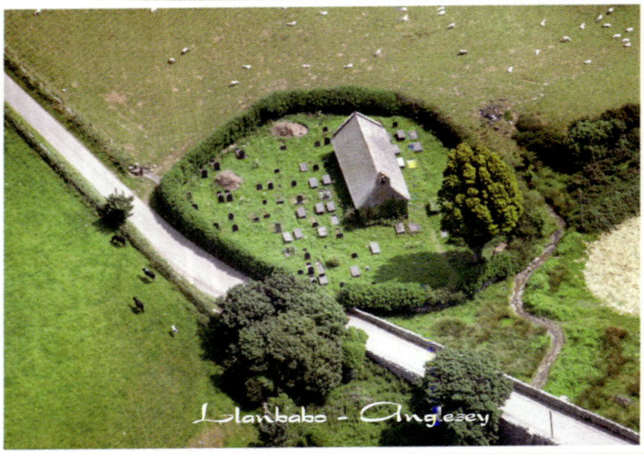

For the Celts, all natural phenomena (including stones, lakes, trees and birds) were sources of divine power. Their religious leaders were the druids, who learnt their craft over twenty years by word of mouth. They dressed in white robes and conducted human sacrifices in sacred oak groves. On laylines of quartz they erected circles of moon-coloured rocks where they worshipped the sun and made further offering to their gods. Greece was not the only culture that knew of these powers, and the druids were experts in these long forgotten ways.

In 61 AD the druids inspired resistance against the invading Romans. However, the druids were forced to retreat to Anglesey. Backed by warriors and women carrying firebrands, the druids cursed the immaculate Roman soldiers across the Menai Strait. Eventually, the awestruck legionaries crossed over the water. It's then that the druids disappeared from our history. Together with men, women and children, they were burnt alive, wrapped in their own torch-flames.

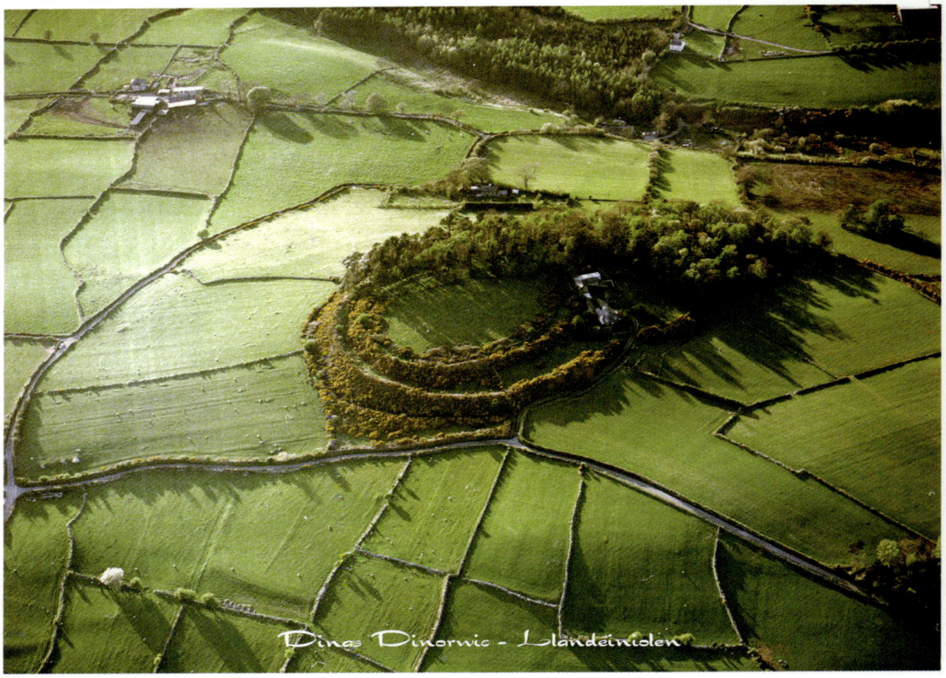

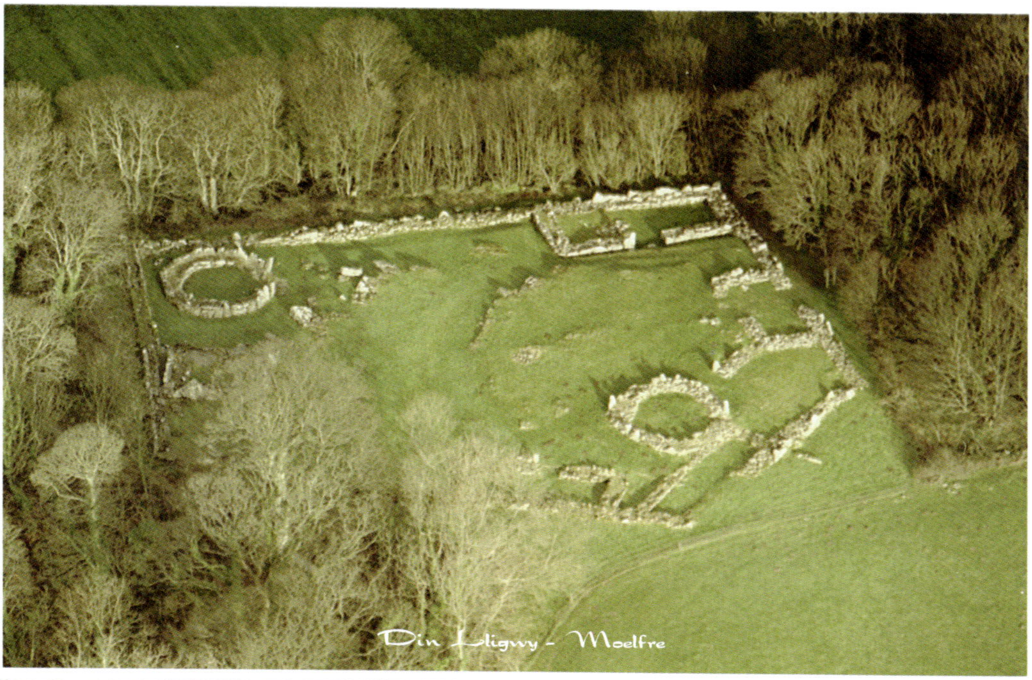

• Sheltered by sunlit woods, the round stone buildings at Din Lligwy were the homes of cultured Roman-Britons in the 4th century. These people used imported pottery, wore silver jewellery and made iron tools.

• Thomas Telford lived on the crescent of Trearddur when he was building his road, now the A5, across Anglesey. In his time it was sparsely populated but it became an emerald haven for the wealthy Cheshire Set.

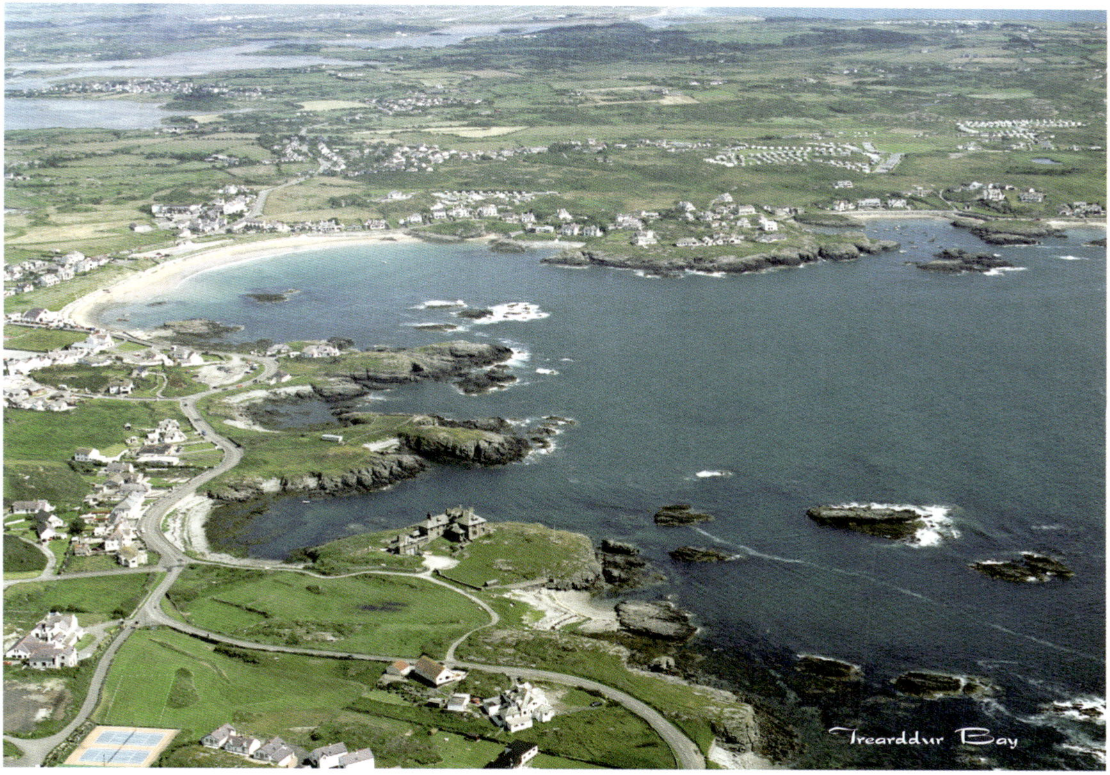

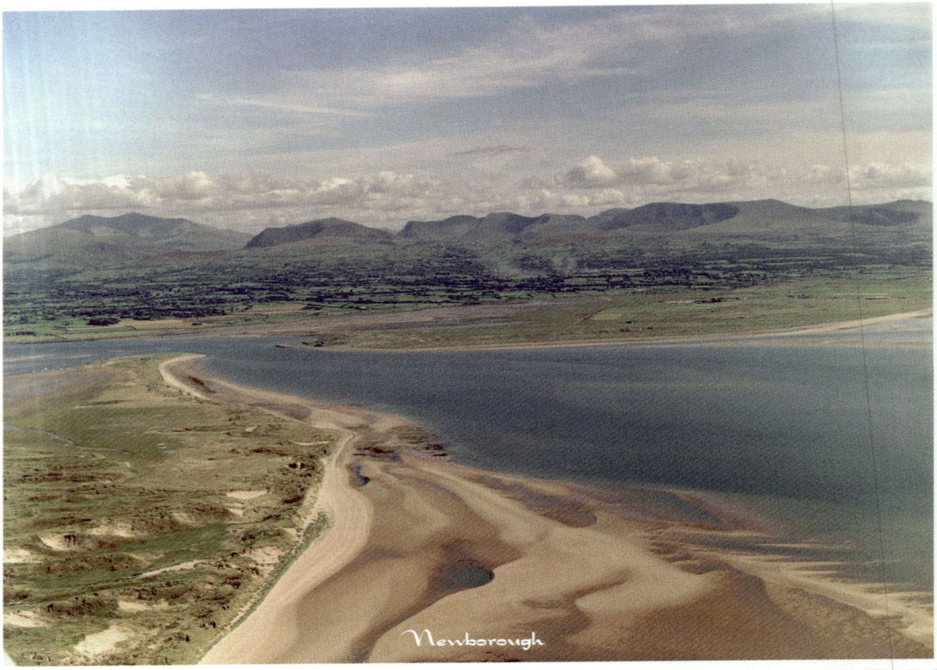

Tranquil Corners

- The golden sands of Newborough reach out at Aber Menai for Fort Belan across the Menai Strait. This is the gateway for lazy seals and leaping porpoises takes the quickest route to Liverpool Bay.
- For years a ferry plied between Menai Bridge and Bangor. The University's slick new research ship, the Prince Madog, moored up in 2001. Its predecessor was well known for making marine scientists seasick.

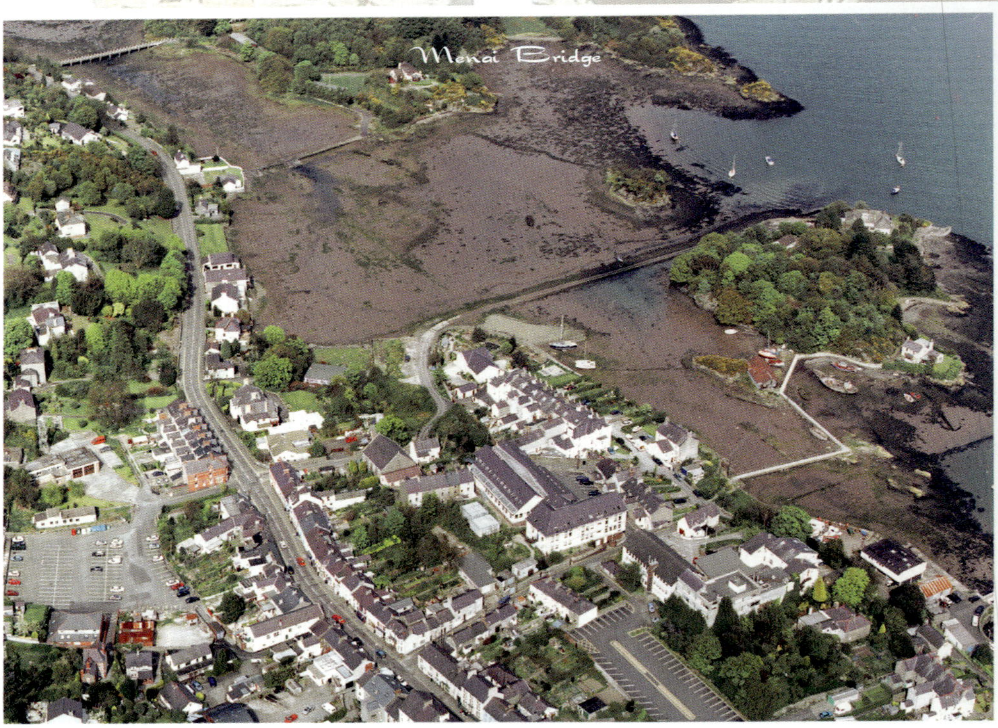

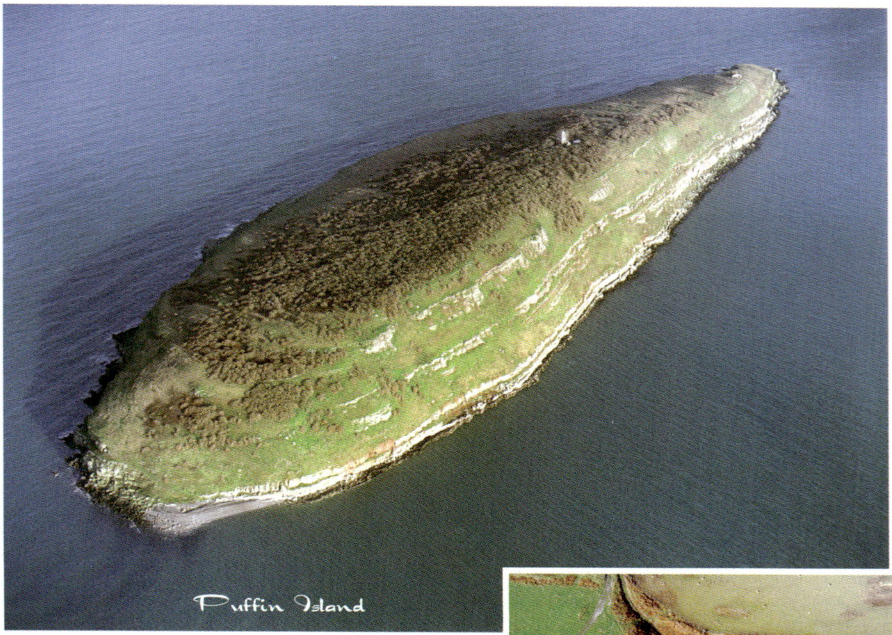

Puffin Island

- The food in St Seiriol's monastery on Puffin Island was spoiled by mice whenever the monks squabbled. When holy peace returned, the mice disappeared.
- A lighthouse was built at Penmon after the wreck of the Rothesay Castle paddle steamer from Liverpool. Over 100 people were drowned.

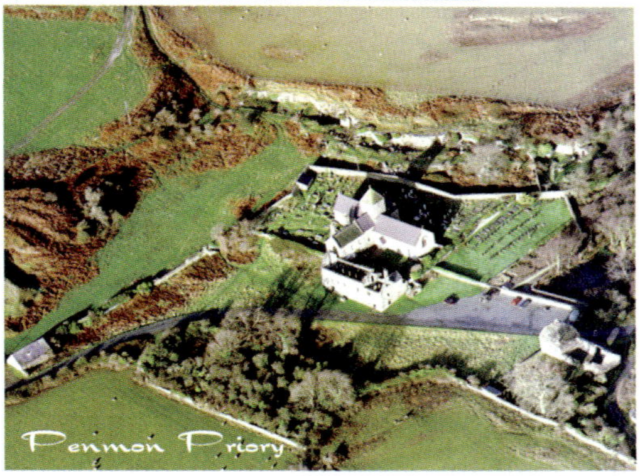

Penmon Priory

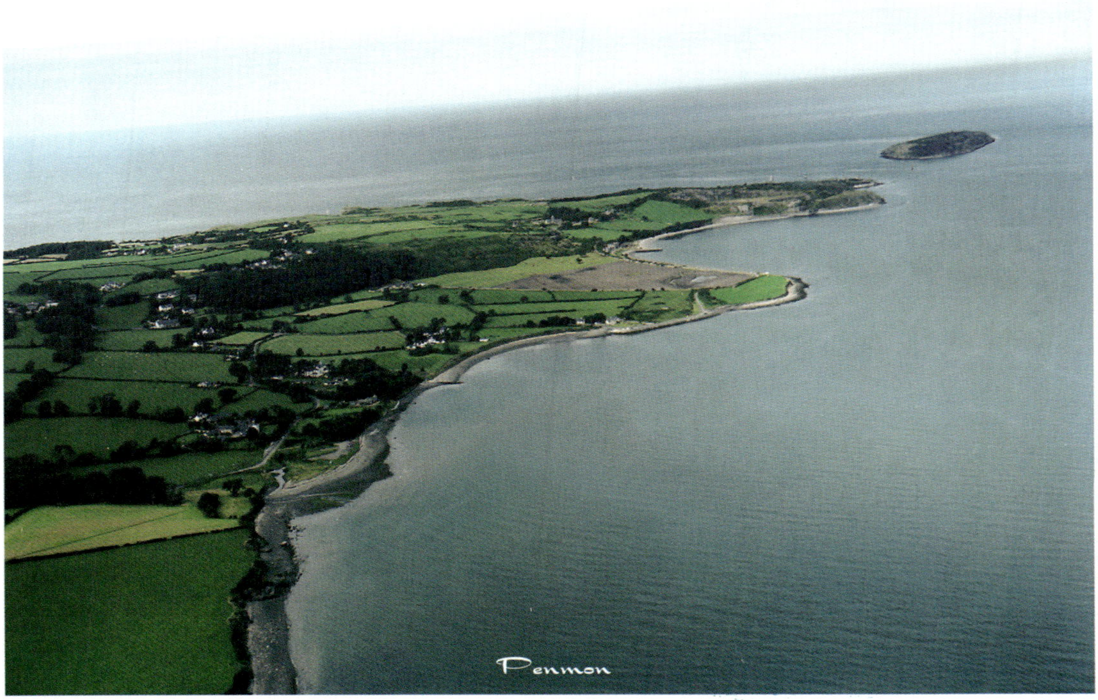

Penmon

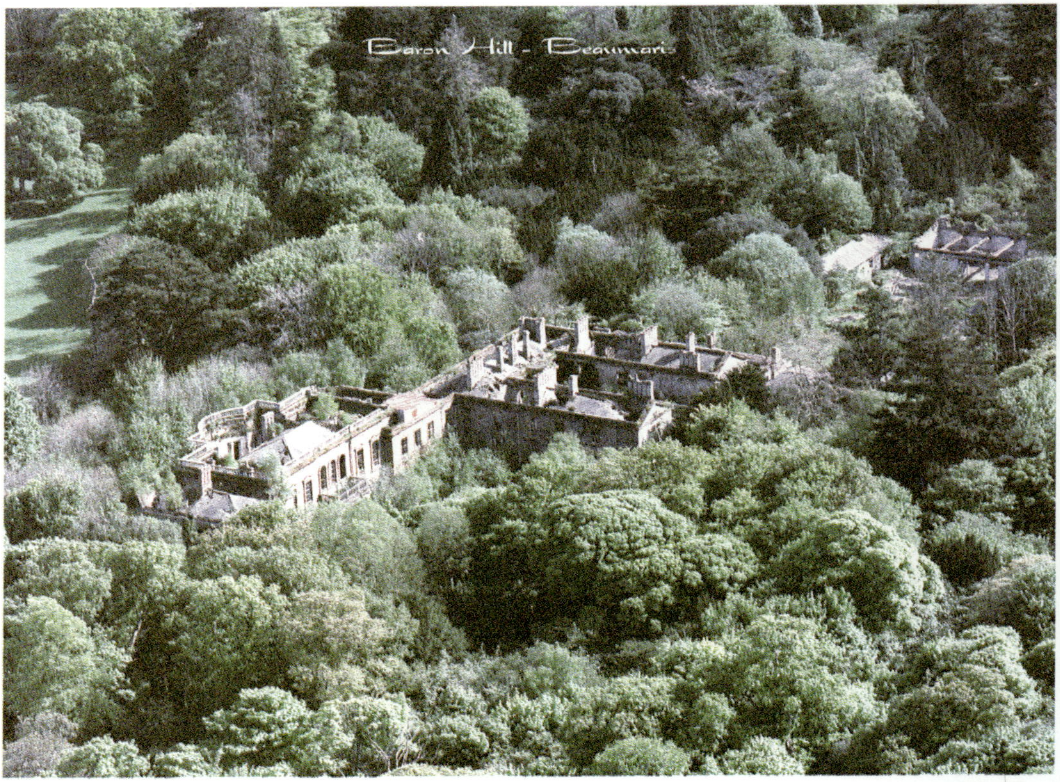

"Sir, the Funny Windmills Have Arrived"

● Near Beaumaris the skeletal ruins of Baron Hill are being engulfed by ravenous trees. Sadly, the once majestic mansion burnt down in 1836. It was the stately seat of Lord Viscount Bulkeley and was designed by Samuel Wyatt in 1776.

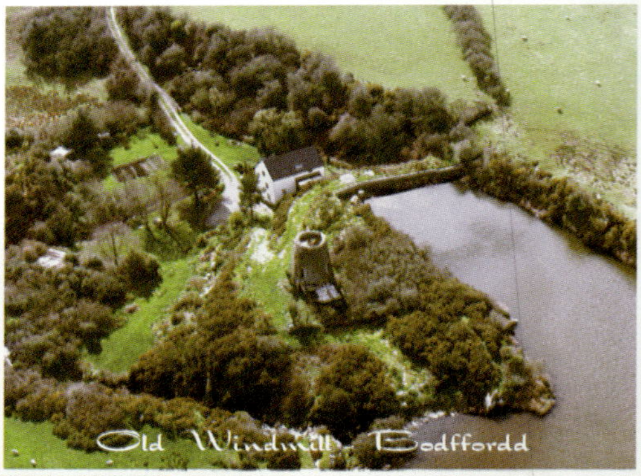

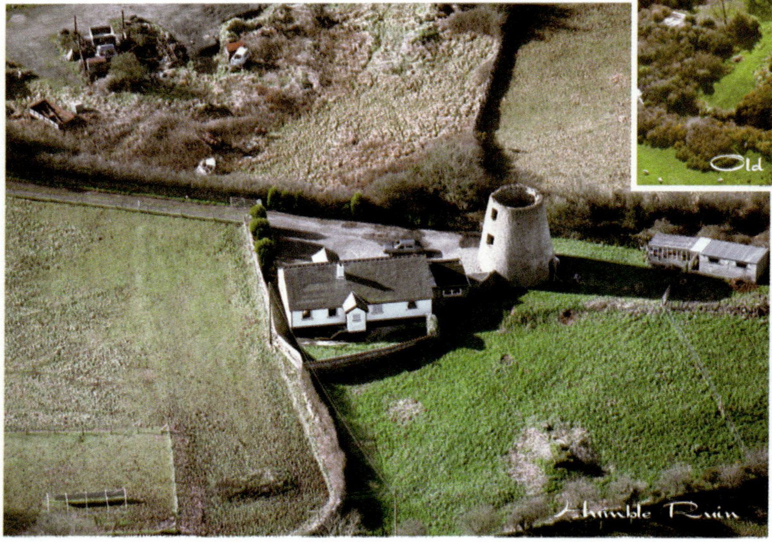

● Anglesey was called Mam Cymru (the Mother of Wales) because of her fertile land for growing barley and oats. It was an ideal location for mills powered by strong winds to grind the grain into flour for the hungry mainland .

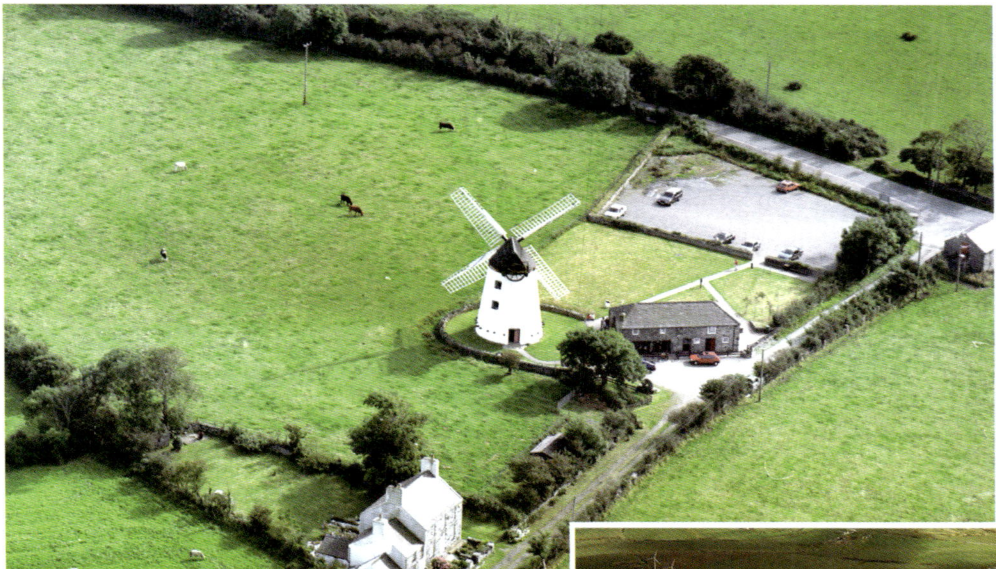

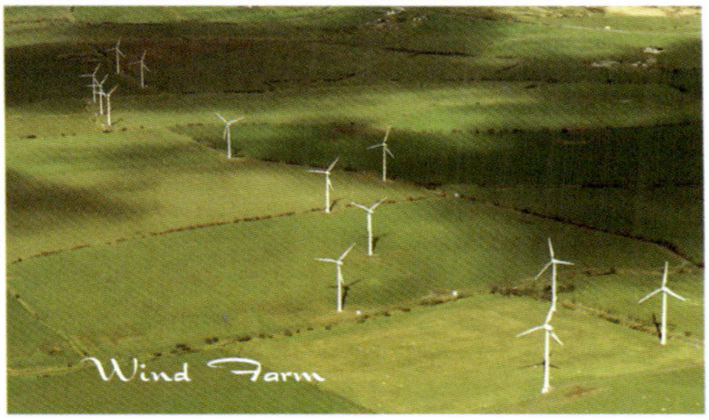

- Llynnon Mill is one of only two working windmills on Anglesey. Many remain, although without sails, including the mill at the end of Mona Airfield at Bodffordd.
- In contrast to traditional crop farming and the nuclear power station at Wylfa, Anglesey now has several windfarms performing out-of-step gymnastics in fields near Holyhead, Amlwch and Llyn Alaw.

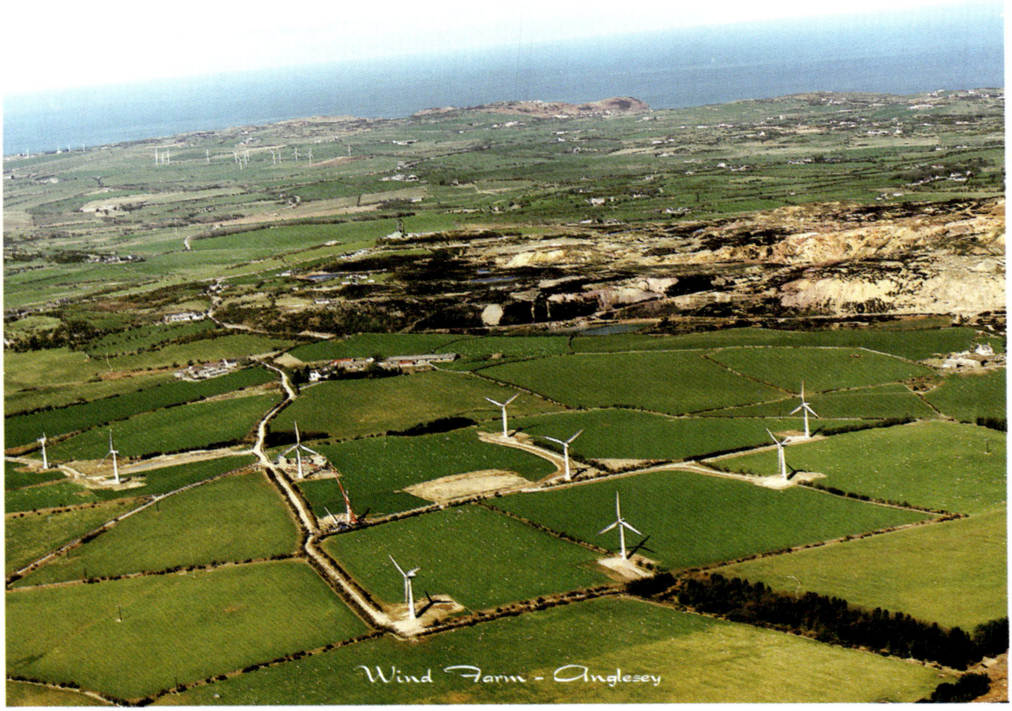

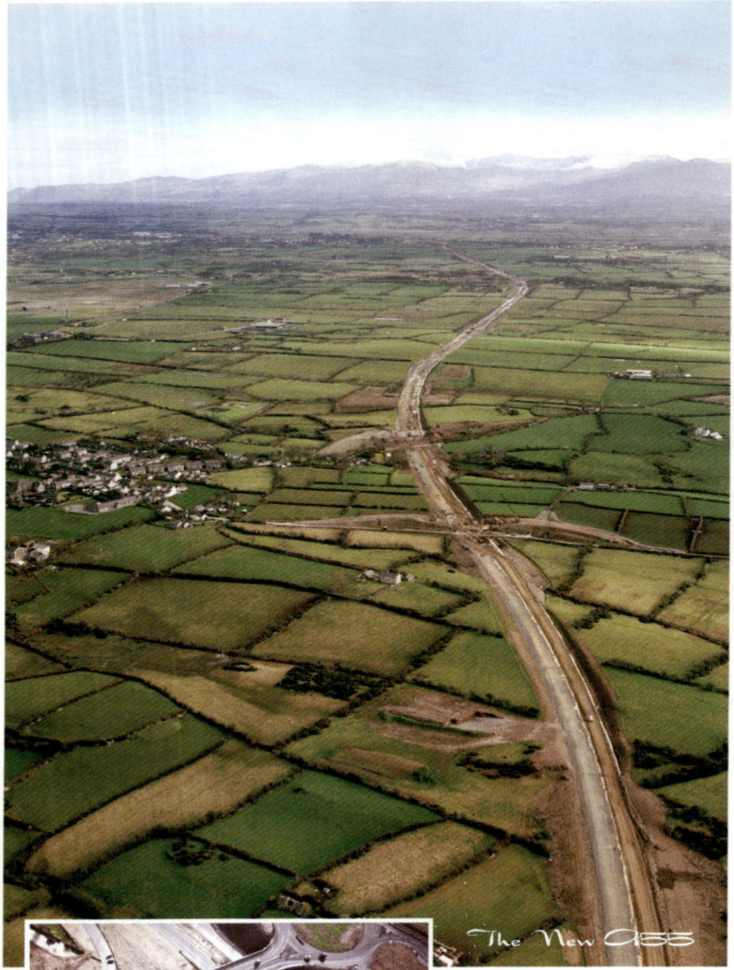

The New A55

Telford

Thomas Telford's Great Irish Road (A5) was built to appease Irish MPs who had complained about the badly made roads linking London to Anglesey.

Telford's road ran from the small fishing village of Holyhead across Anglesey, over the Menai Strait, down through Betws-y-Coed and onto Shrewsbury, before a long haul to London. It was used by Royal Mail coaches carrying the Irish Mail to Dublin.

He built many stunning snaking roads and swaying bridges, including the Menai and Conwy Suspension Bridges and the Aqueduct at Froncysyllte

Telford was the only man in Britain at the time who could carry out such constructions. Now they stand as timeless monuments to his genius.

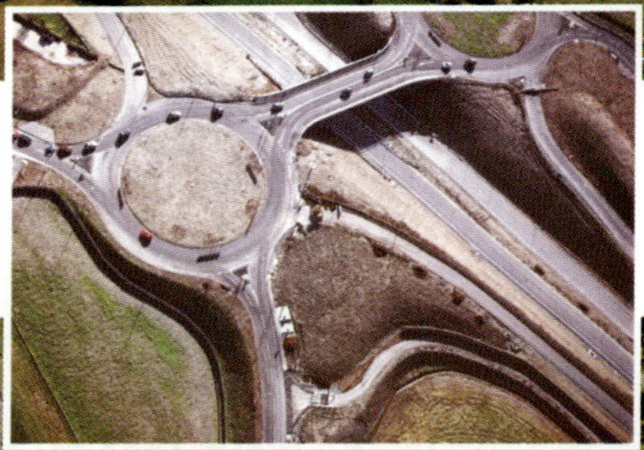

A Herd of Hues

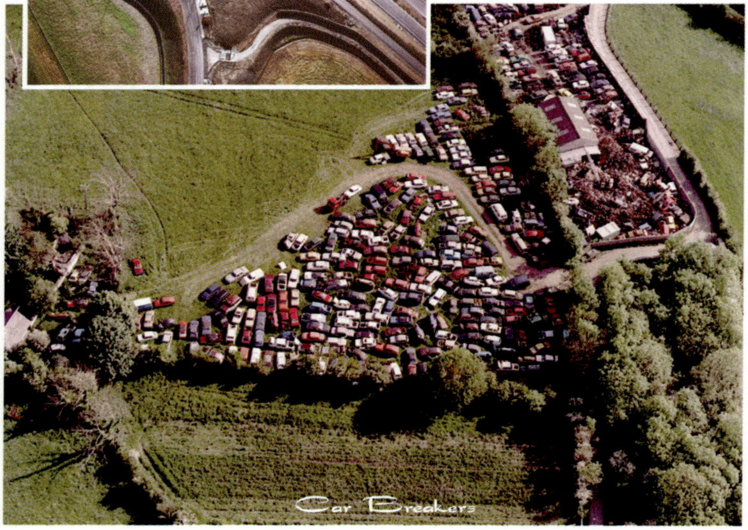

Car Breakers

At Gaerwen a Roman mosaic of scrapped cars are put out to grass, worn out by Telford's road. The scar of the A55 during construction twists across the patchwork landscape. It's part of a worldwide picture, the E22 Euroroute, which runs from the Baltic coast to Dublin. During construction care was taken to create new habitats for badgers and shy Welsh otters, which have been making a comeback on the Island after years of near extinction.

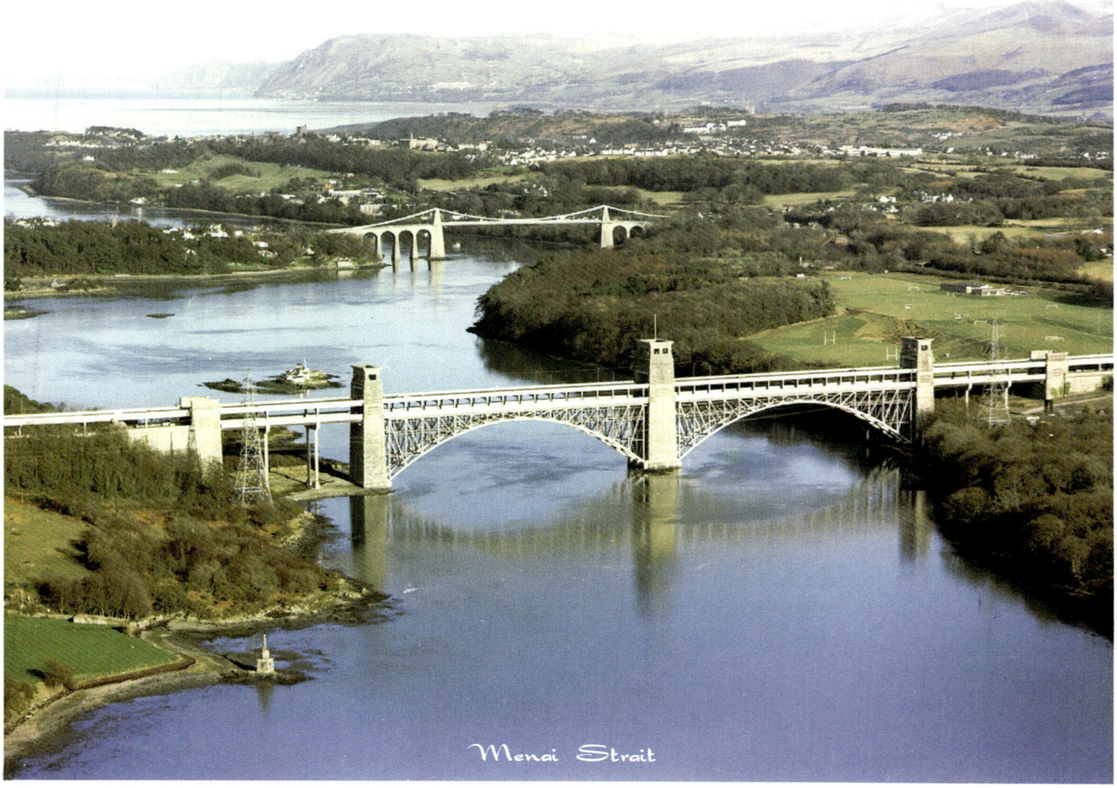

Deep Reflections

For thirteen dangerous miles racing tides surge through the Menai Strait between Anglesey and mainland Wales. Down the centuries ferries carried passengers to Beaumaris whilst cattle in droves had to swim across.

Eventually, two bridges were, as George Borrow put it, "flung over the Menai". At the completion of Telford's Bridge in 1826 bagpipes played in celebration, Telford prayed on his knees, and the Irish Mail was the first to dash across. Stephenson's Britannia Bridge, carrying the railway, was perched midstream on a rock which had sunk the Britannia ship only a few years before. Originally, four limestone lions guarded his Bridge. Then in 1970 teenagers started a fire, burning the timber structure, which had to be rebuilt. Today the half-hidden lions wear glum faces and can only be seen by walkers from below.

Between the bridges and the banks are many islands. Ynys Gorad Goch, the Island of the Red Weir, still flings out its arms to catch unwary fish; in older times they were smoked in its own small curing tower. Church Island was the peaceful retreat of St Tysilio. In 1188 the Archbishop of Canterbury stopped at the Church, drumming up money and volunteers for the Third Crusade to the Holy Land. Today, the Island's reached by a causeway built by Belgian refugees during World War I.

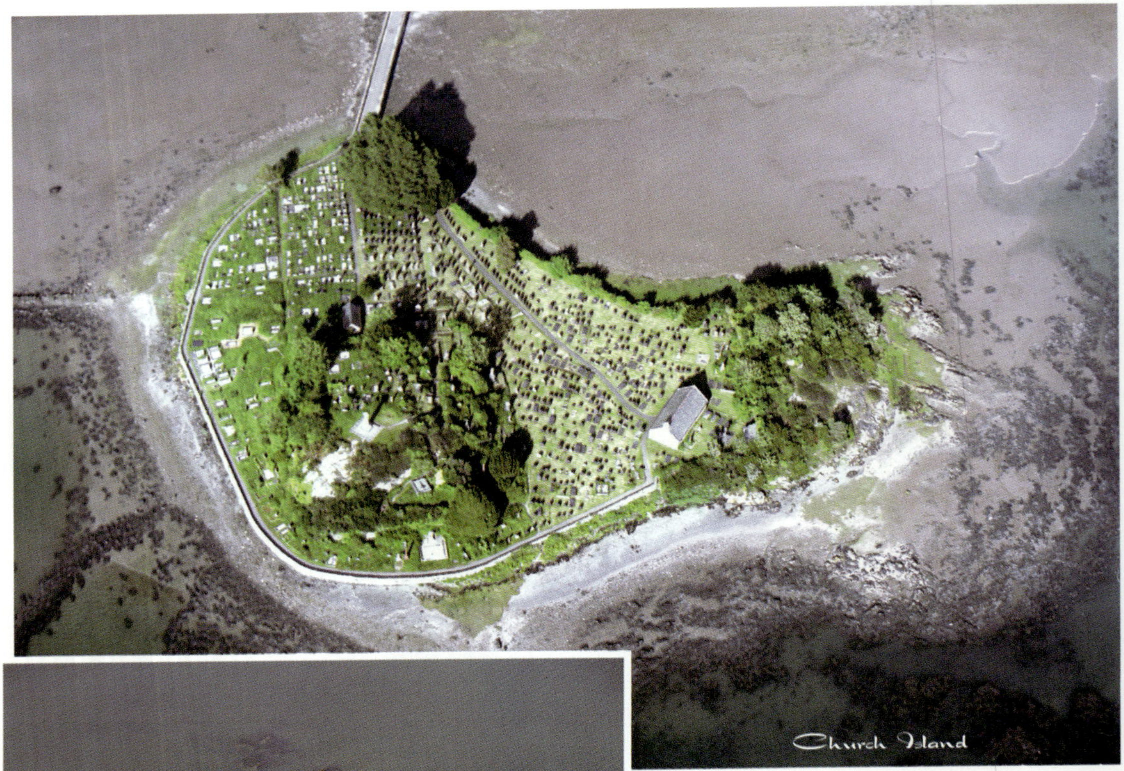

Church Island

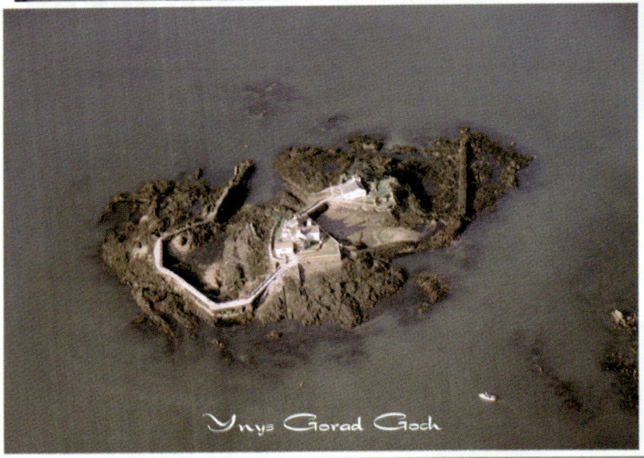

Ynys Gorad Goch

● The Cockle Poet of Church Island sold cockles and wrote poetry. "Four fat lions, without any hair, two on this side here, and two over there" concerned Britannia Bridge.

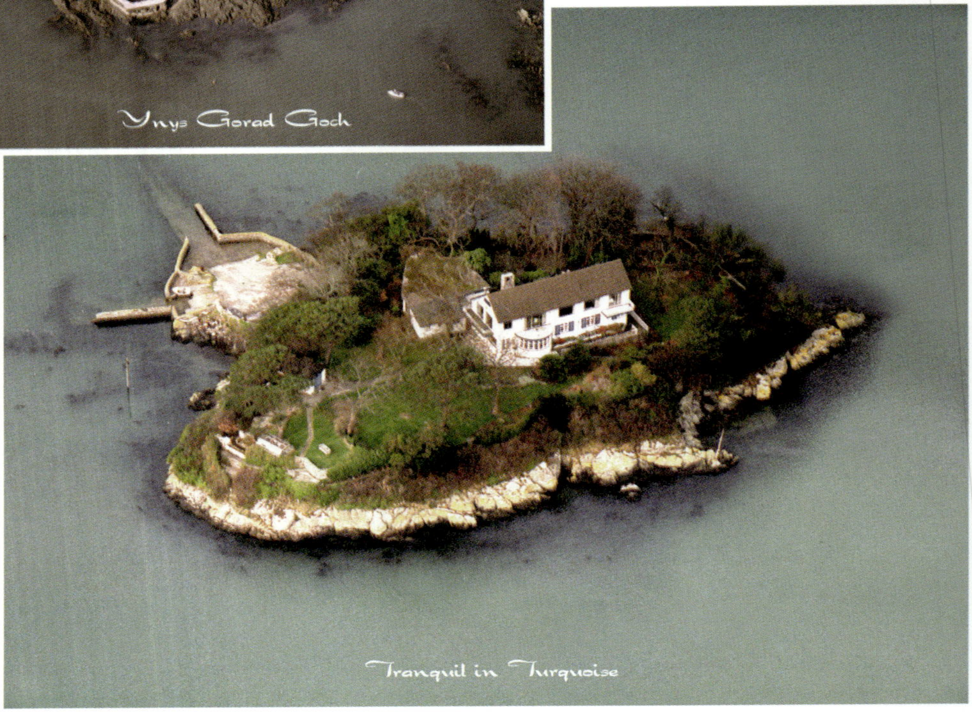

Tranquil in Turquoise

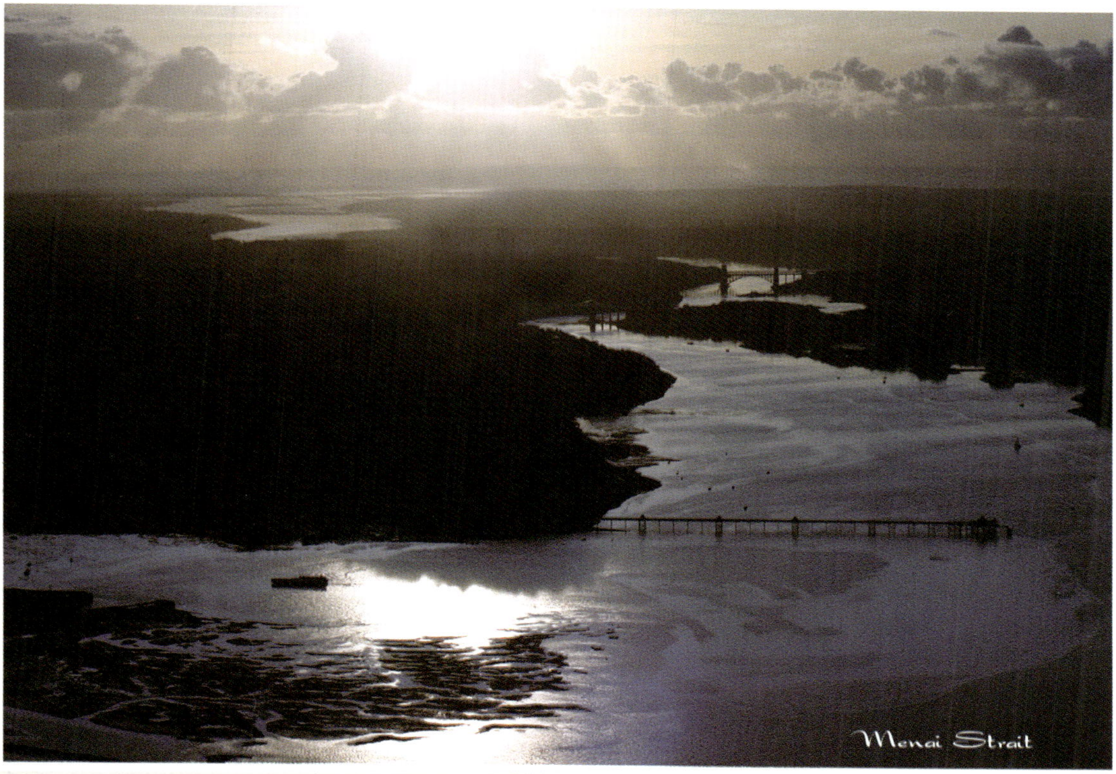

• The Menai Suspension Bridge was built 100' (30m) above the Strait to allow for tall ships to sail under it. During WW2 an ace fighter pilot (W Ross-Jones) flew his Battle of Britain Spitfire under the bridge also.

• Bangor grew up around the monastery of Deiniol, who was the spiritual leader of reprobate Maelgwyn Gwynedd. Its Cathedral contains the bones of 3 Welsh princes and lazy tongs to remove energetic dogs.

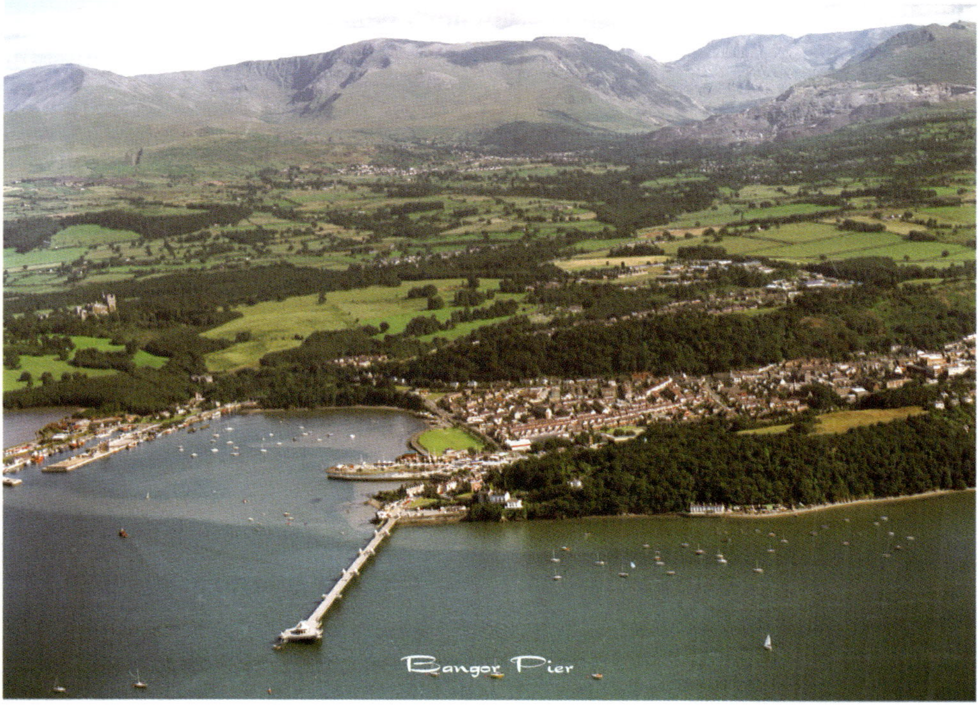

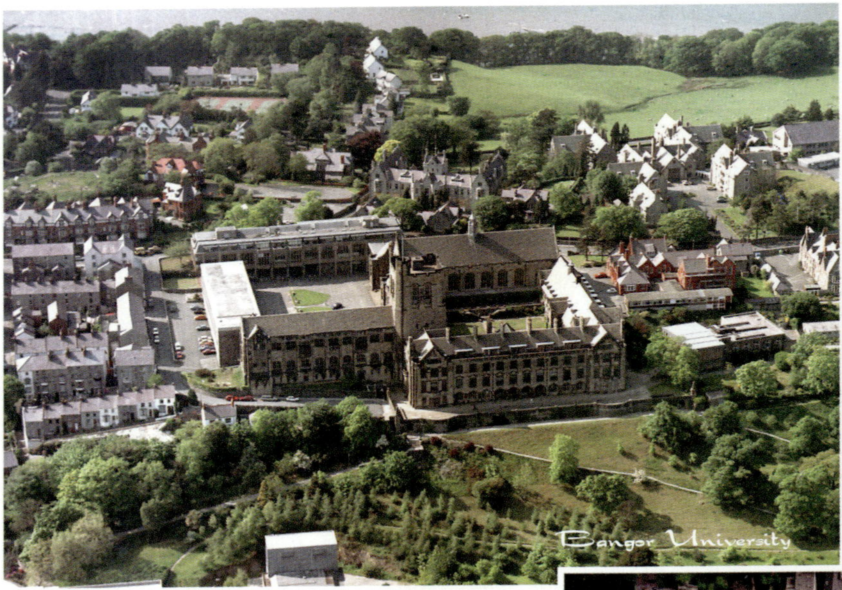

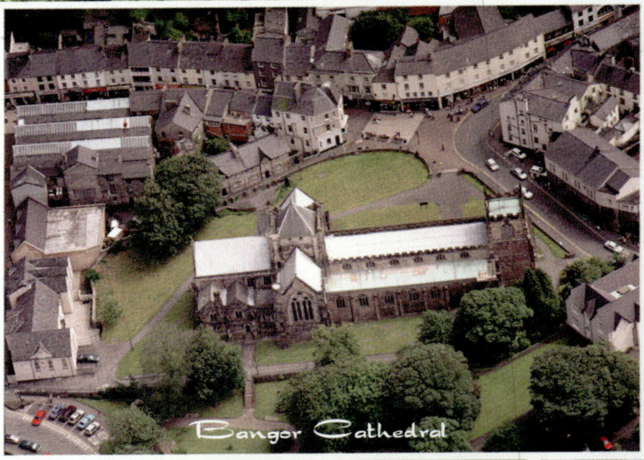

- Quarrymen from Penrhyn made voluntary contributions from their wages to set up the University at Bangor in 1884. The first building was a former coaching inn called the Penrhyn Arms. Locals celebrated by closing their shops and wearing Sunday best.
- Before Port Dinorwic developed to ship slate from the lakeside of Llanberis a ferry ran between here and Moel y Don on Anglesey.

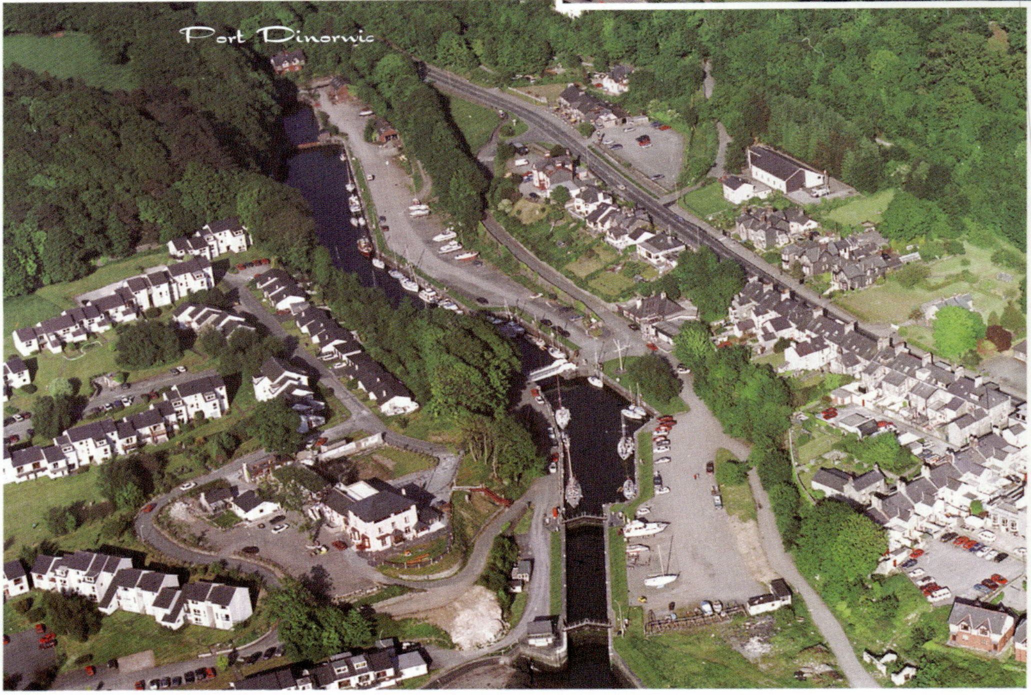

Slate Drivers

Penrhyn Castle looks like the perfect Norman castle but it was built 700 years later with the profits from the Bethesda slate quarries. Hewing slate from the mountains had been a village industry since Elizabeth 1st. Then Baron Penrhyn bought up all the rights and hired back local men as his labourers. Penrhyn Quarry paid them 12 shillings (60 new pence) a week. It also made the fortune that financed the limestoned Castle for its owners, providing the slate for the billiard table and one-ton bed. Meanwhile, the quarrymen lived in barracks, with bare stone walls and battered roofs to keep off the wind and rain.

A rival quarry by Llyn Peris exported its slate from Port Dinorwic. The Lord of the Manor of Dinorwic was a Master of Hounds, a cricketer and a gentleman. He enclosed 4/5ths of the common land to establish the Dinorwic Quarry, depriving the villagers of their rights. They could work for him though in their thousands, and they lived in the new village of Llanberis.

- Turreted Penrhyn Castle was built around the manor house of the Gruffydds of Penrhyn. Piers Gruffydd fought with Sir Francis Drake against the Spanish Armada and was accused of piracy. He sold off the Penrhyn Estate to buy his pardon.

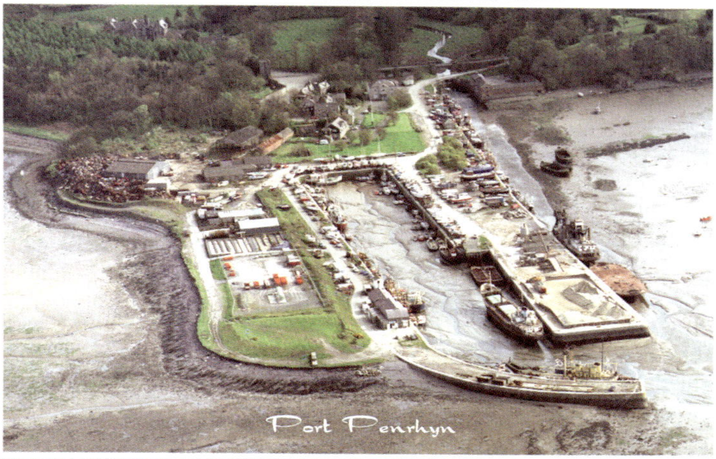

Port Penrhyn

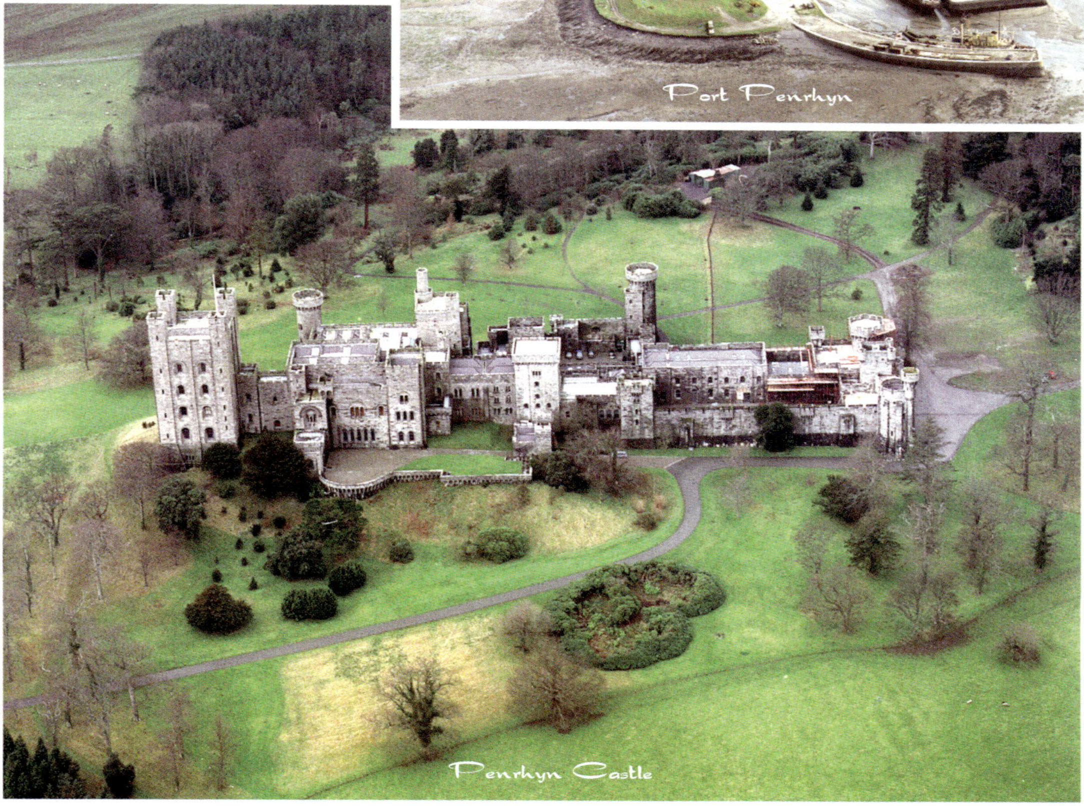

Penrhyn Castle

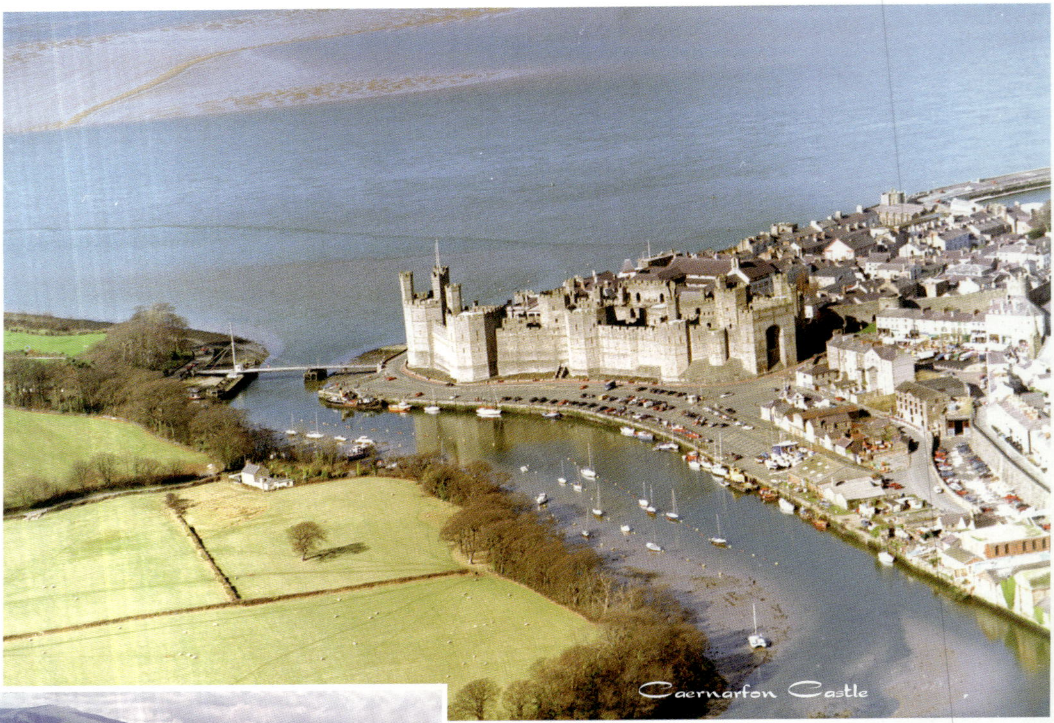

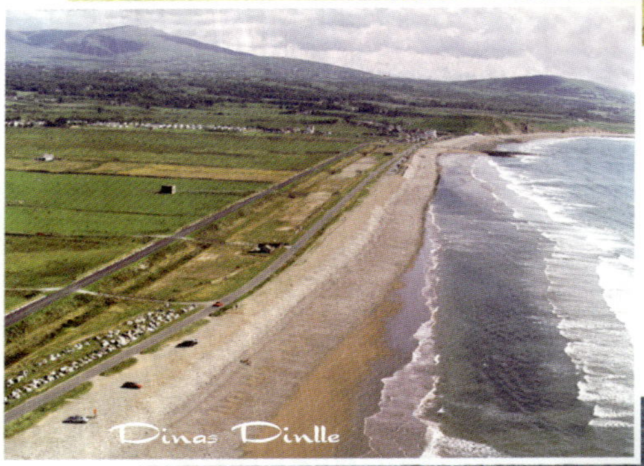

- Eagle-topped Caernarfon Castle was sited near a Roman fort used by Macsen, the last Emperor of Britain. He was a Spanish general who married a Celtic wife.
- During the American War of Independence Fort Belan was built along the same surfline as an Iron Age fort at Dinas Dinlle. It was still being used during WW2.

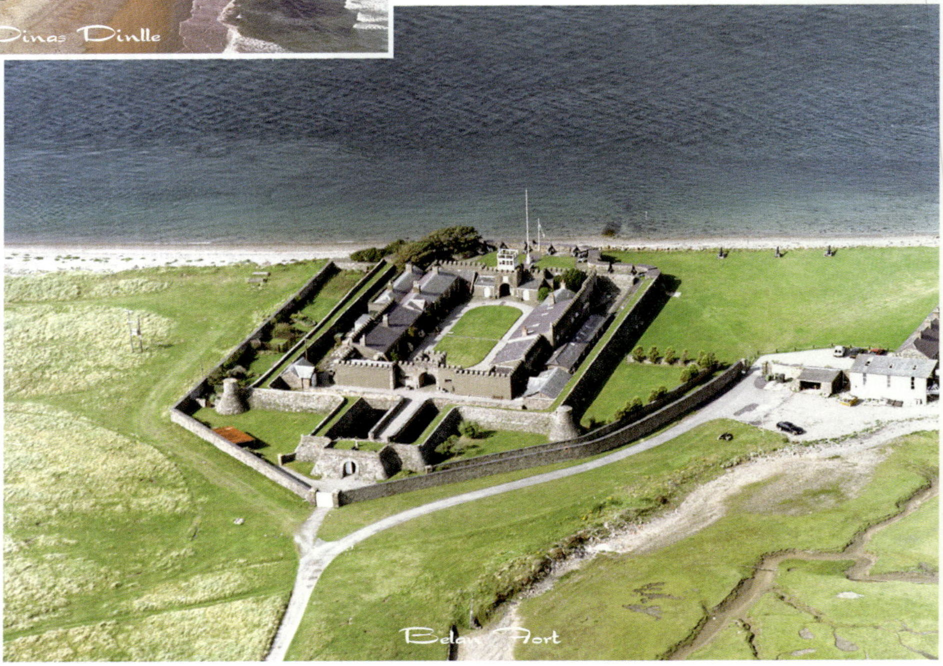

Aber

● The small village of Aber was once the site of a Welsh court lived in by the Princes of Gwynedd. Their other royal houses were at Aberffraw and Trefriw. Aber's real name is Abergwyngregyn, which means the mouth of the river of white shells. In the hills beyond, Aber Falls plummets down a leaf-splashed, tree-lined gorge for 100' (33m).

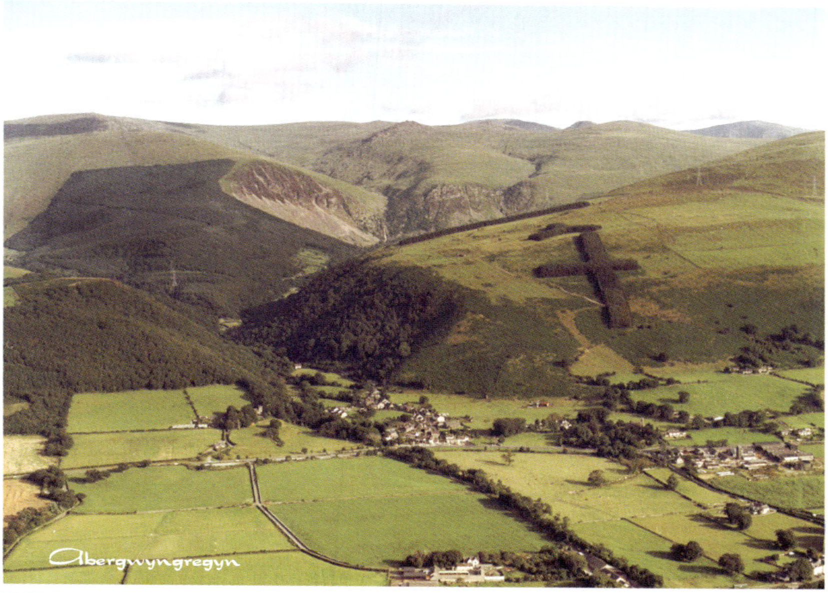

Abergwyngregyn

● Aber lies at the end of an ancient road running over the mountains to the Conwy Valley. It has been used by people for thousands of years, and a "Cairn of the Englishman" lies on its route. Aber was also the starting point for a damp trek across the sucking sands of Traeth Lafan at low tide to reach Beaumaris on Anglesey.

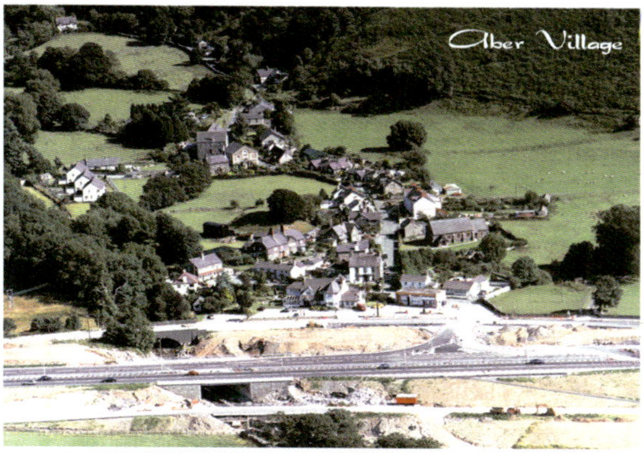

Aber Village

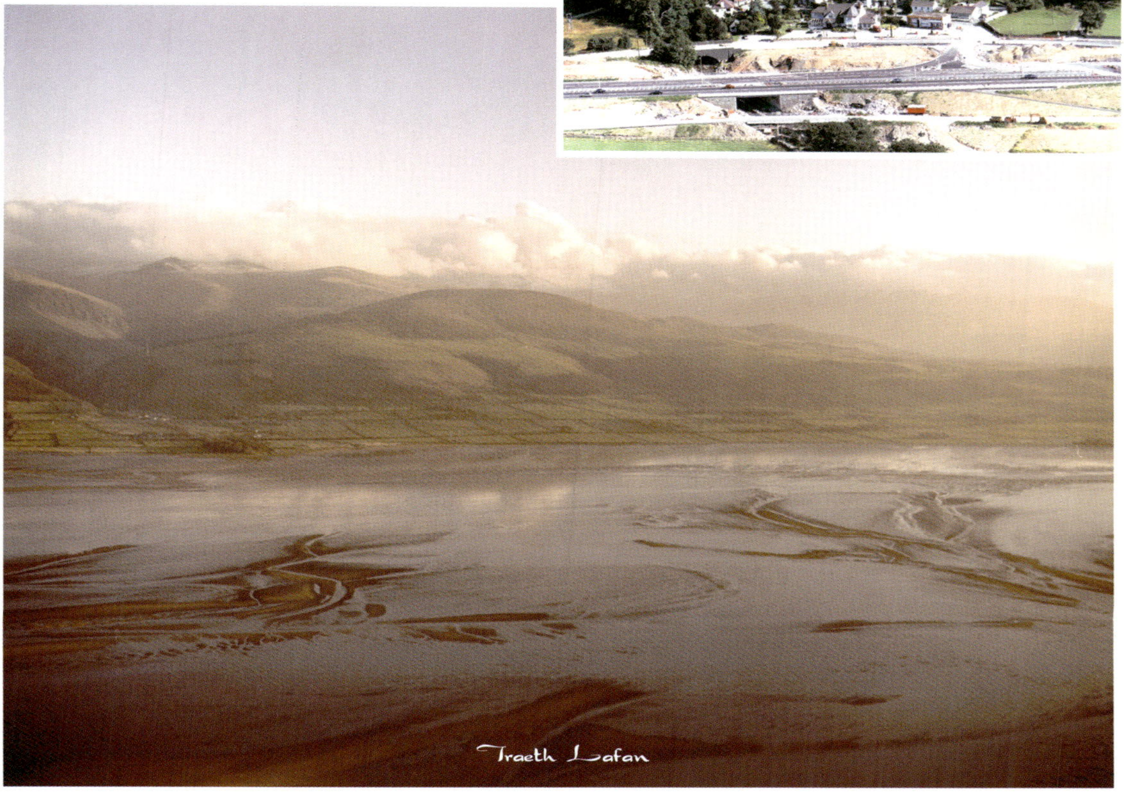

Traeth Lafan

Timeless Motions

Along the north coast of Wales the chiselled face of Penmaenmawr defiantly confronts the Irish Sea. This sheer cliff-face has been a barrier to man since he first arrived over 250,000 years ago. Thousands of years later New Stone Age quarrymen hammered out the hard granite of Graig Lwyd above the town to make their axe-heads and then exported their quality tools all over Britain.

Many of the cairns and standing stones along the ancient roads belong to the Bronze Age from 2,000 years ago. The Roman armies trudged along here also, marching from Caerhun in the Conwy Valley to barren forts on Anglesey or Emperor Macsen's fort near Caernarfon.

In later times Penmaenmawr was beloved by sea-bathing Victorians, including Prime Minister Gladstone, who called it "dear old Penmaenmawr, the most charming watering place in Wales". Even the granite pebbles fallen from the volcanic headland above were gathered from its tide-washed beaches and shipped to Liverpool and Manchester to line the grimy cobbled streets.

Beyond the headland at Llanfairfechan the Church of St Mary gave its Welsh name to the town, and her saint's day was celebrated with dancing on the village green. Hopefully, St Mary gave the frolickers courage when walking around the rockface to Penmaenmawr since it was always formidable, even when a road was built in 1772 and glowing inns with flickering log fires were located at either end of it. Today it still takes skill to navigate, not around the jagged rocks but passed the speed cameras that flash more times than the South Stack Lighthouse at people going about their daily chores. It's a great shame Prince Llywelyn isn't around today, for he would have flashed his mighty sword and swifty behead cameras galore, including their chieftain and his flat cap.

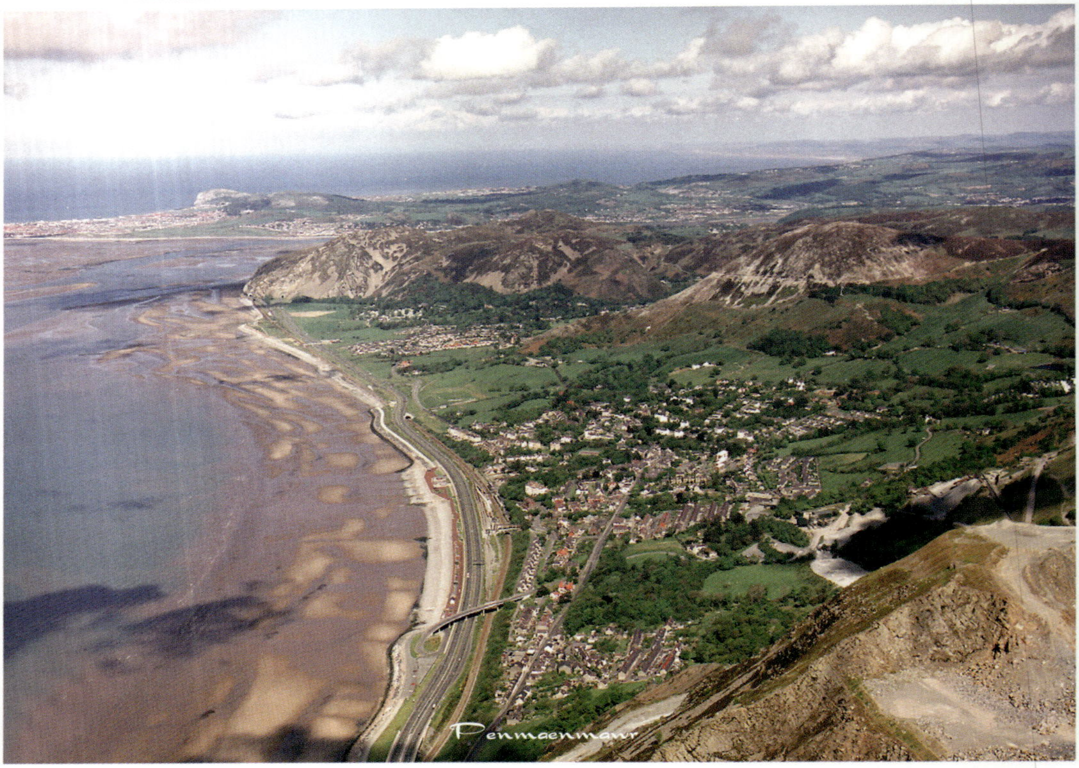

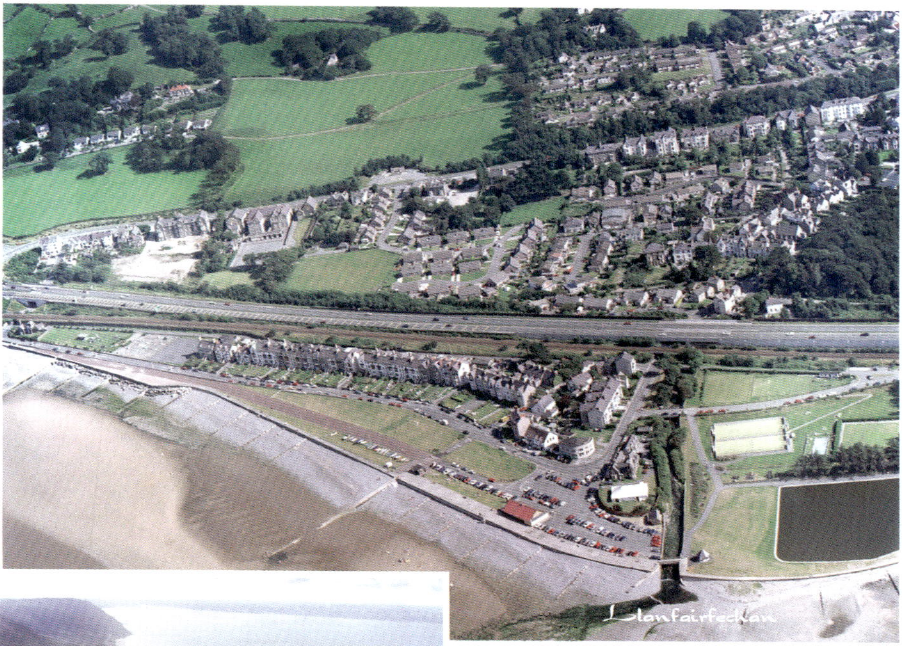

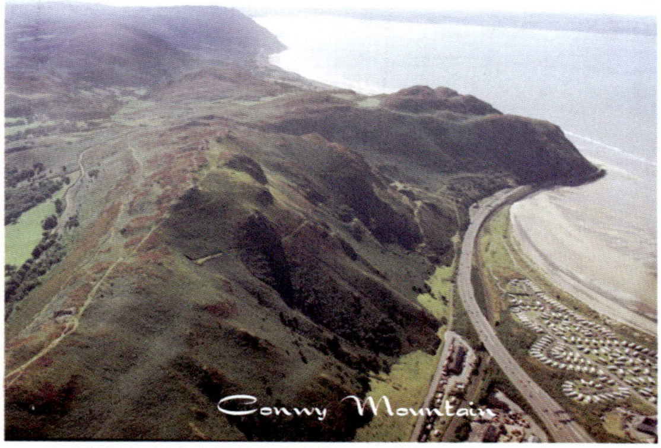

• A pint of frothing Guinness, beloved by the Irish, may have originated in Llanfairfechan. A local malt house was already producing thick black wine when Arthur Guinness stayed in the village on his way to Ireland. His brewery in Dublin developed an "extra stout porter".

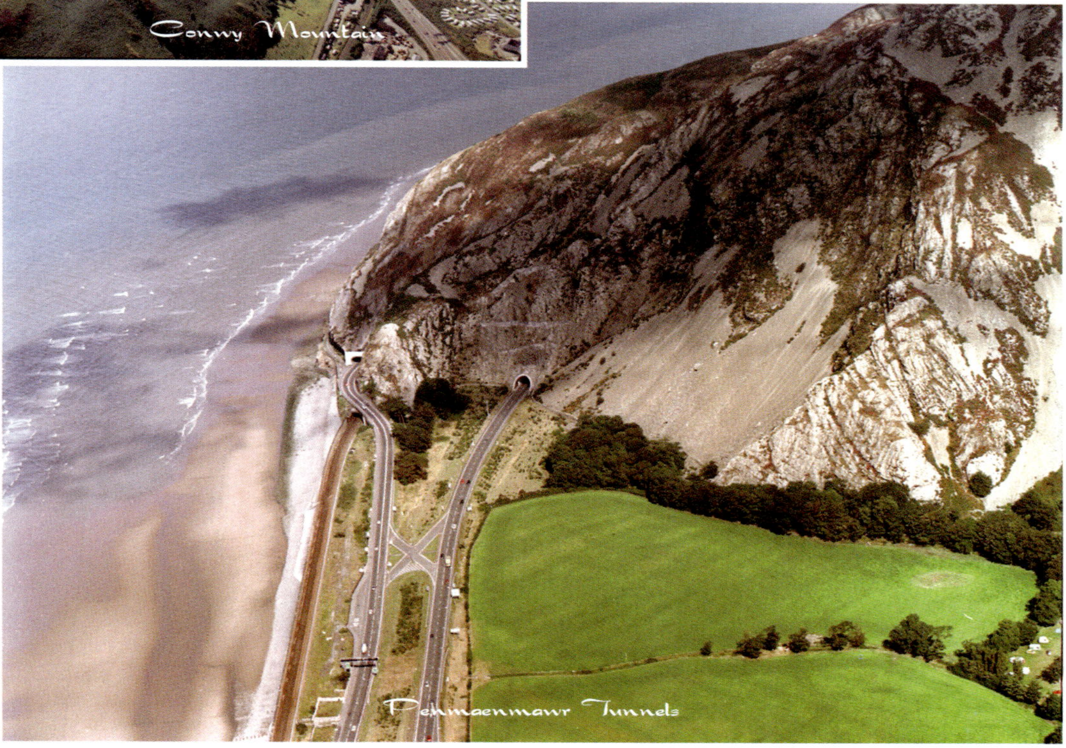

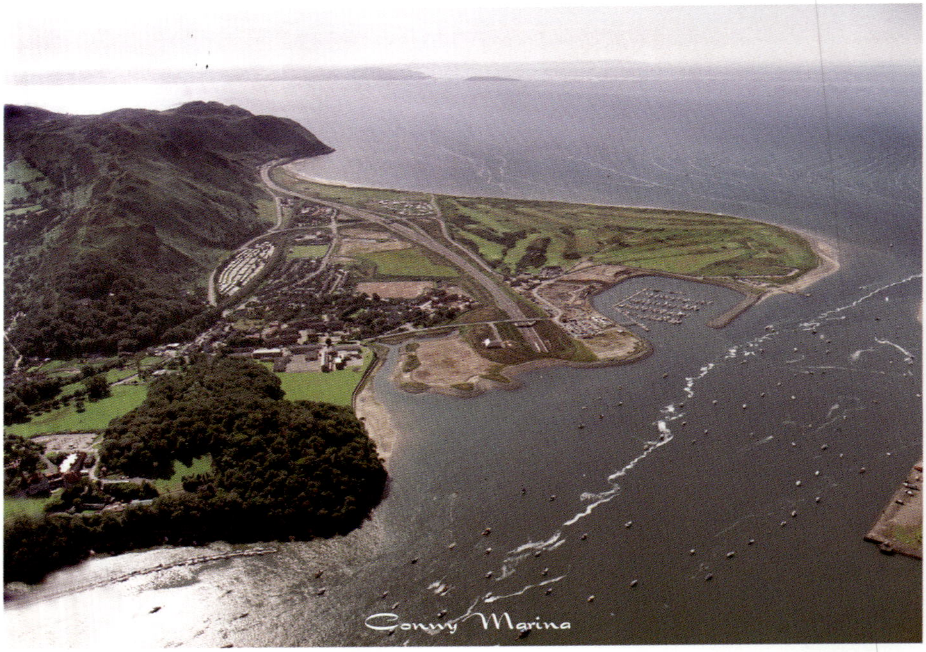

• One Good Friday most of the garrison of Conwy Castle were in church. Knowing this, a carpenter talked his way in through the gates and then admitted the rebellious cousins and "children" of Owain Glyndwr. They held the castellated Castle for 2 months. The iron-chained Suspension Bridge was built by Thomas Telford, who was the jovial son of a Scottish shepherd and was called "Laughing Tam".

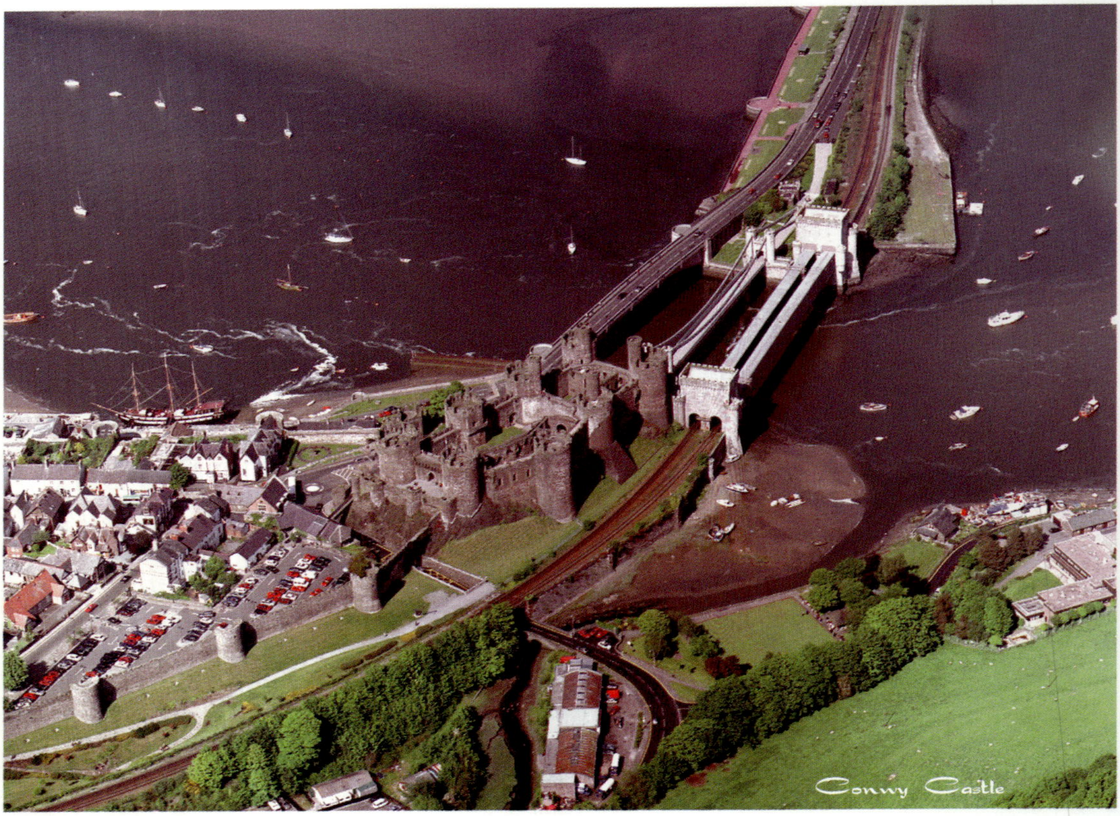

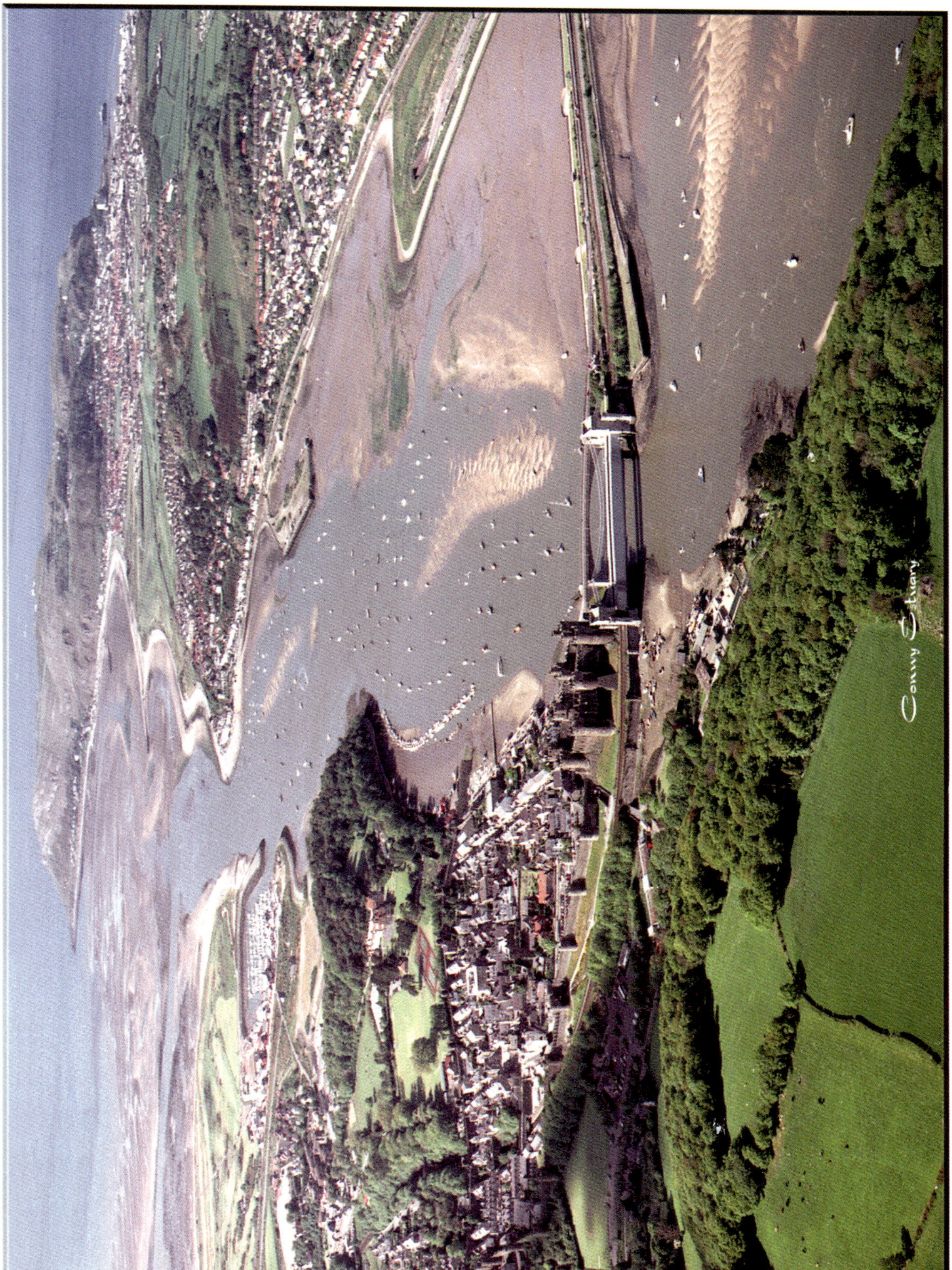
Conwy Estuary

The Dragon's Tunnels

Conwy Tunnel cost nearly £200 million to build beneath the muddy brown waters of the Conwy Estuary. It was begun in 1986 and opened by the Queen in 1991.

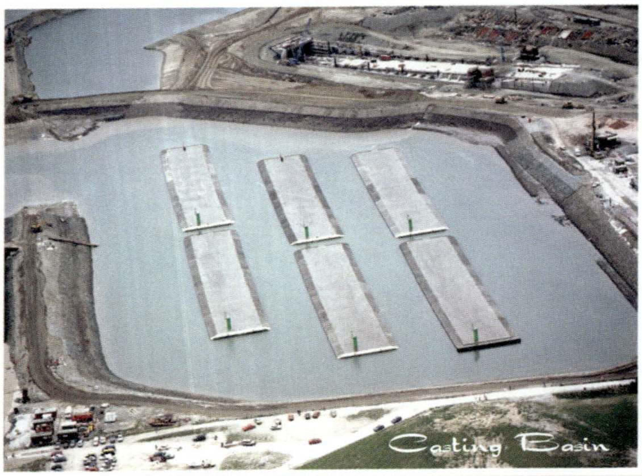

Casting Basin

Six concrete tubes 400' (120m) long, each weighing 30,000 tonnes and plated with shining steel, were prefabricated in a deep dry basin beside Penmaenbach. The basin was flooded, then each tube was floated out, one behind the other, and sunk into a trench beneath the riverbed. This created an immersed tube tunnel beneath the Estuary, and impatient drivers were soon hooting in celebration and on their way. Finally, the casting basin was recreated into Conwy Marina with safe moorings for 300 stately yachts.

Between Penmaenmawr and Llanfairfechan the 3030' (930m) long tunnel which was bored through the crumbling rockface was built by contractors specialising in mountaineering techniques. Keeping to train timetables meant only 20 minutes at 8 pm each evening were available for blasting out the rock, using gelignite packed into holes. Each explosion cut through 12' (3.5m). High retaining walls on the tunnel's sides were built of concrete panels and took 18 months to fix in place.

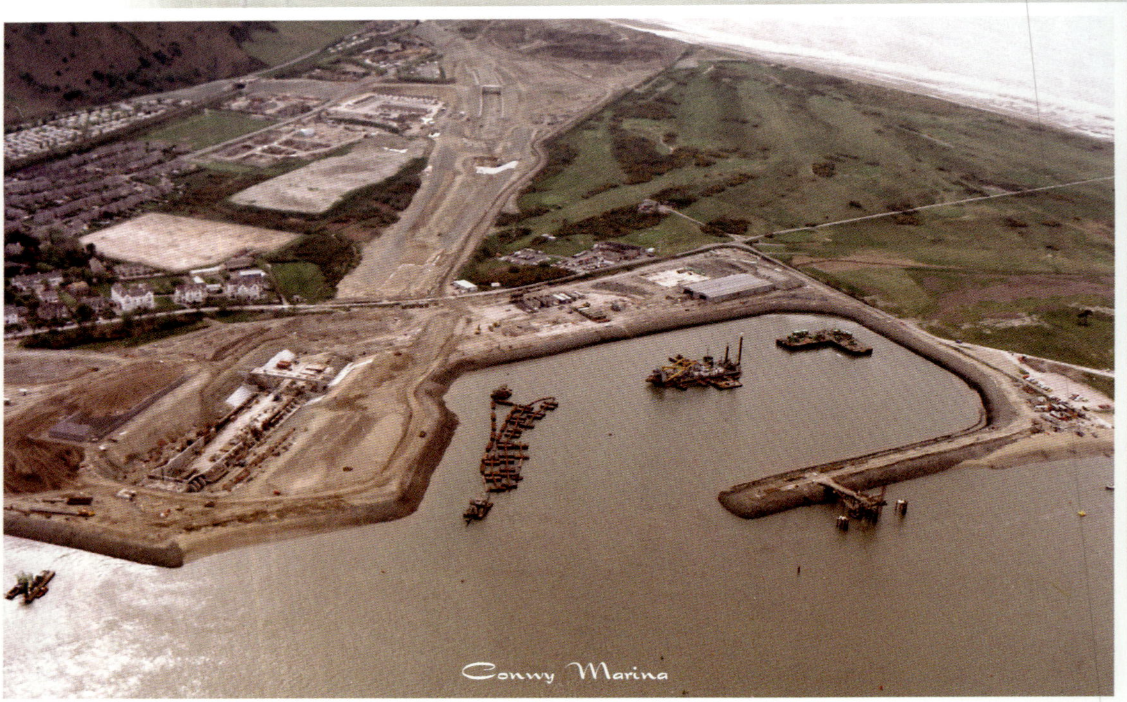

Conwy Marina

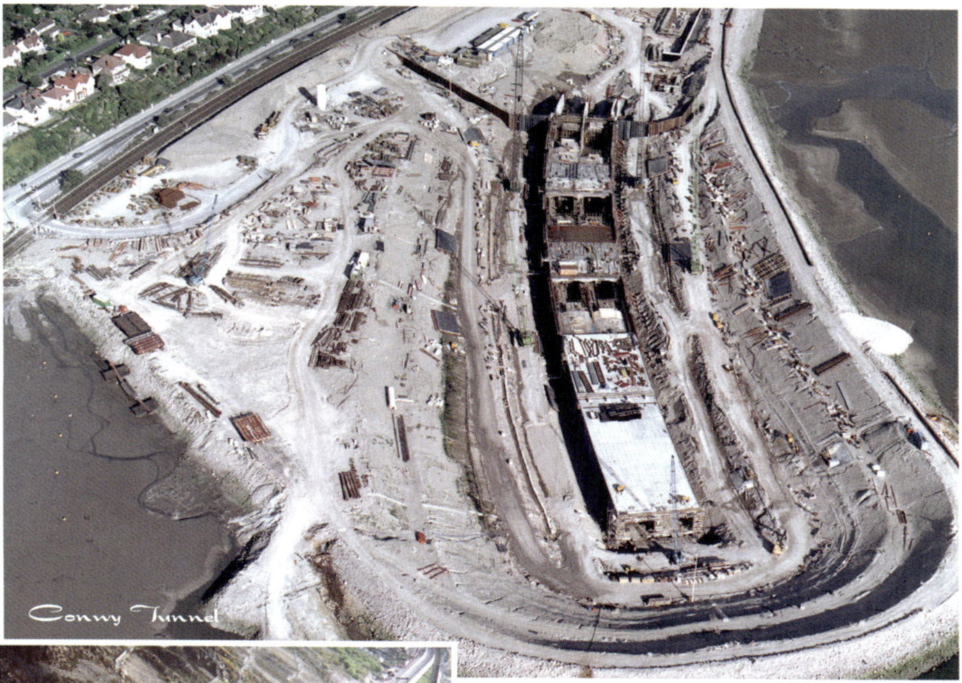

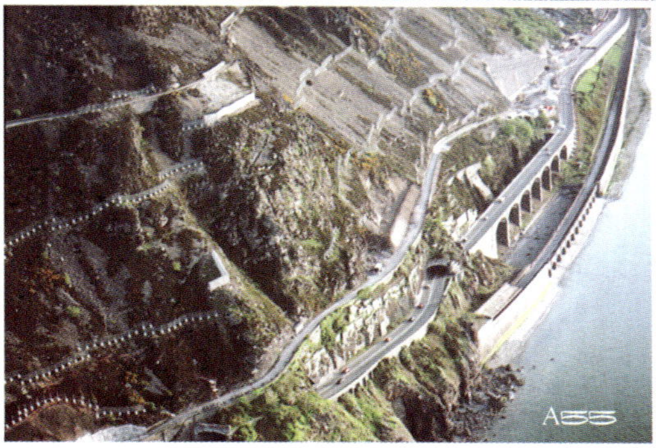

- The Pen-y-Clip Tunnel between Penmaenmawr and Llanfairfechan was bored into shattered volcanic rock. The rockface is secured by 5100 rockbolts, smooth steel and cold concrete.

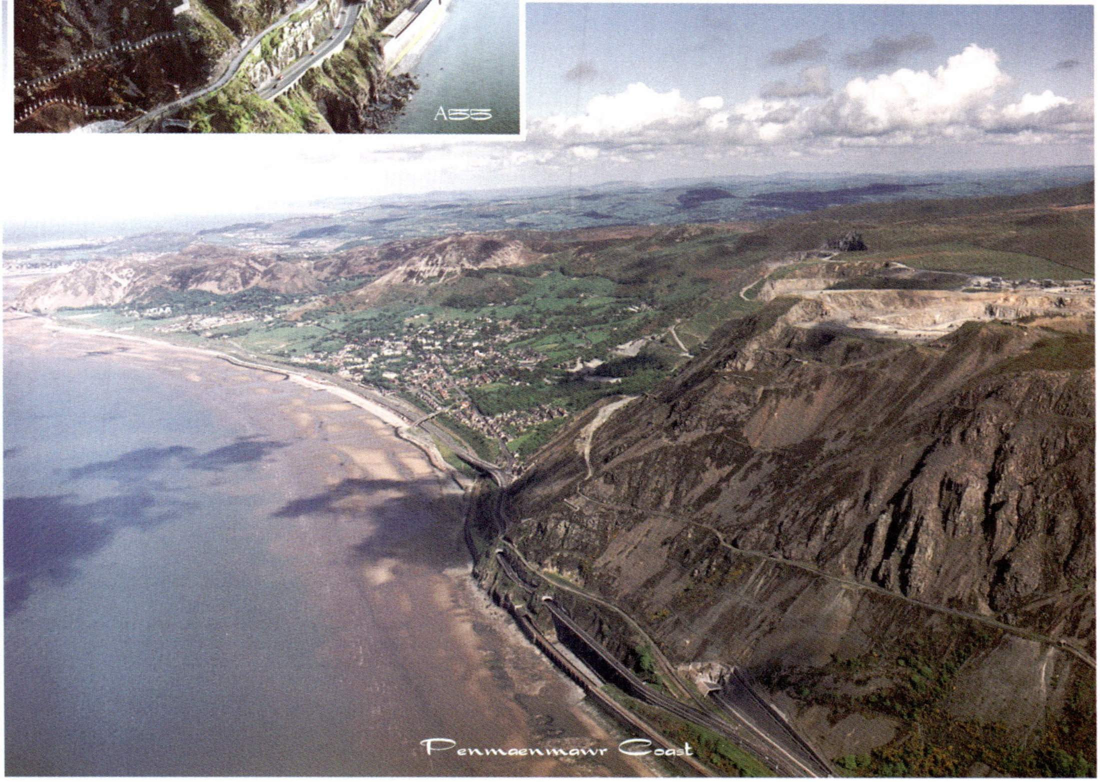

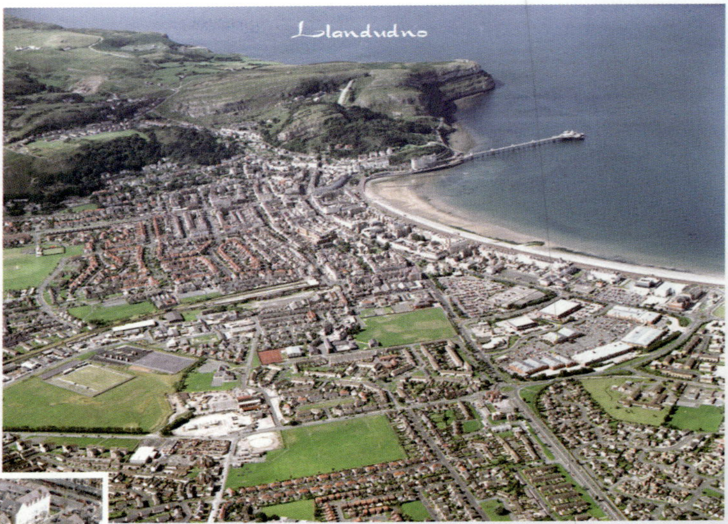

● Llandudno is called the "Queen of Resorts" because of the graceful Victorian hotels sweeping the wide sandy bay. On the Great Orme a herd of wild shaggy goats roam which were presented to Queen Victoria by the Shah of Persia. The goats were used as mascots for the Royal Welsh Fusiliers. Walkers on the sea-girdled Orme need not worry as they are said to be rather shy and not at all aggressive!

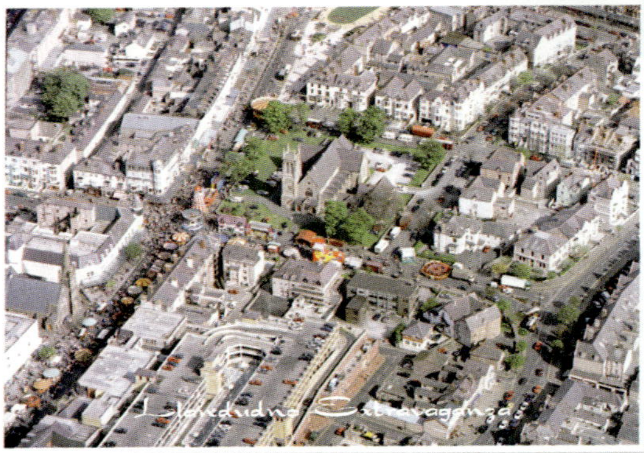

Queen of Shades

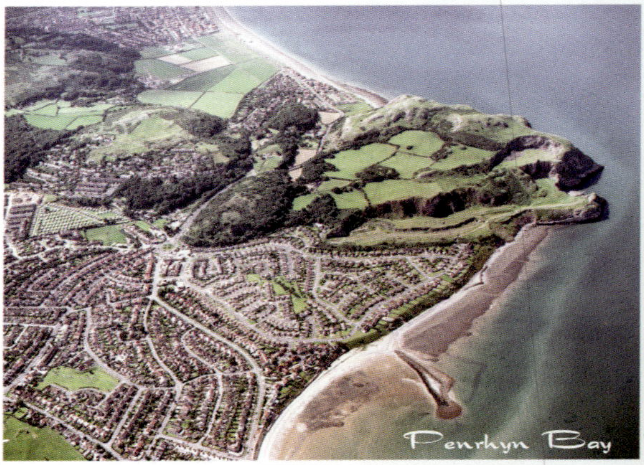

● For three razzle-dazzle days every May bank holiday Llandudno erupts into a Victorian Extravaganza. Retailers and residents wear Victorian dress, and a Victorian fairground takes over the streets, creating a sense of days gone by.

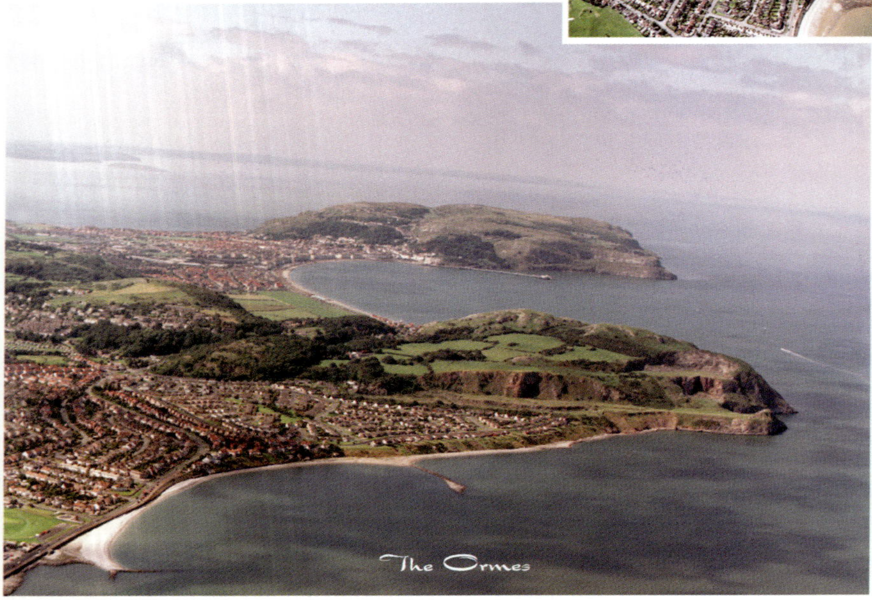

● Stone Age people lived in limestone caves on the Great Orme 30,000 years ago. During Victorian Times a couple and their 13 children also lived in one of the caves. They were very happy there but were evicted when Marine Drive was built.

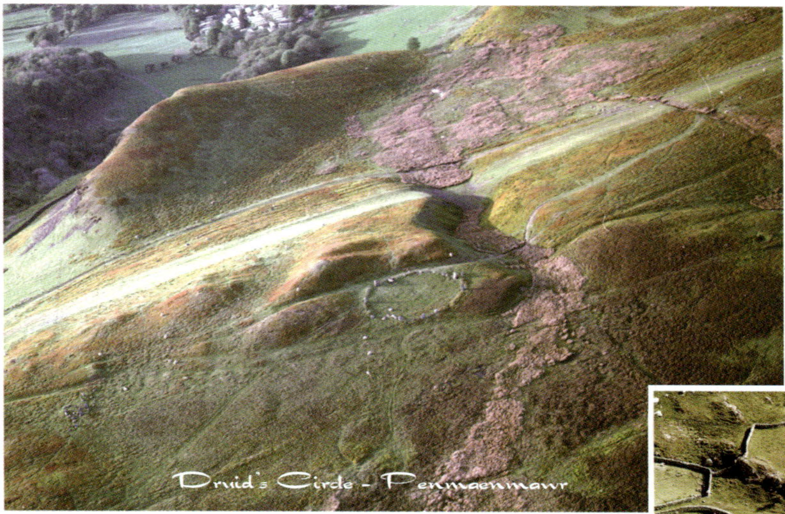

Druid's Circle - Penmaenmawr

• The Druid's Circle was erected by Bronze Age people, not druids. One hollowed flat stone is called the Stone of Sacrifice because the cremated bones of children were found in the Circle. The Deity Stone is shaped like a human; do not swear near it or it will lean over and hit you!

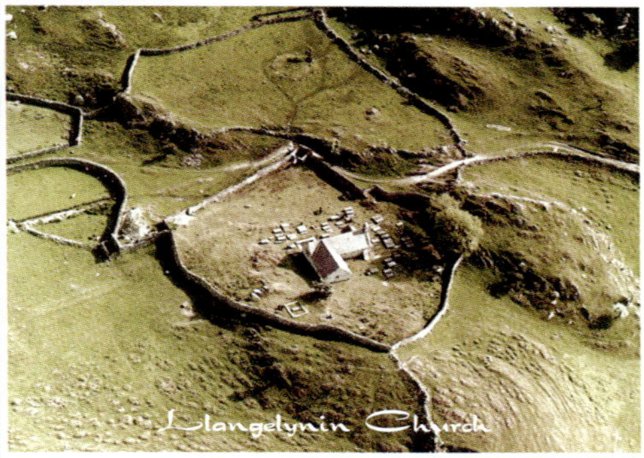

Llangelynin Church

• Our earliest churches were founded in the 5th to 7th centuries during the Age of the Saints when many holymen wandered the land. The churchyards were circular, and the church was aligned with the shadow of a cross held up at sunrise.

Serene Effects

• Like many Welsh villages, Bethesda's name has its origins in the religious revival which swept North Wales in the 1800s. Glan Ogwen it used to be called, after the river which runs through the Ogwen Valley, but the chapel's name of Bethesda took precedence in the end. Above the town, the rollicking mountains of the Carneddau loom. Carnedd Llywelyn and Carnedd Dafydd take their names from two Welsh princes.

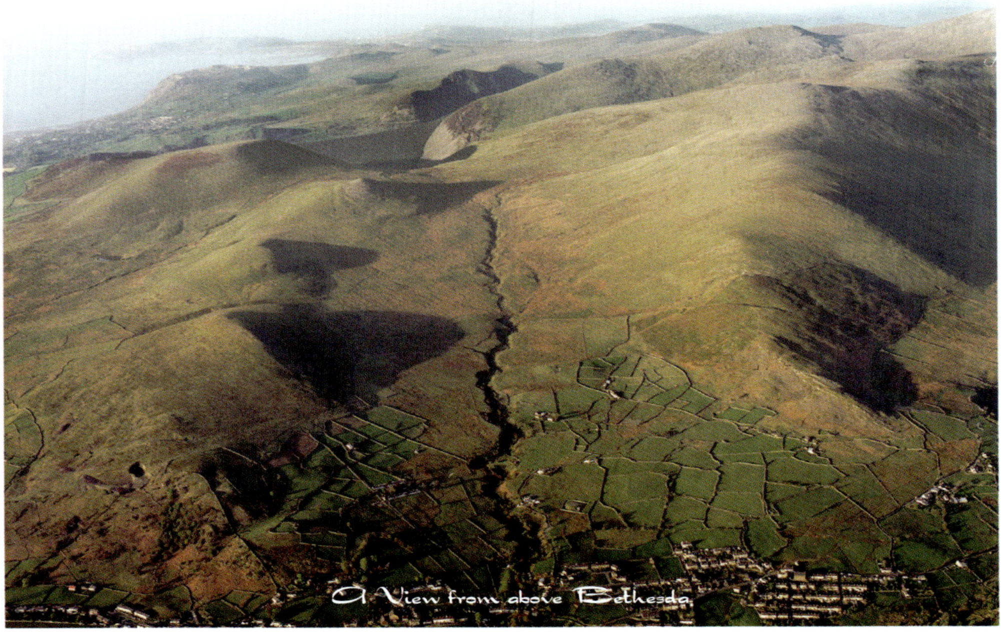

A View from above Bethesda

Splashes of Green

The River Conwy begins its life bubbling from a still grey lake amongst the purple Migneint moors. Then it curls and wanders, sometimes sleepily, sometimes hurtling over rocks and waterfalls, between the harsh mountains of the Carneddau and the gentler Clwydian hills.

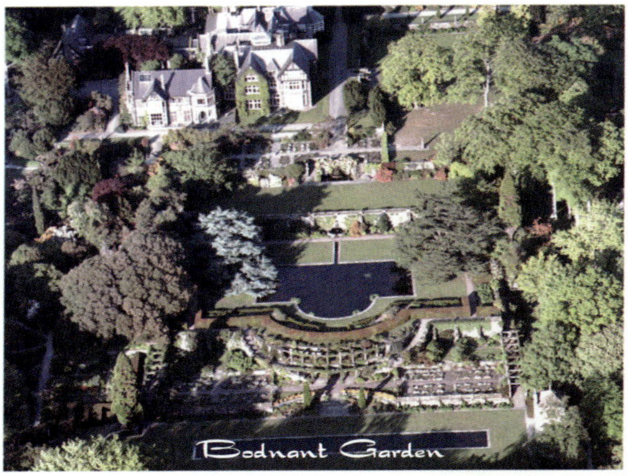

Bodnant Garden

An outlaw named Dafydd ap Siencyn lived in a cave in the woods above Gwydir Castle. Dafydd was a fine archer with bow and arrow, and he took from the rich to give to the poor. Once he fired an arrow to split a pudding about to be eaten by reapers on the other side of the Conwy! Downriver Bodnant Garden is a mosaic of summer colours, helped by generations of green-fingered gardeners, cleverly born with the apt surname of Puddle.

Sailing ships came on the tide as far upriver as Trefriw, and paddle steamers chugged up during Edwardian summers. Earlier still, Roman galleons moored up by Caerhun fort. Their ships brought good wine from Spain and Italian glasses. In return they exported the warm red woollen cloth of the Celts and smooth pearls scooped up from the riverbed.

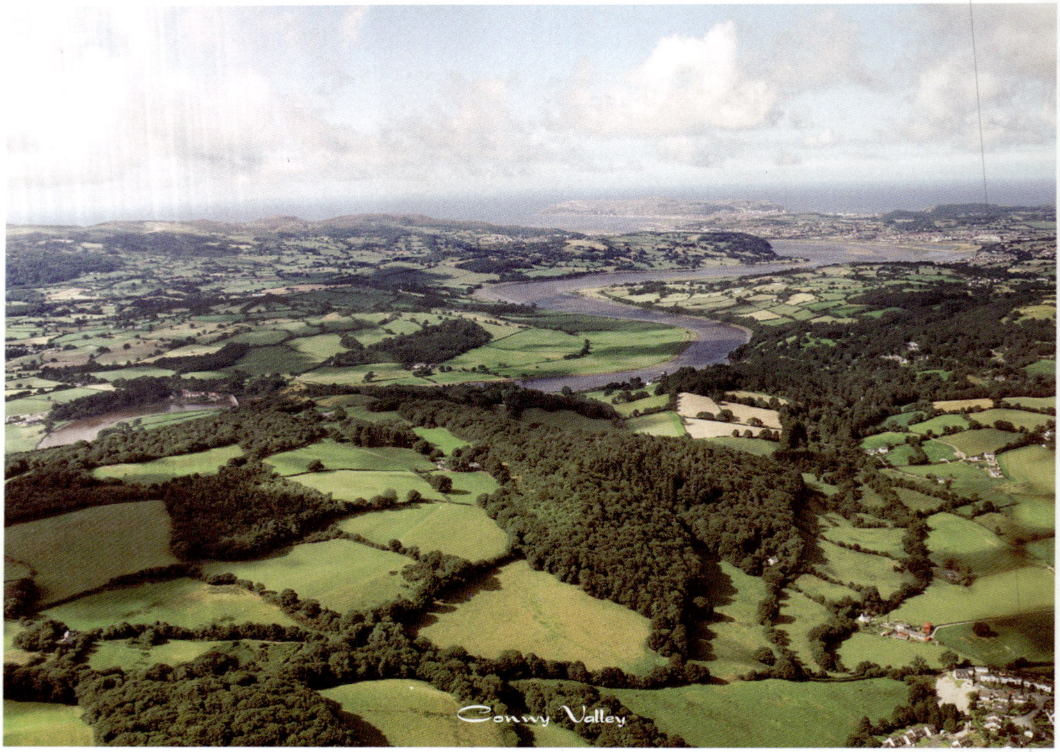

Conwy Valley

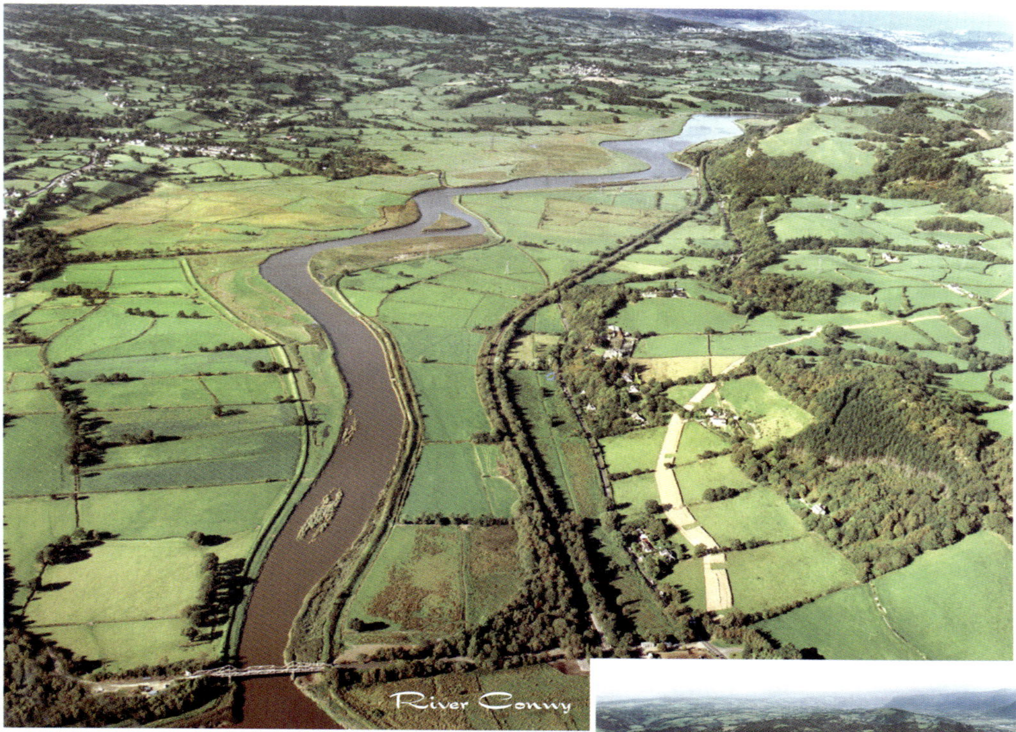
River Conwy

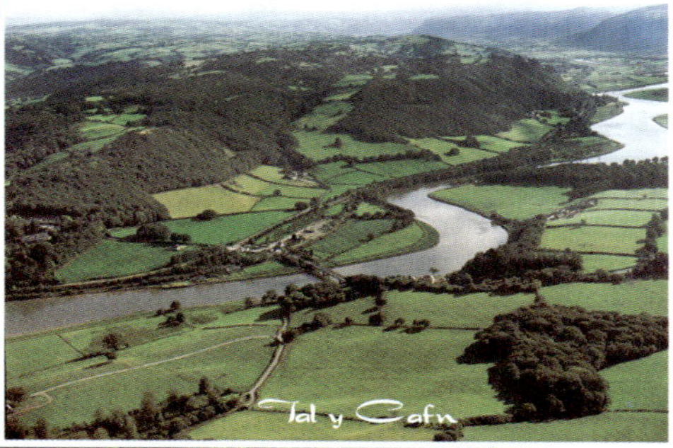
Tal y Cafn

• Llanrwst was famous for harpmakers and clockmakers. One elderly craftsman lived in the almshouses of Llanrwst but would never finish a harp there. He said that the chatter of the old women would ruin the mellow tones of his instruments.

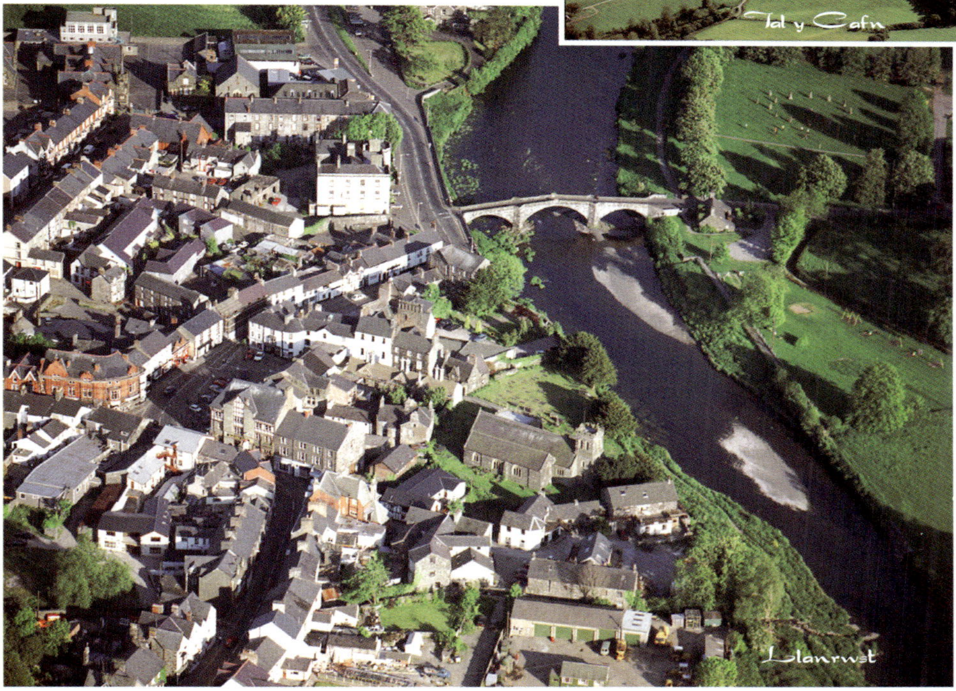
Llanrwst

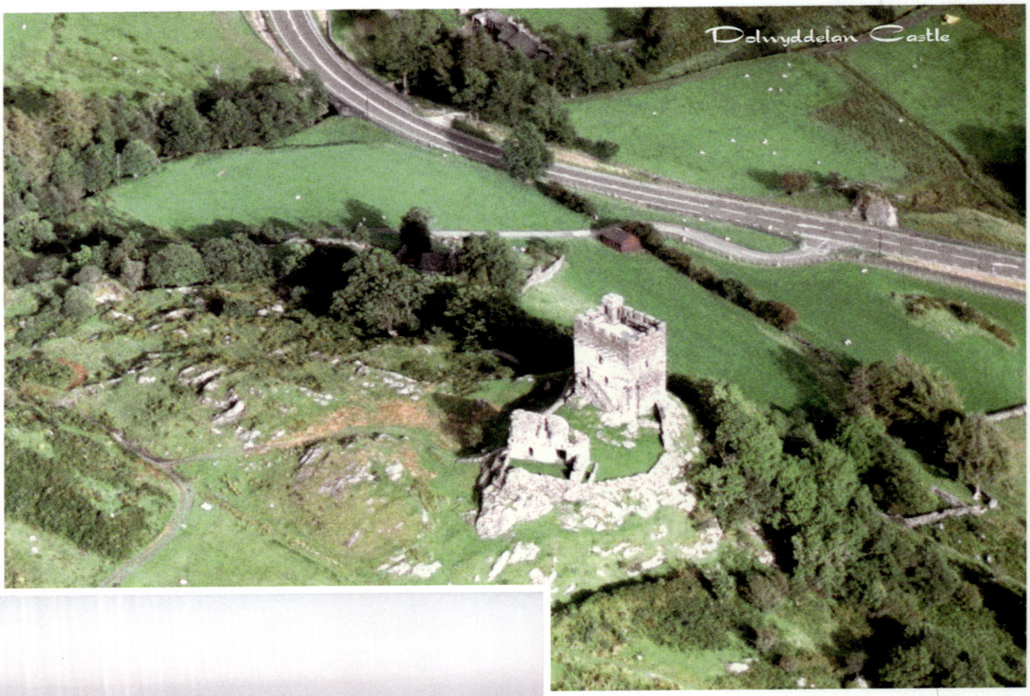

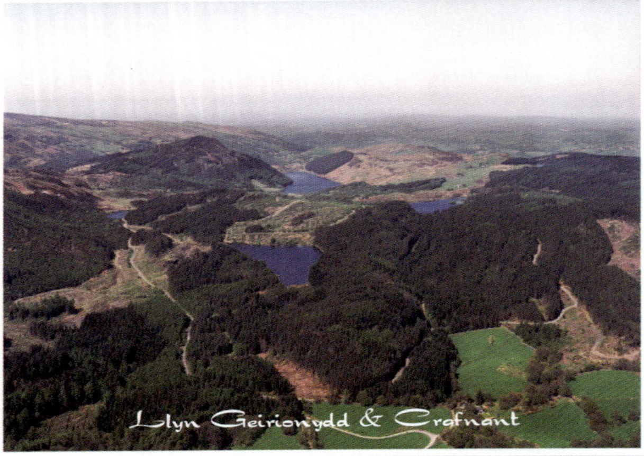

In the 12th Century Llywelyn the Great, Prince of Aberffraw and Lord of Snowdon, built his remote and lonely castle on a craggy rockface beneath the shadows of Moel Siabod. He was born in the green-meadowed Dolwyddelan valley below and died in 1240.

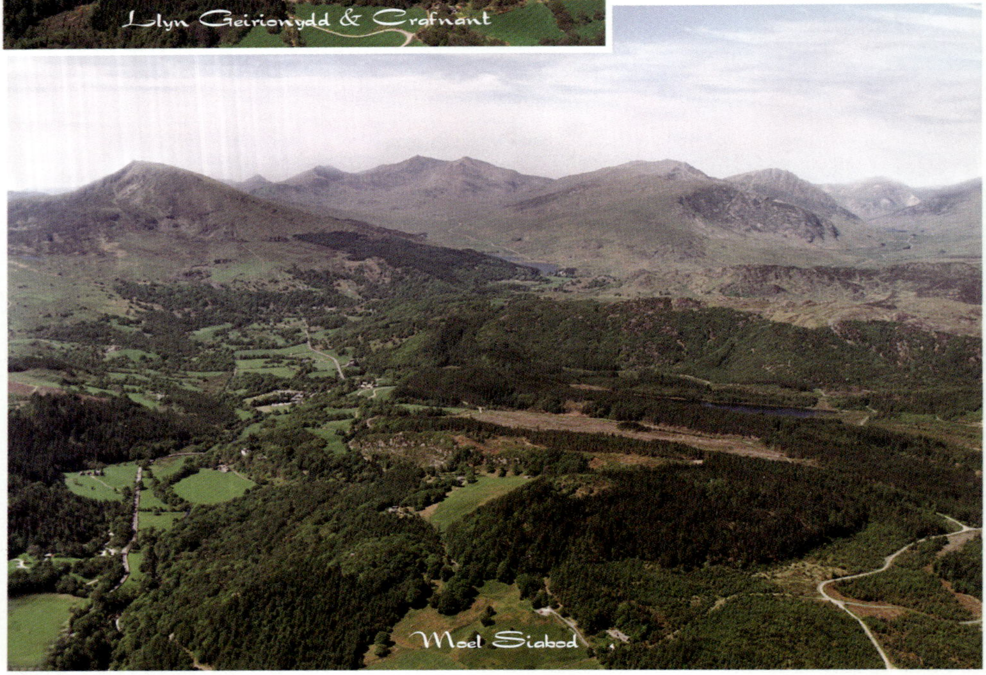

Rustic Moods

- Capel Curig lies at the heart of Snowdonia and was a welcome break for Romans travelling from their villas on the Llyn. A small fort on flat land by the riverbank had a guest house well supplied with jars of wine.

- The Royal Bridge across the twin lakes of Mymbyr offers rainbow views of Snowdon and leads on to the fir-treed slopes of Moel Siabod.

- Beneath the purple Migneint moors the Afon Machno winds along the valley from Penmachno. It's an ancient settlement, and the village church contains five 5th/6th century gravestones enscribed in Latin.

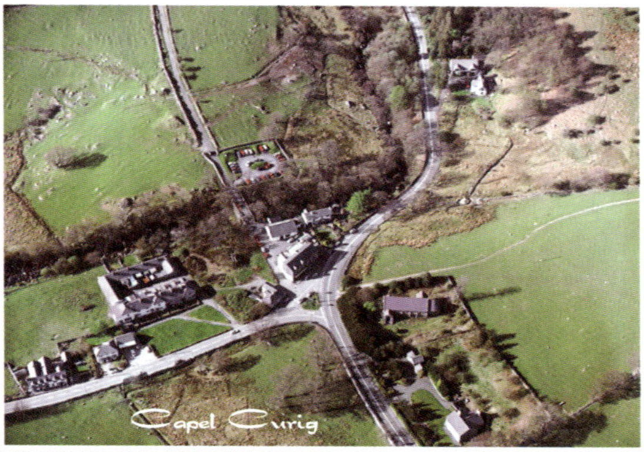

Capel Curig

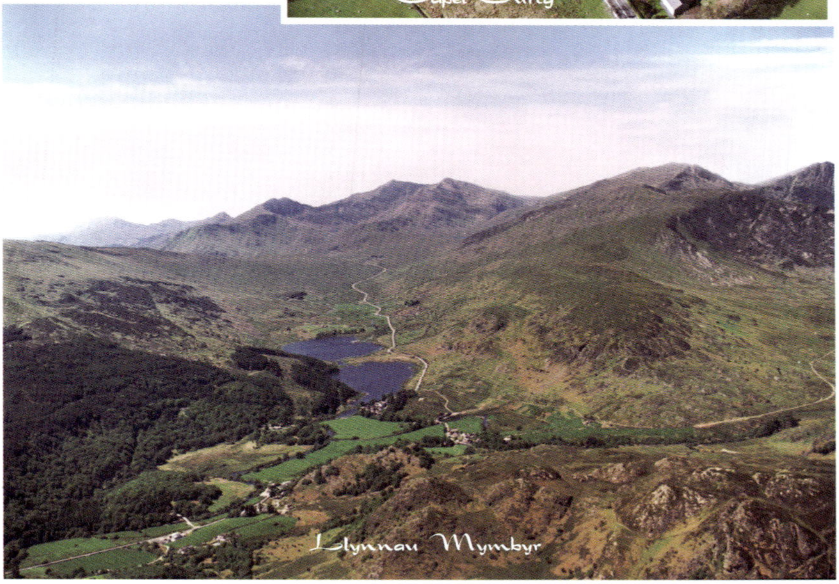

Llynnau Mymbyr

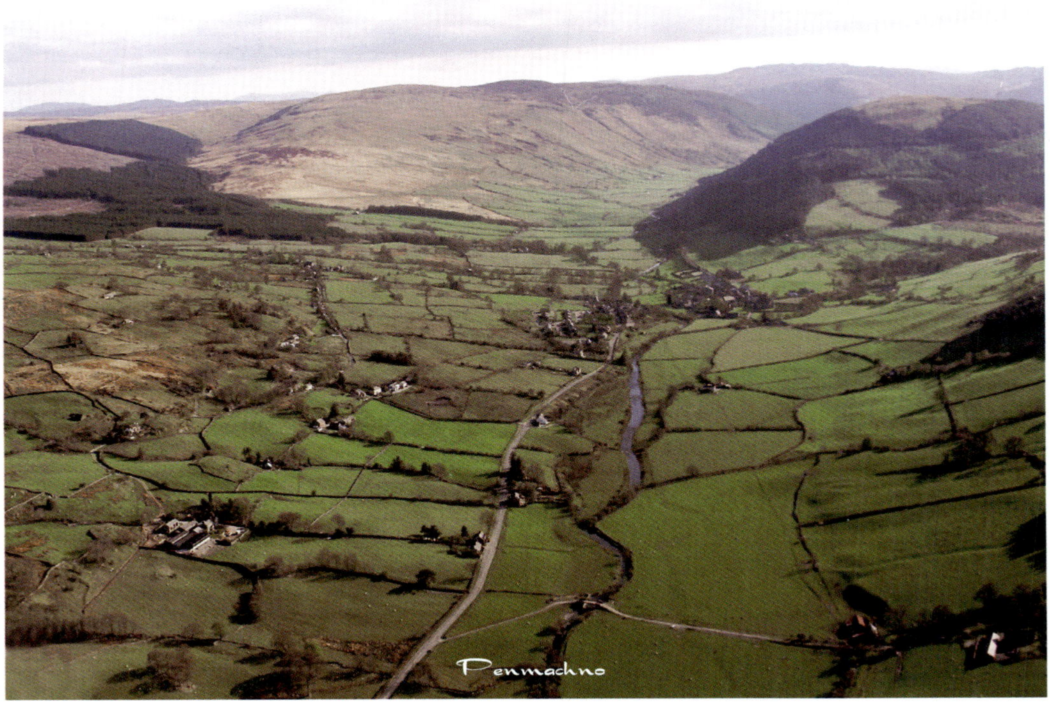

Penmachno

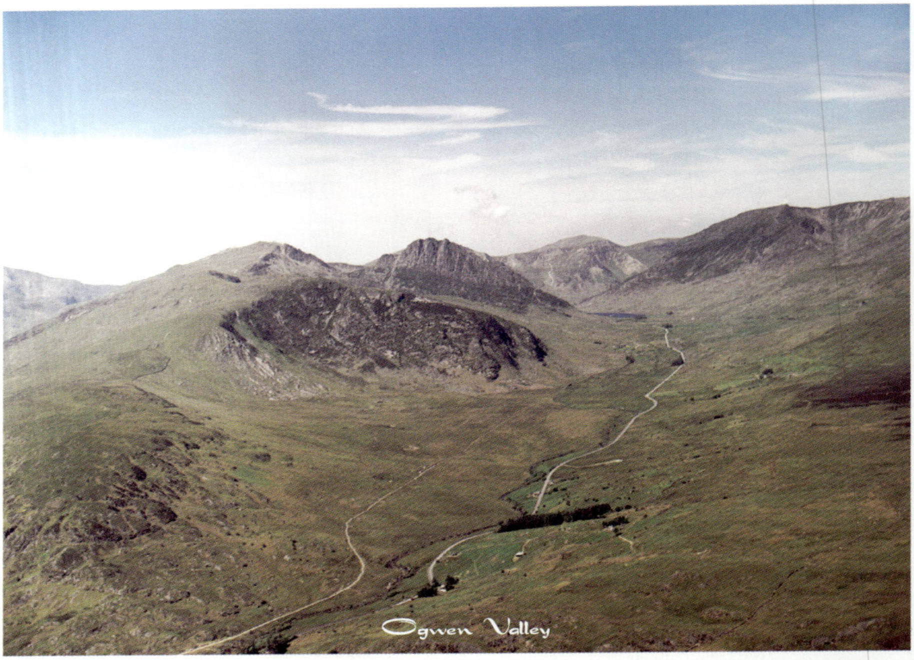

Ogwen Valley

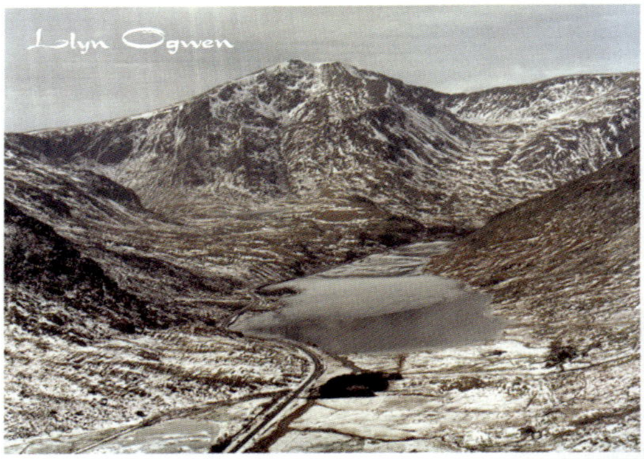

Llyn Ogwen

● During the last Ice Age glaciers 2,000' (600m) thick overlaid Wales. One glacier scooped out the basin of Cwm Idwal and inched its way northwards, rounding out the Nant Ffrancon Valley. The ice retreated, leaving the white Snowdon Lily isolated in the mountains.

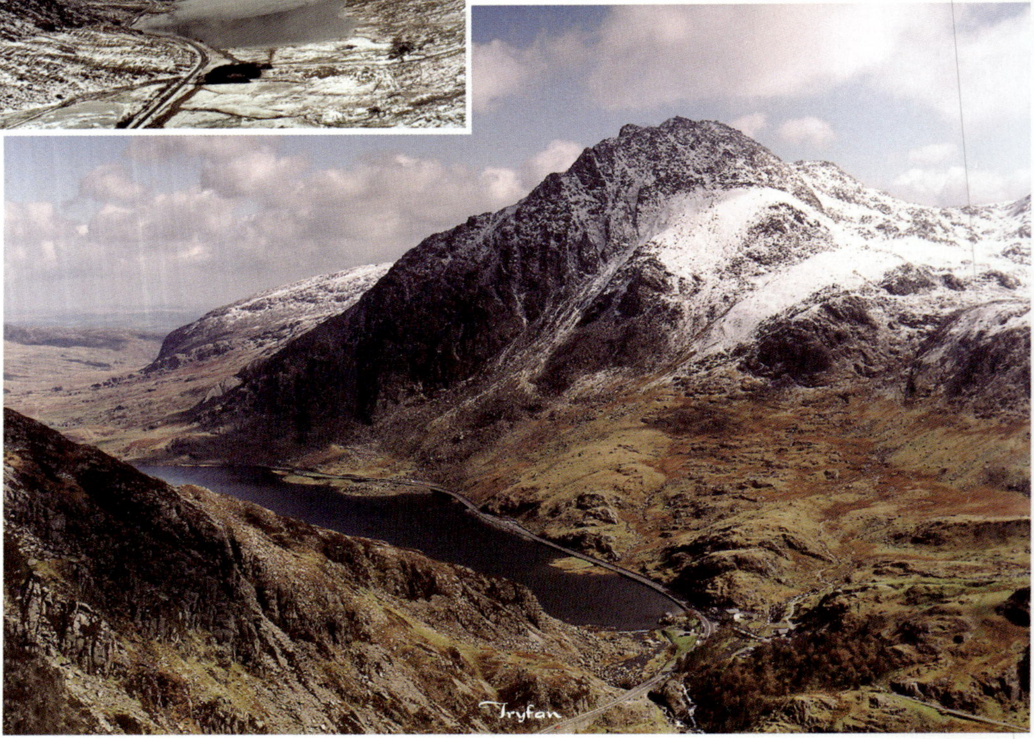

Tryfan

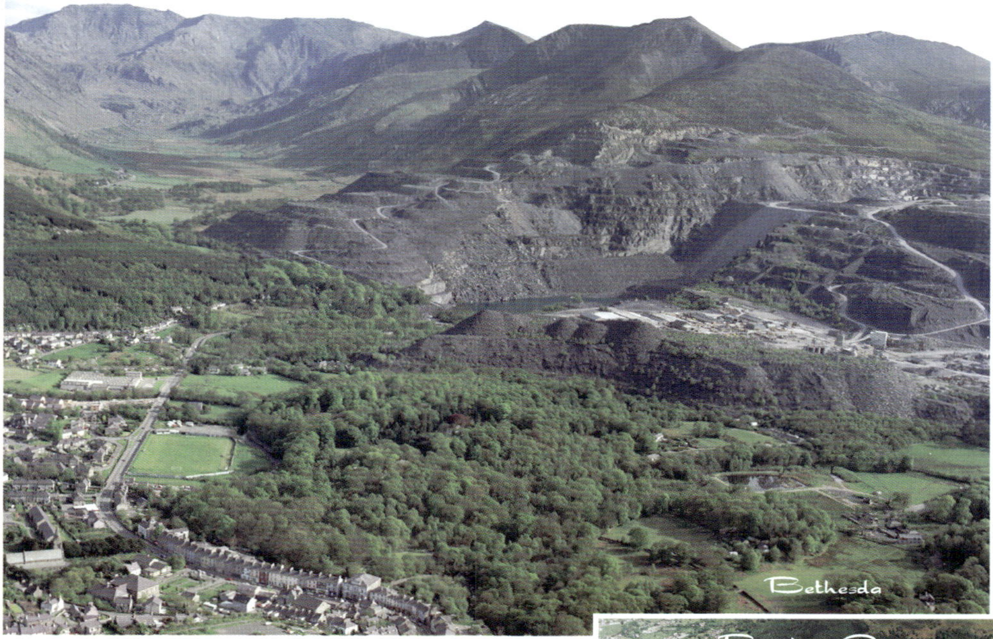

Bethesda

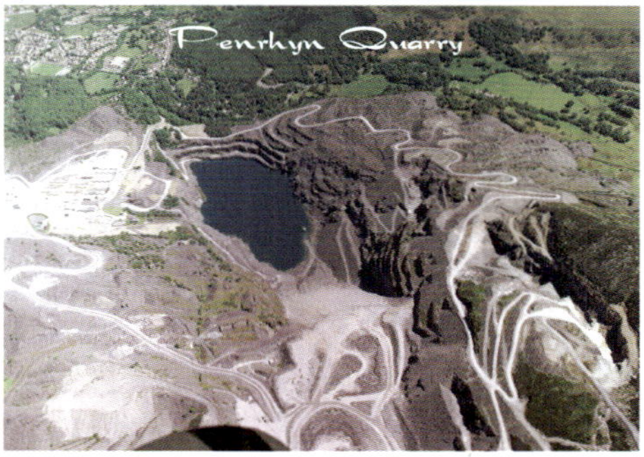

Penrhyn Quarry

• Nearly 3,000 quarrymen walked out from their silver-trailed quarry over Lord Penrhyn's attempt to squash the Union. When some men were tempted back, their house windows were broken. Troops were sent in, the Riot Act read, and the strikers were forced to return after 3 years.

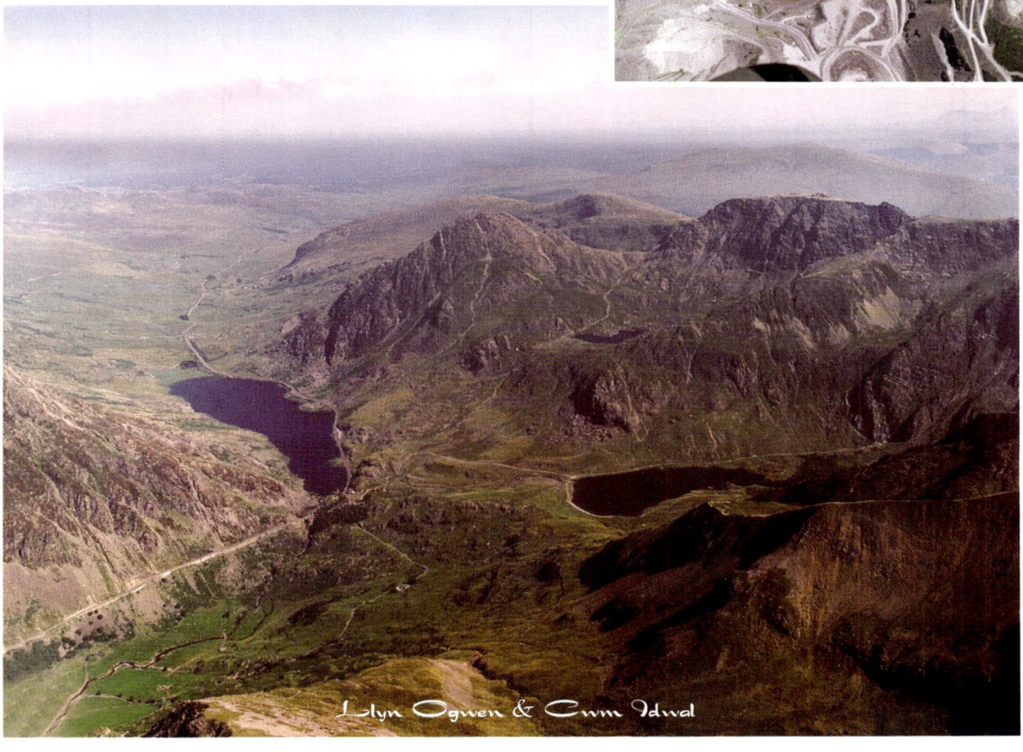

Llyn Ogwen & Cwm Idwal

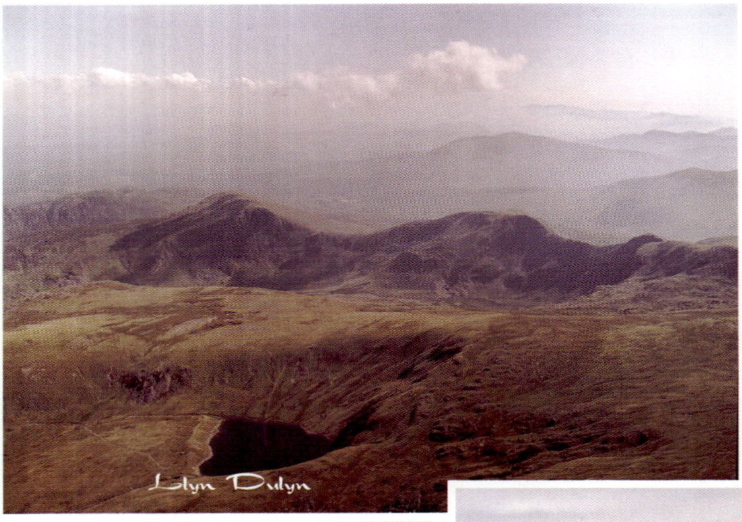

● The Carneddau Range includes many mountains between the Ogwen Valley and the coast, but it takes its name from two of the highest ones. Carnedd Llywelyn was named after Prince Llywelyn, and Carnedd Dafydd after his brother. They were the last Princes of Wales and were beheaded by Edward I, but their memories live on forever in the minds of Welsh people.

● Within the Carneddau mountains are several lakes, such as Crafnant and Geirionydd. Others, like Eigiau and Cowlyd, are reservoirs. Llyn Dulyn (the Black Lake) lies 600' (180m) at the base of Foel Fras and supplies water to Llandudno. Dulyn's sheer cliffs have been the downfall of many aircraft during WW2, and their wrecks can be found beneath the metallic blue water.

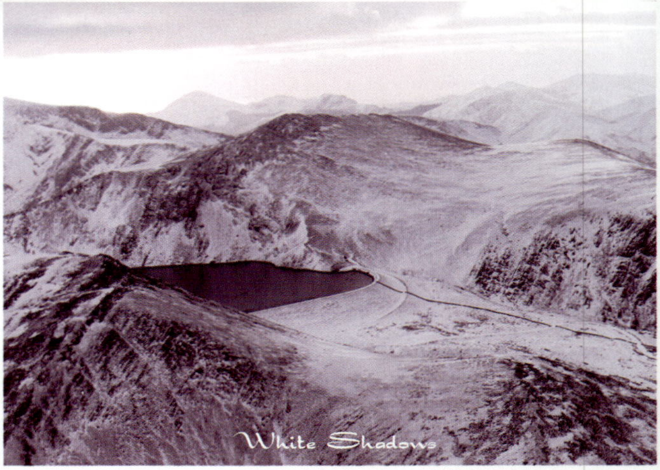

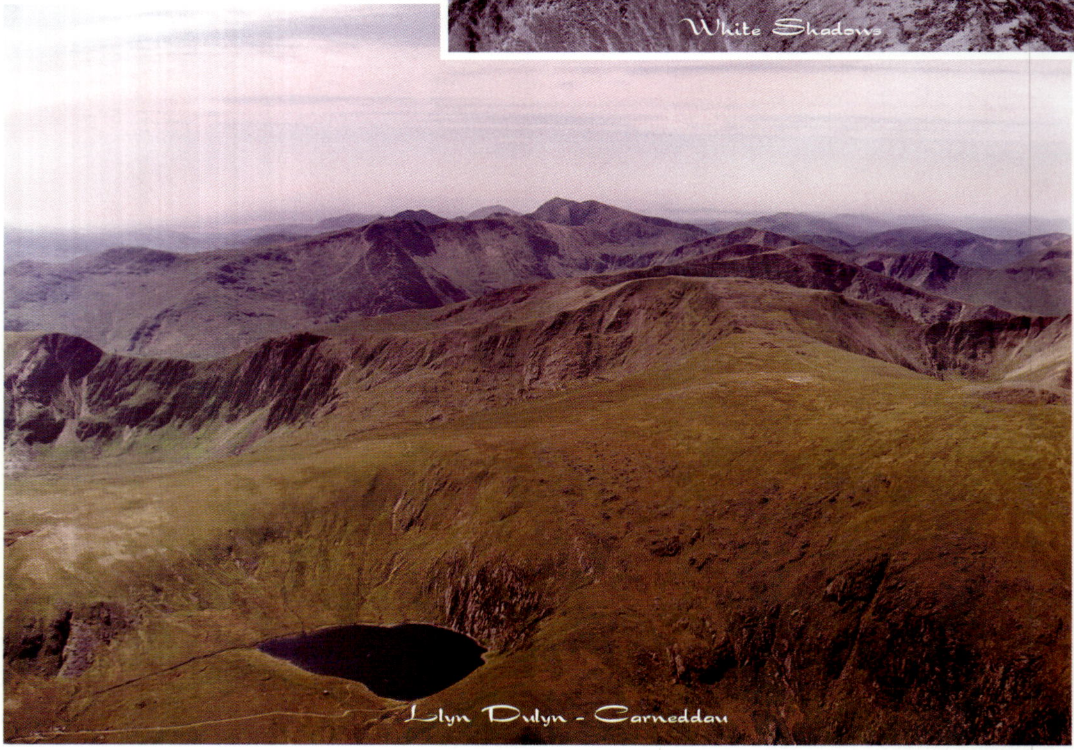

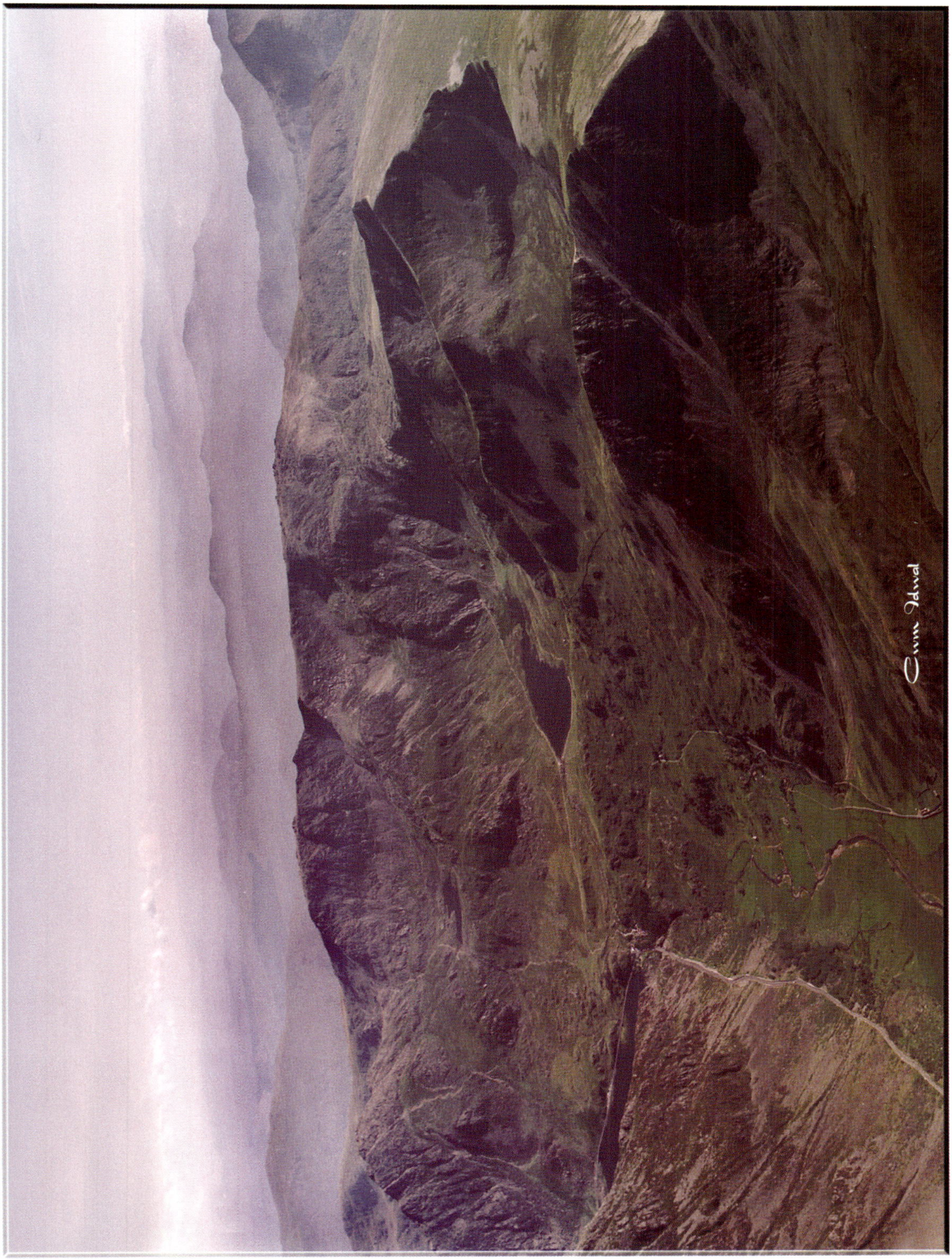
Cwm Idwal

Grains of Time

Imagine North Wales 540 million years ago. The climate was warm because Wales lay where South Africa is today. It was part of a large landmass, and an ocean separated the Welsh continent from another one. Periodically, seas deposited thick layers of sands and muds. Into the mudstone volcanoes injected copper and gold, or it was metamorphosed into the slate of Llanberis and Bethesda.

After fifty million tides the two continents moved towards each other, and submarine volcanoes and volcanic islands were thrown up into the narrowing ocean. Many of Snowdonia's mountains are made of rocks from this explosive age but none were ever volcanoes themselves.

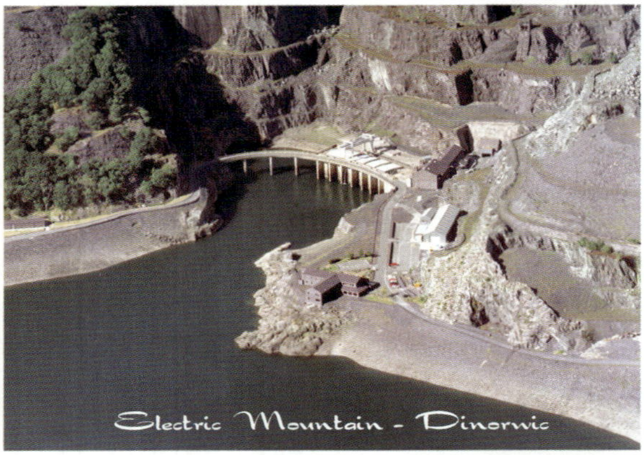

Electric Mountain - Dinorwic

The two continents collided, then Wales drifted northwards over the Equator. The Ice Ages came and went. Neanderthal Man walked into Britain with the warmer weather and walked out again in colder times. The ice melted and sea-levels rose, cutting off Britain from Europe. The ice left a trail of erratic rocks and u-shaped valleys. Lakes formed in the valleys and cwms, and on the mountainsides Stone Age man hunted deer and wild boar amongst the trees.

- Landscape artist JMW Turner was a Londoner from Covent Garden but he loved painting the natural palette of Welsh castles, rivers and waterfalls. His picture of Dolbadarn Castle by Lakes Padarn and Peris beneath Mount Snowdon gained him membership of the Royal Academy at the age of twenty six.

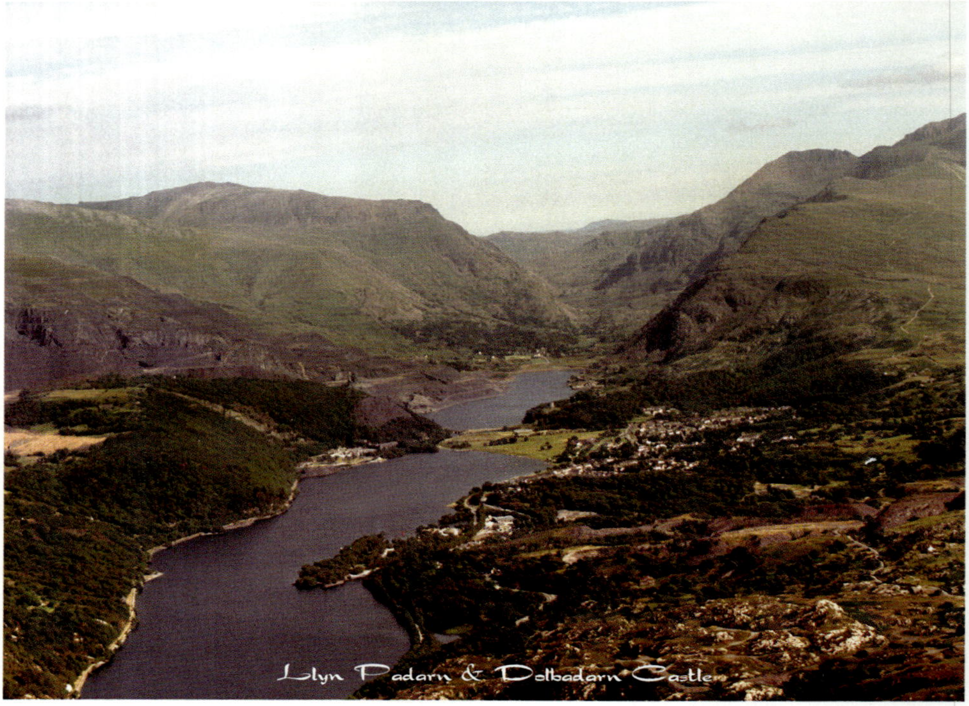

Llyn Padarn & Dolbadarn Castle

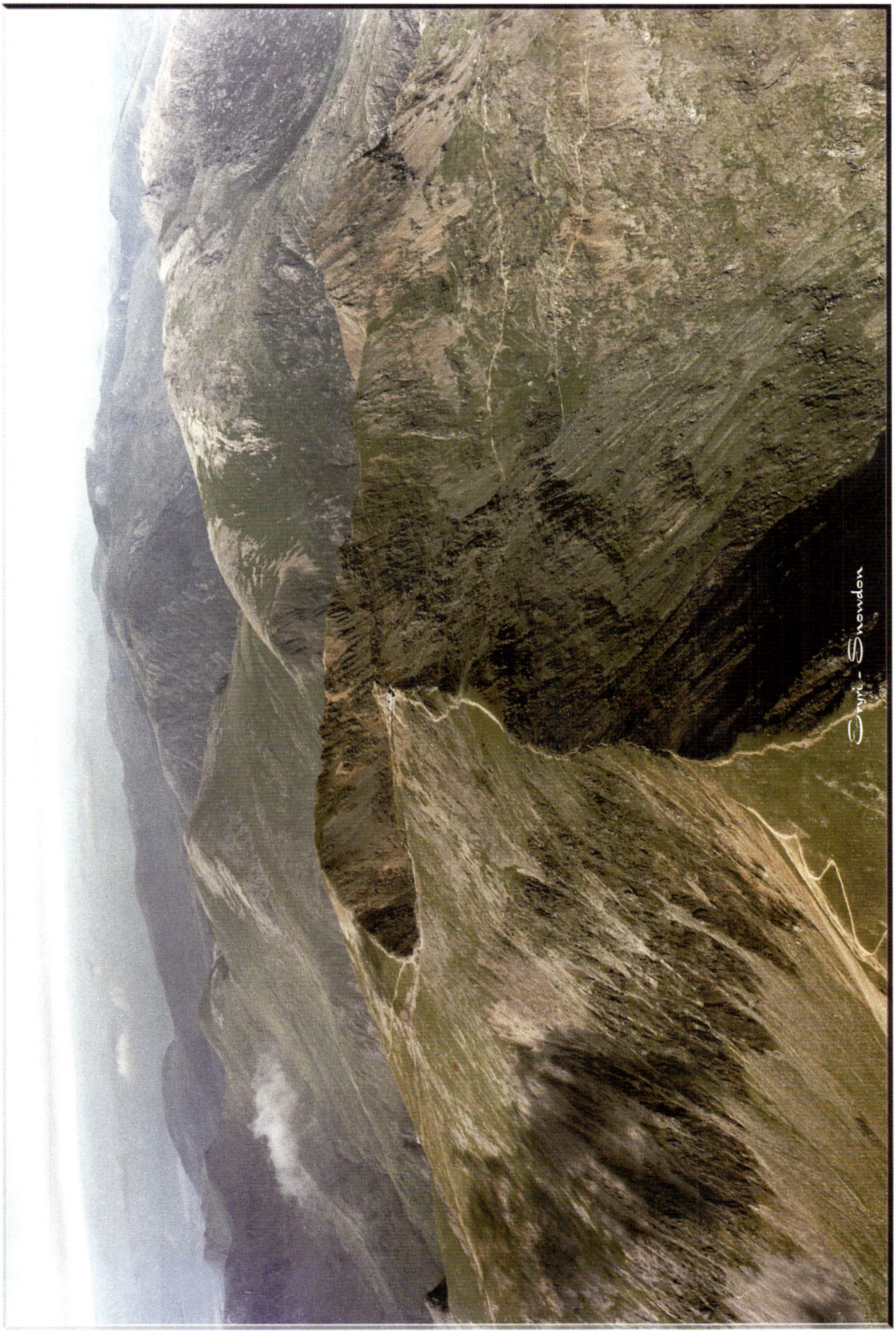
Eryri - Snowdon

● On the Glyders the wind moans among the cotton-wool rocks of the Castle of Winds.

● Victorians would pay 12 shillings (60 new pence) for a pony ride up Snowdon. The guide would take any luggage, and there would be brandy or sherry along the way. Today the Snowdon Mountain Railway takes passengers in comfort. The only accident happened to the first train on the first morning. The steam engine overturned and one passenger jumped to his death. Since then, no engine has been called Number 1.

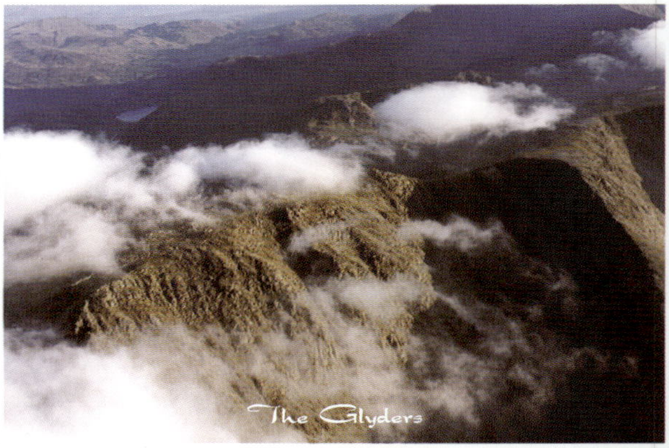
The Glyders

Creeping Shadows

● The Miner's Track up Snowdon crosses Llyn Llydaw. The Watkin Path passes blue-ice waterfalls and was made by Sir Edward Watkin of Beddgelert. He also built a mini version of the Eiffel Tower on the future site of Wembley Stadium. His was demolished, as were the Stadium's twin towers in 2003.

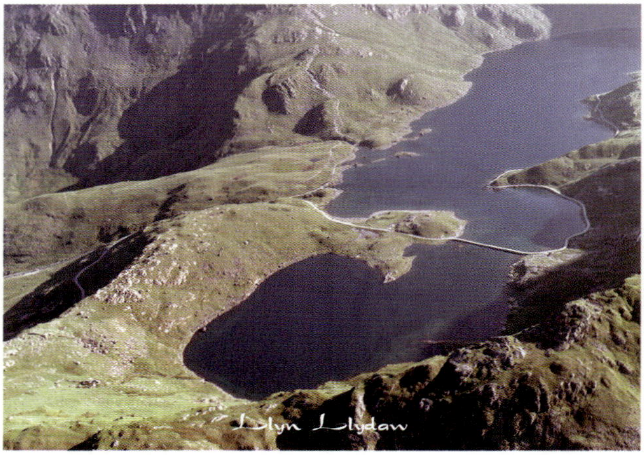
Llyn Llydaw

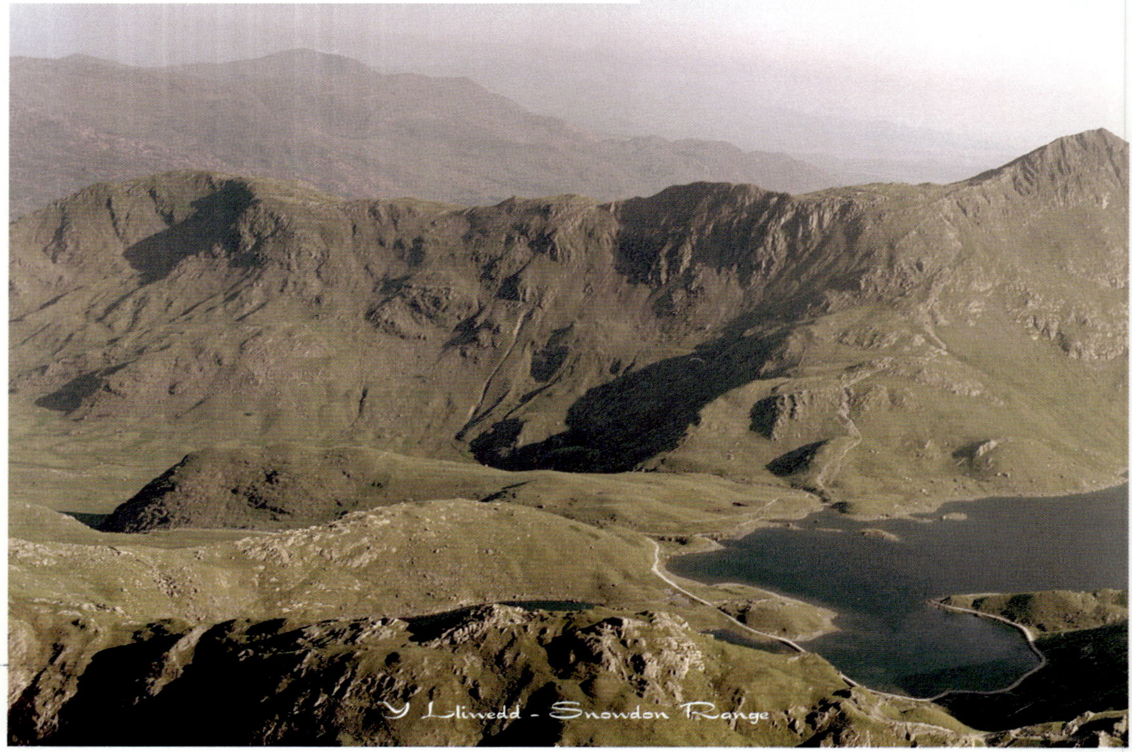
Y Lliwedd - Snowdon Range

Purple Crumble

At the head of the Nantlle Valley the Great Elephant (Mynydd Mawr) stands guard over purple slate tips and flooded blue quarries. Unlike the vast slate quarries of Bethesda, Llechwedd and Llanberis the ones in Nantlle were small and many, and now numerous open pits scar the sides and valley floors.

Cooling the feet of Mynydd Mawr is Llyn Dywarchen, which is famous for its floating island, one of the Wonders of Wales. The astronomer Haley climbed aboard its soggy turf, reporting it to be about 6 by 4 yards (5.5 by 4.5 metres) wide. Cattle have been seen wandering lazily on to the island, grazing unconcernedly, then strolling off the next time it hit shore.

Beyond the Nantlle Valley the Llyn Peninsula narrows its pointing finger at Bardsey Island, the site of pilgrimage for all Welsh saints and sinners.

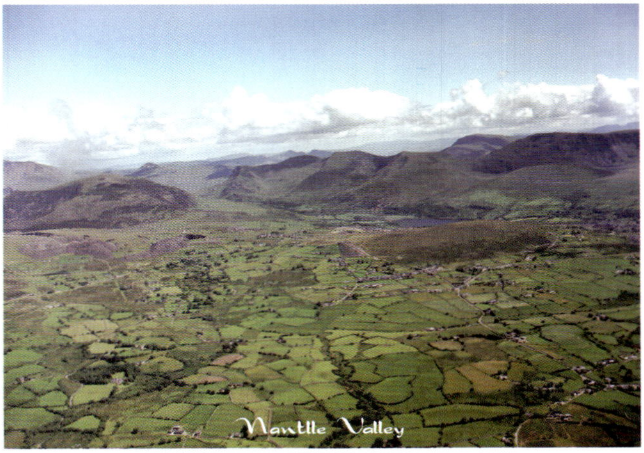
Nantlle Valley

Both sides of the Llyn have fine golden beaches and rocky coves around a backbone of craggy mountains. There are also small villages with centuries of history and mysterious legends attached to their names.

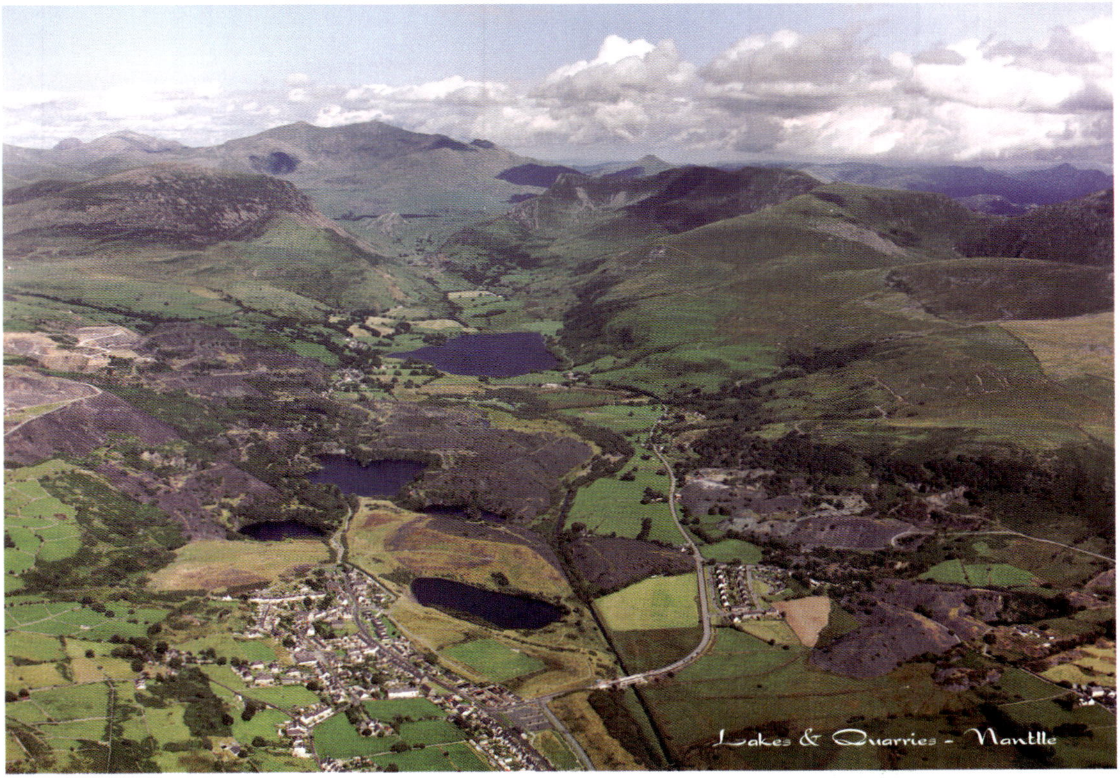
Lakes & Quarries - Nantlle

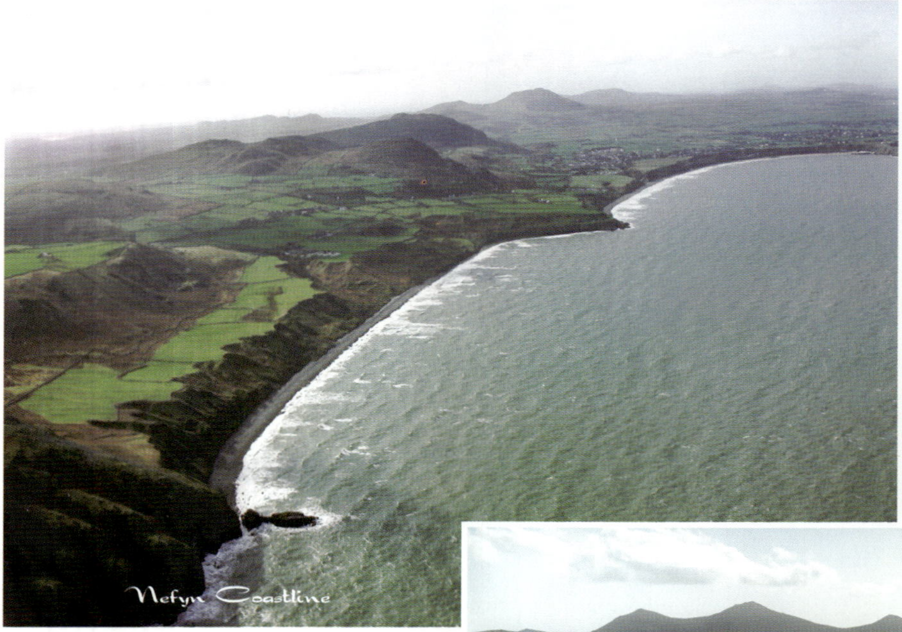

Nefyn Coastline

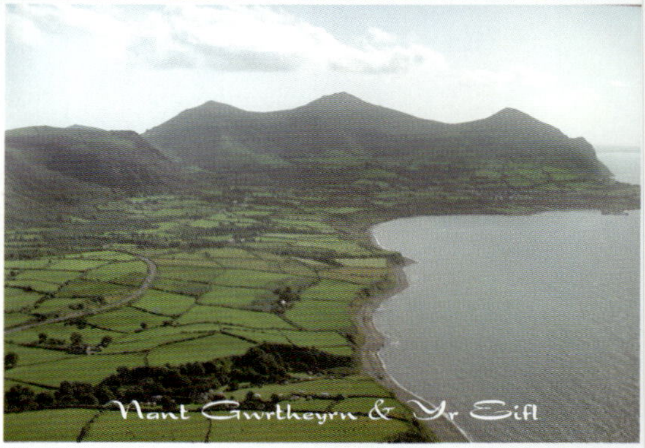

Nant Gwrtheyrn & Yr Eifl

• Nant Gwrtheyrn means stream of the super king, and it's named after Vortigern. He was a king who invited the Saxons to Kent but was forced to flee. He built his castle on an isolated rockface rising sheer above the sea. Today, it's the site of the Welsh Language Centre.

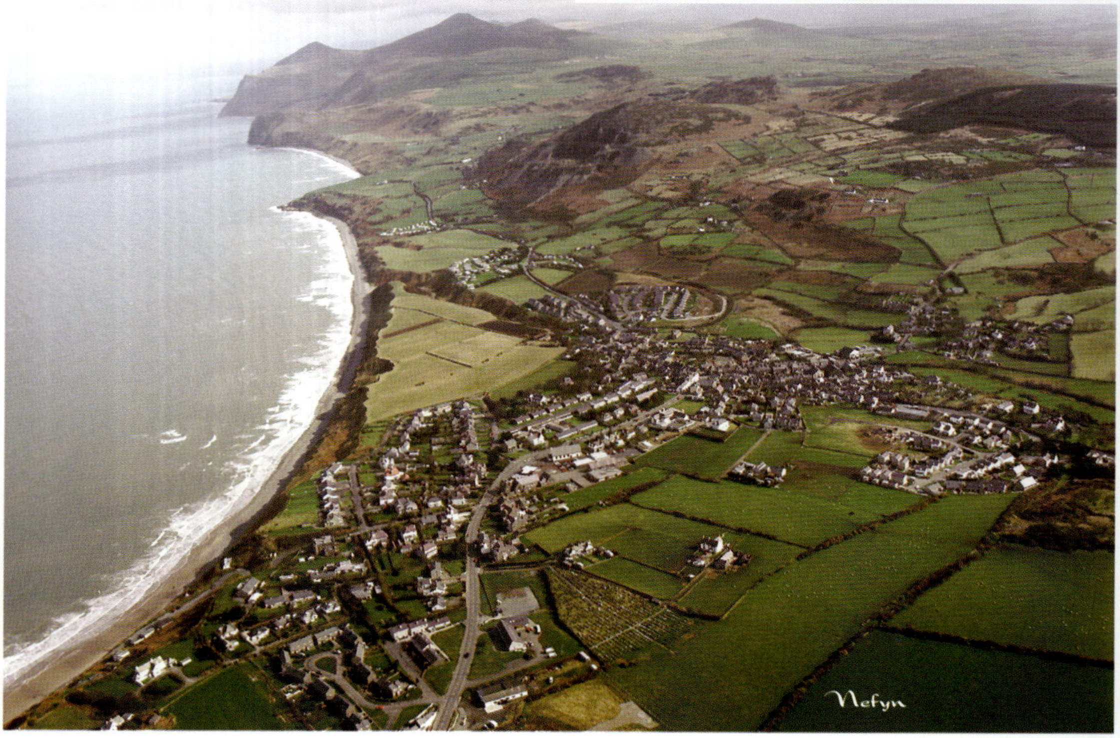

Nefyn

● For a giant it was just a few strides to reach Tre'r Ceiri, the Town of Giants, on top of Yr Eifl (The Rivals). The Celts, however, had to climb over 1500' (460m) before they could settle down snugly in one of the stone huts beneath a turf roof. They were rewarded with views to South Wales and across to Ireland.

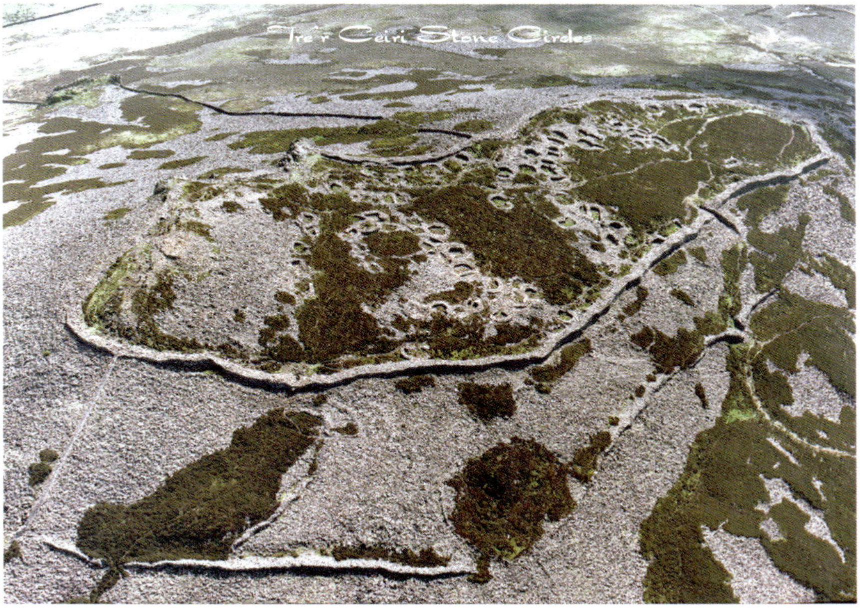
Tre'r Ceiri Stone Circles

Greatness in Grey

● The village of Nefyn was the choice of King Edward I to hold a Round Table (jousting tournament). Alas, he was celebrating his victory over the Princes of Gwynedd. Today the sandy beaches of Morfa Nefyn and Porth Dinllaen are loved by golden-brown sunloving holidaymakers.

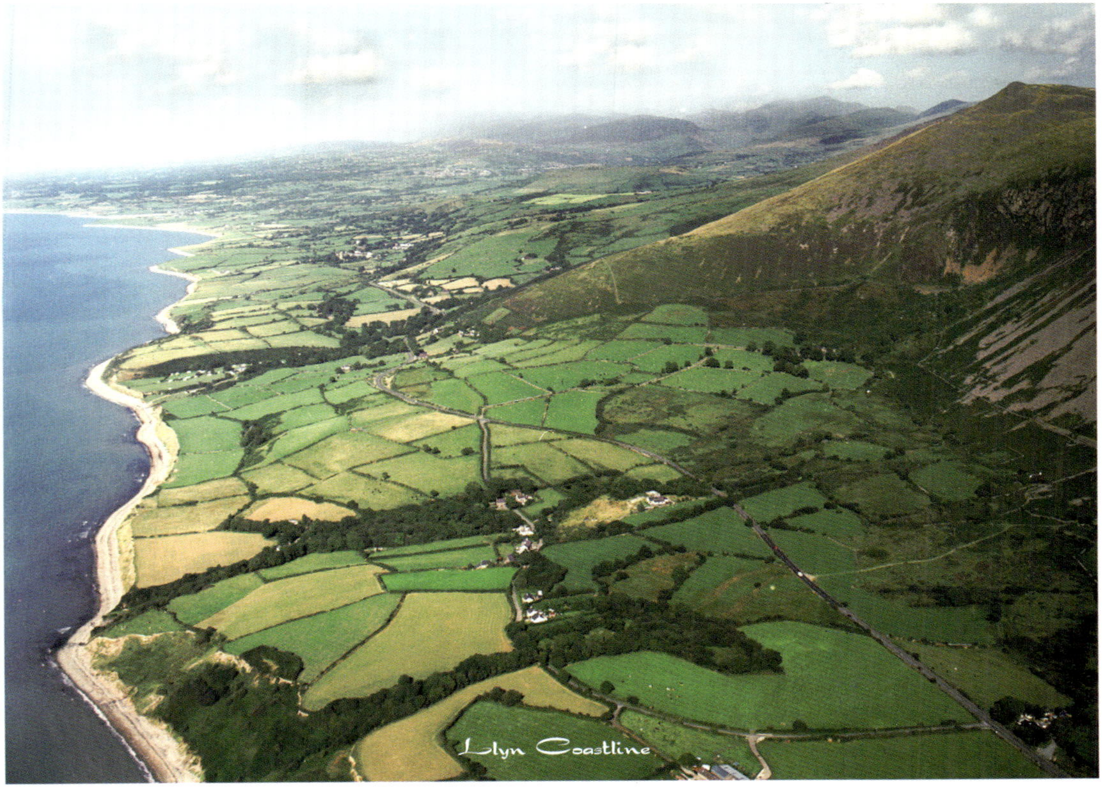
Llyn Coastline

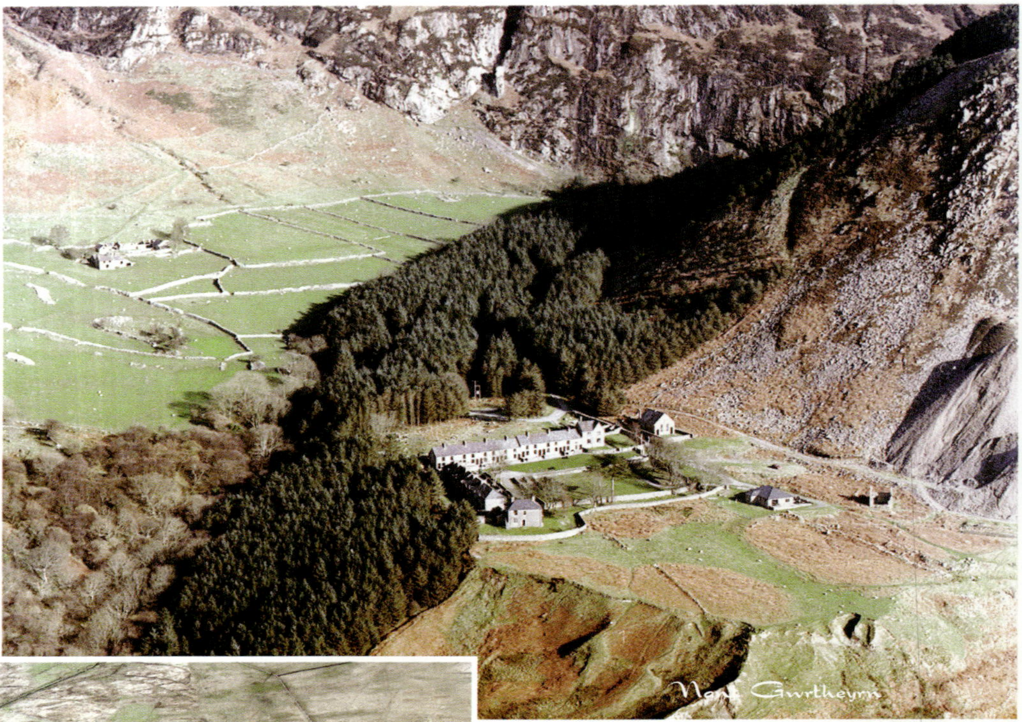

Nant Gwrtheyrn

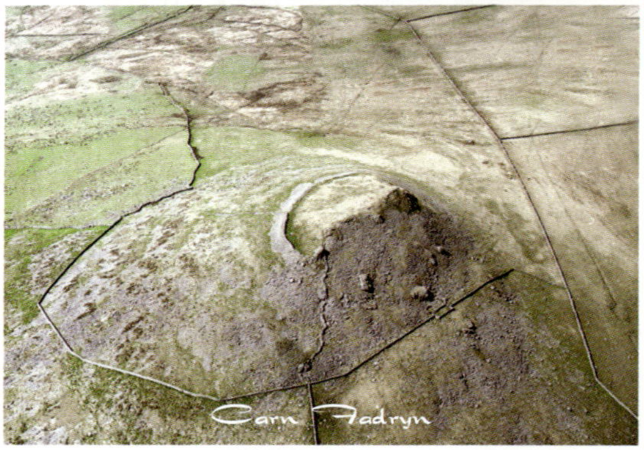

Carn Fadryn

- On the peppermint rock of Carn Fadryn at over 1200' (370m) is a Celtic hillfort consisting of stone huts protected by a defensive wall. The mountain may be named after Modrun, granddaughter of Vortigern the Thin.

In the 12th century the Princes of Gwynedd built a citadel on the site which is one of the earliest stone castles; previously, they were made of timber and packed earth.

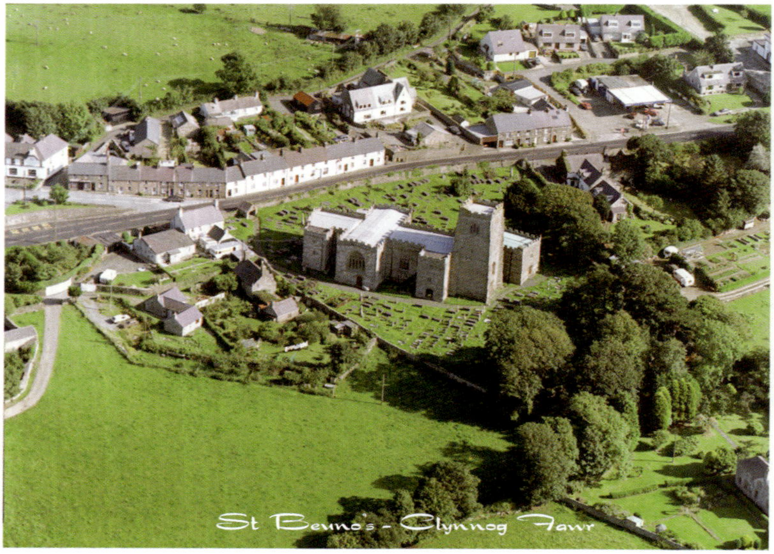

St Beuno's - Clynnog Fawr

- St Beuno, who founded his square-towered Church at Clynnog Fawr, could walk on water. Once he dropped a book into the sea but a curlew rescued it. The grateful saint blessed the bird, which is why its nest on the heather moors can never be found. This was the church of Edgar Christian, who died at 18 years old of starvation in a Canadian log cabin. His adventure to the see the world had gone horrible wrong.

The natural harbour of Porth Dinllaen was the chosen setting for a fort by Iron Age people 3,000 years ago. No wonder, as there are terrific views to the mountains of Ireland and the snowcapped peaks of Snowdonia.

In the 1830s railway engineer Brunel had plans to link Porth Dinllaen to Newtown on the west coast. Other proposals were to run trains from Carmarthen and Worcester.

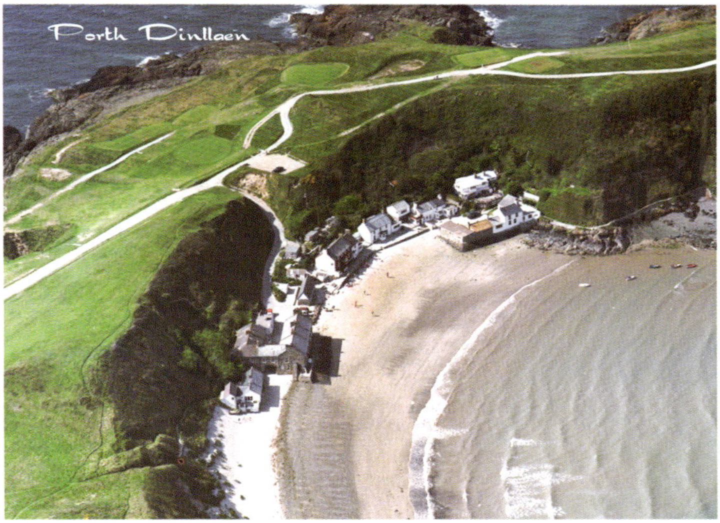
Porth Dinllaen

Edges of Jade

For centuries the harbour was a beehive of shipbuilding, and there were hopes of turning it into the main port for Dublin. In 1834 the House of Commons heard that it was "well situated for a packet station" to carry Irish mail. Thankfully, the Commons opted for Holyhead by one vote and left the harbour to its tranquillity. Apart, that is, from the sound of cursing golfers and golf balls soaring into the sea.

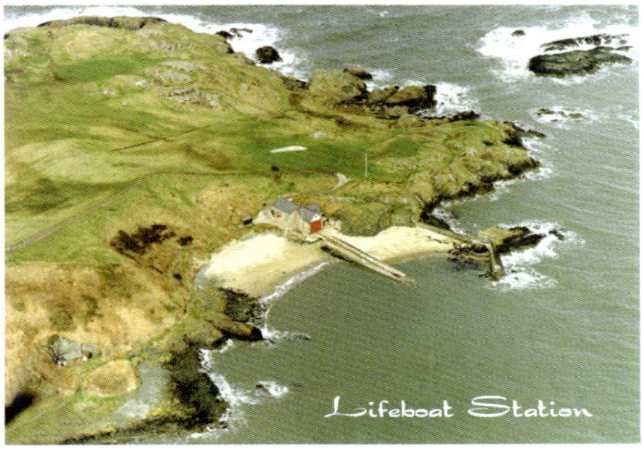
Lifeboat Station

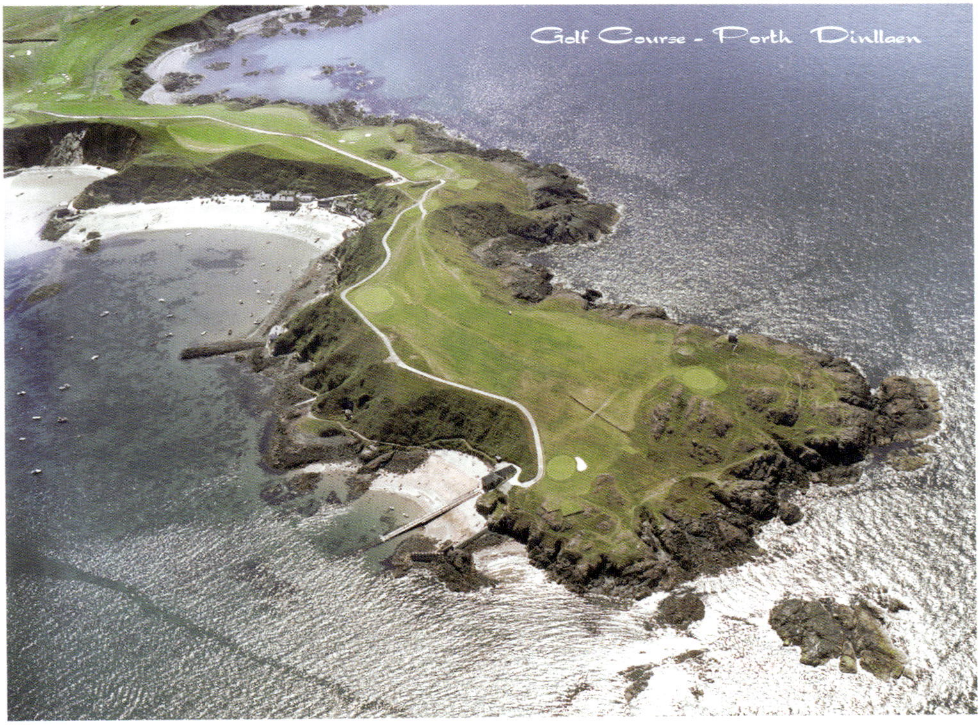
Golf Course - Porth Dinllaen

Effects of Light

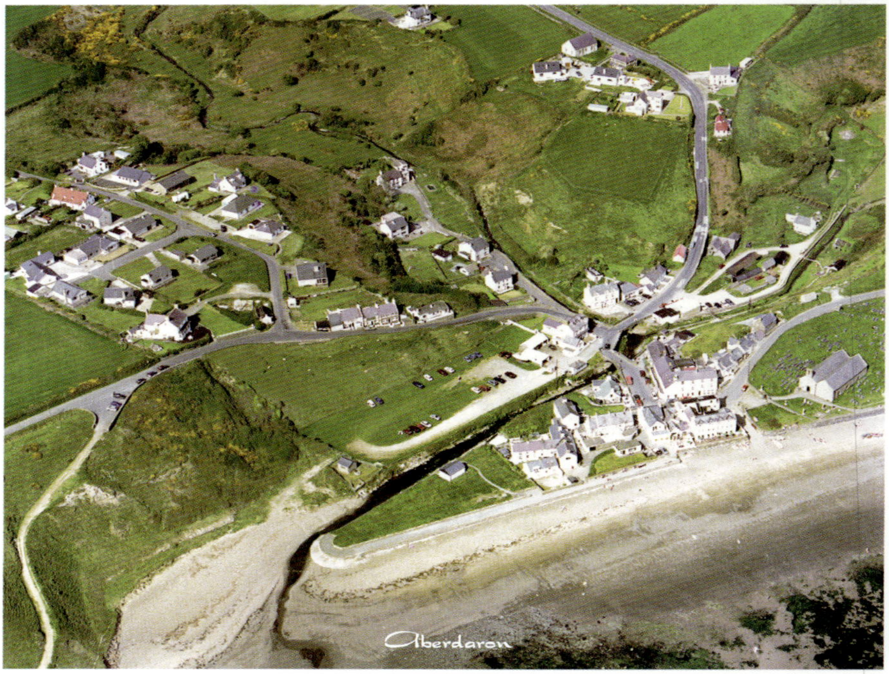

Emperor Constantine made Christianity the religion of his Roman Empire, which included Britain. Two hundred years later, missionaries arrived here from Ireland and Gaul, and monasteries developed in Wales. The monks lived in wattle and daub huts, all grouped around a larger hut which was used for worship and dedicated to a saint. The fenced area containing the huts and its burial ground was called the llan, meaning enclosed land. The saints and their llans gave their names to many Welsh villages, such as Llanberis from the Llan of St Peris, Llandudno (Llan of St Tudno), and Llangollen (Llan of St Collen). One of the most important monasteries was on Bardsey Island, at the tip of the Llyn Peninsula. It was founded by St Cadfan and attracted pilgrims from miles around. In fact, three trips to Bardsey were worth one to Rome. Among the 20,000 saints buried there is Elgar the Hermit from Devonshire who was captured by pirates and sold as a slave in Ireland. Elgar escaped to Wales but was shipwrecked on the Island and lived peacefully into old age.

Another holyman, St Seiriol, settled at Penmon on Anglesey, whilst St Cybi went to Holyhead. The two men were good friends and met each other every day. St Cybi always walked fifteen miles eastwards into the sun and thus, being tanned, he earned the name 'Cybi the Dark'. St Seiriol walked fifteen miles westwards, away from the sun, and he was called 'Seiriol the Fair'.

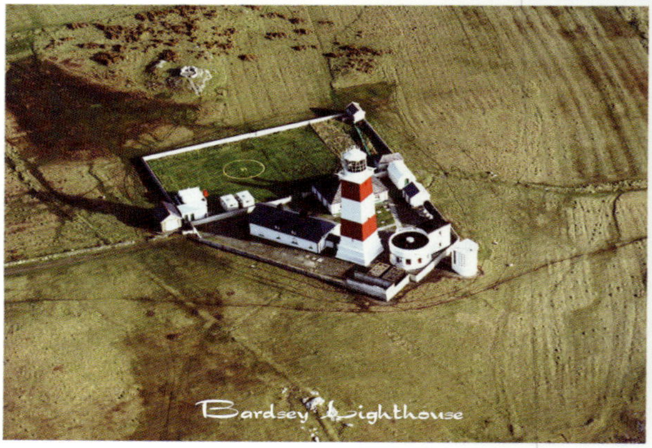

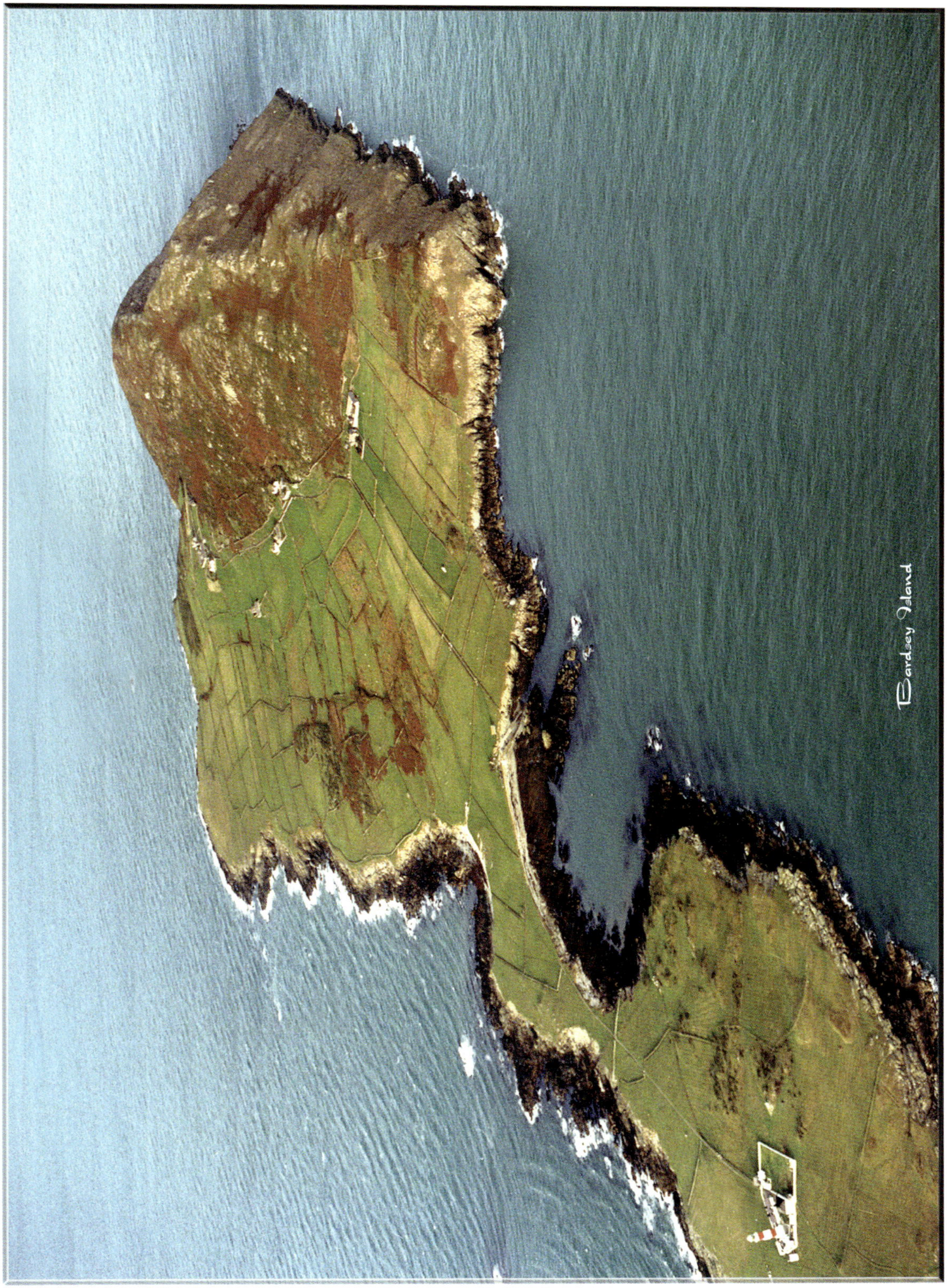
Bardsey Island

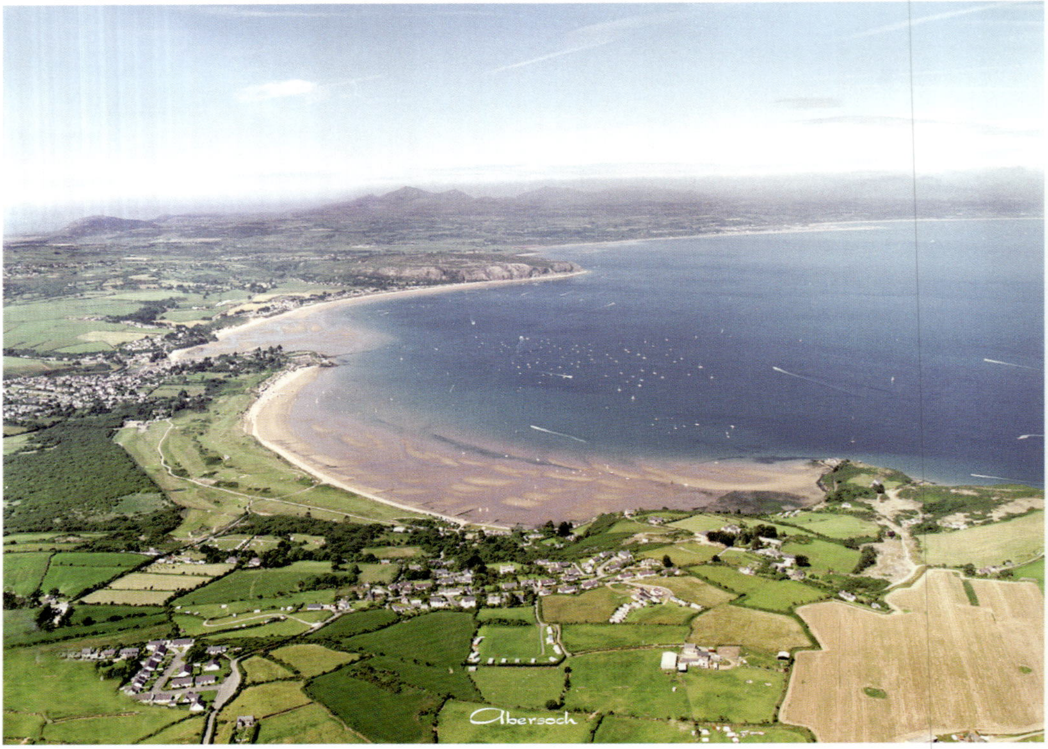

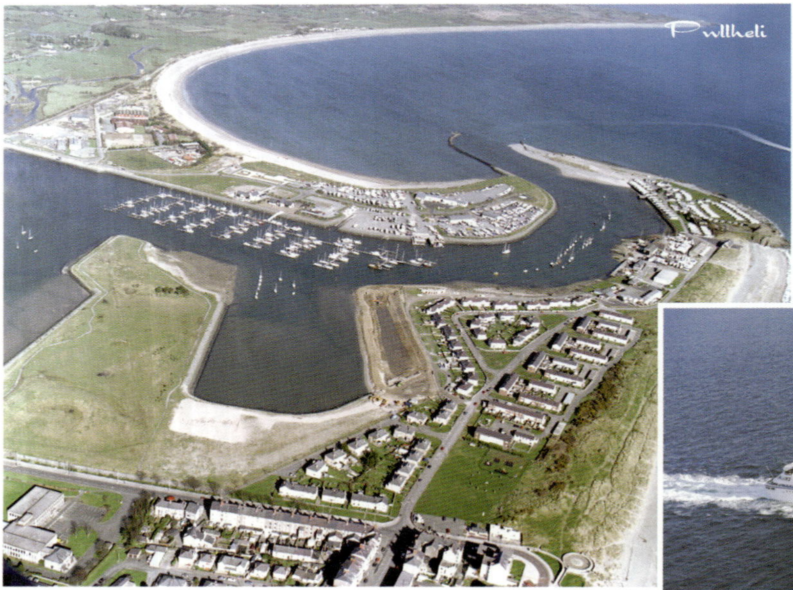

● The golden beach of Abersoch has views towards the mountains over a peaceful stretch of sapphire water called St Tudwal's Road. The two islands of St Tudwal were bought by Sir Clough Williams-Ellis and are now a bird sanctuary.

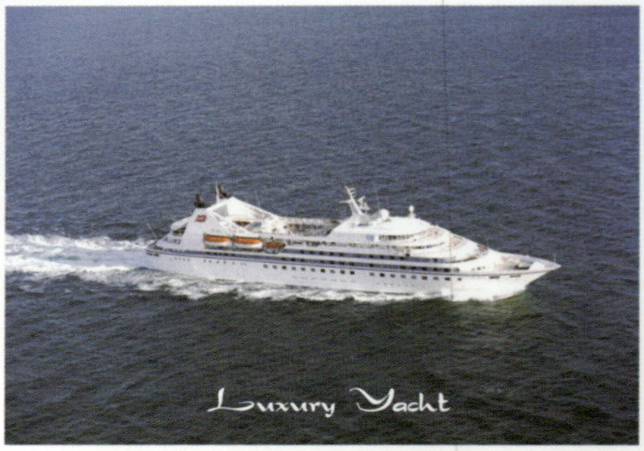

● Pwllheli's Marina is the place to find silver waterboatmen. When Billy Butlin was called on by the Government to find a base to train the Navy he discovered Pwllheli. Land-based HMS Glendower was built here during WW2, and one of the sailors was Prince Philip. Afterwards, Billy developed the site as a holiday camp. He had brought the idea of such camps to the UK from the lakesides of Canada. Future Beatle Ringo Starr, sparkling with rings, appeared at Pwllheli Butlin's as Rory Storm and the Hurricanes in 1960-61.

● Welsh orator David Lloyd-George was actually born in Manchester but he moved as a child to the shores of Criccieth beside the translucent sea. He became a Liberal Prime Minister during WW1, and was nicknamed "The Goat" because of all his children by different women.

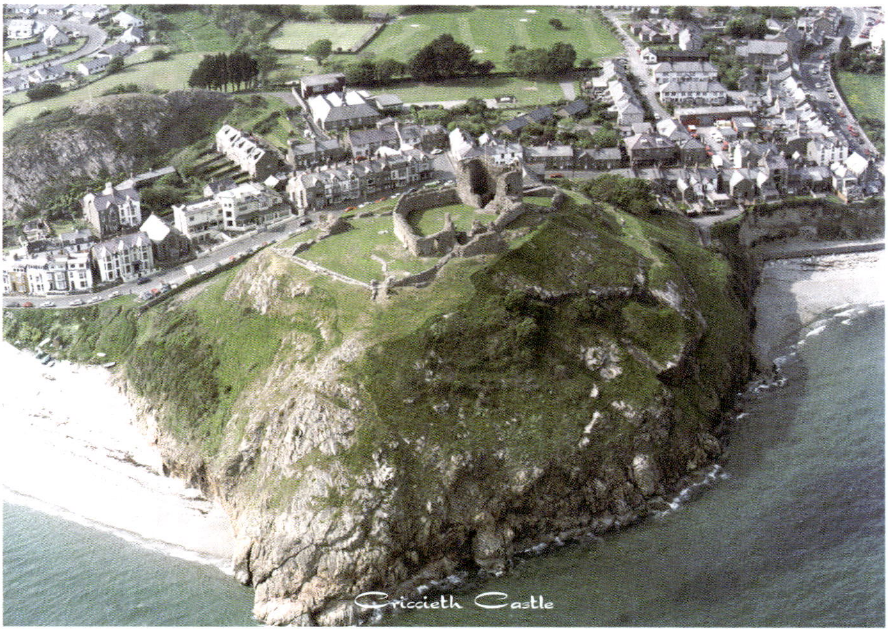

Criccieth Castle

Madocks' Still Waters

● John Greaves, owner of the Llechwedd quarries, exported his slate from the blue lagoon of Porthmadog. Many of the ships built at Borth-y-Gest were named after his family. Unluckily, they were all wrecked at sea.

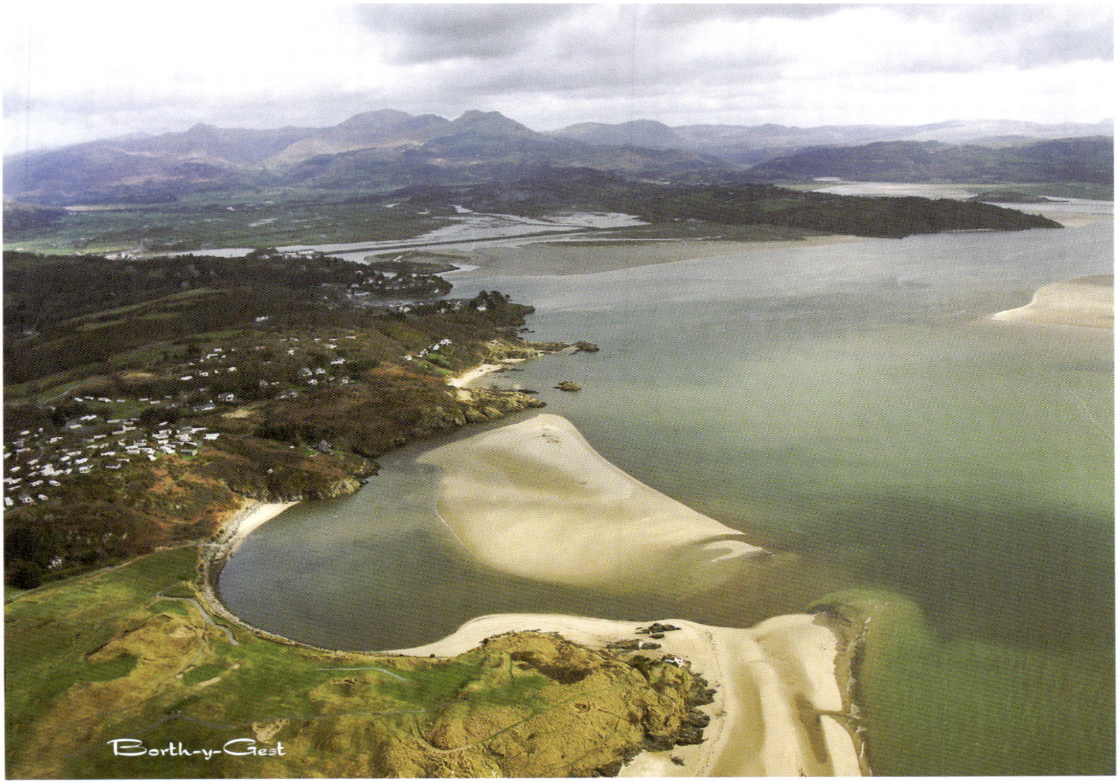

Borth-y-Gest

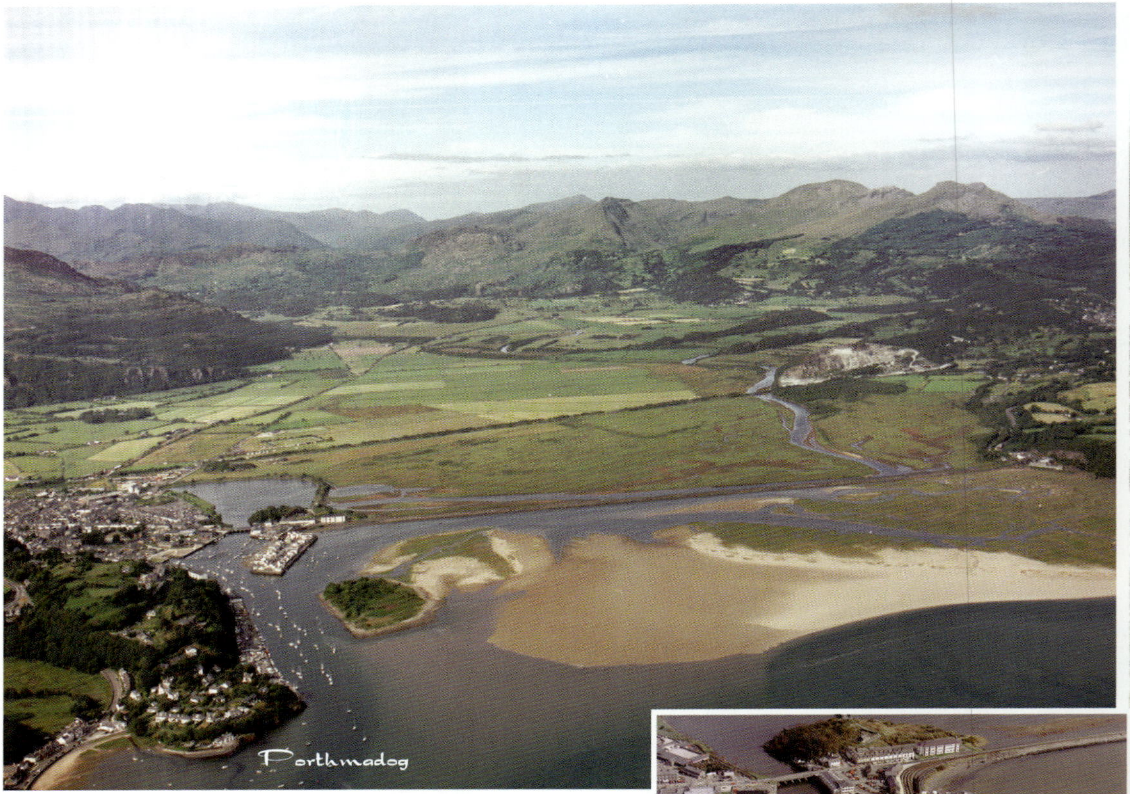

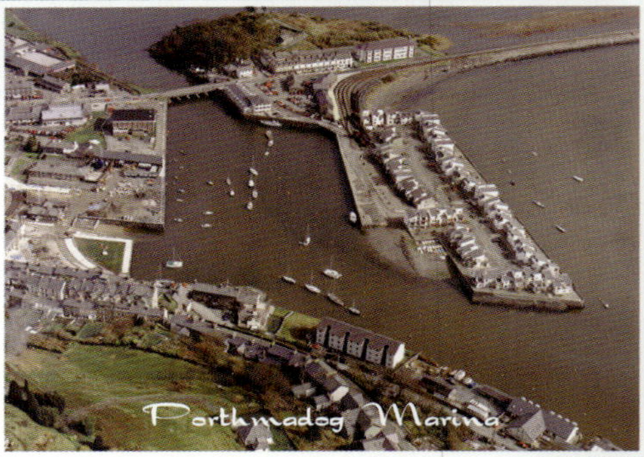

● Dreamy poet Shelley helped Madocks raise funds to build his Cob embankment at Porthmadog. However, Shelley was unpopular as he was a vegetarian and criticised local farmers.

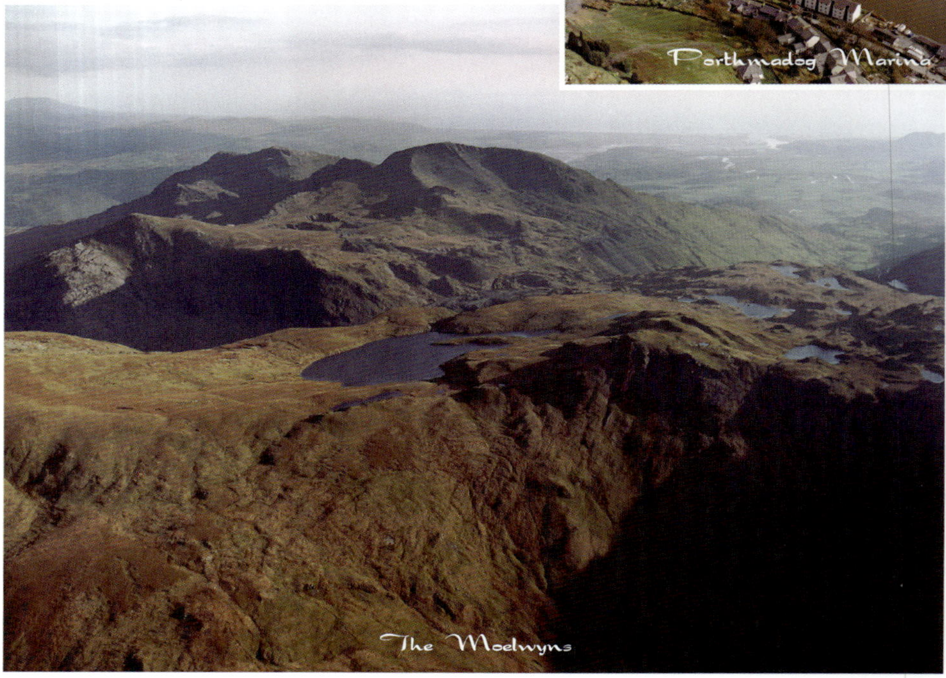

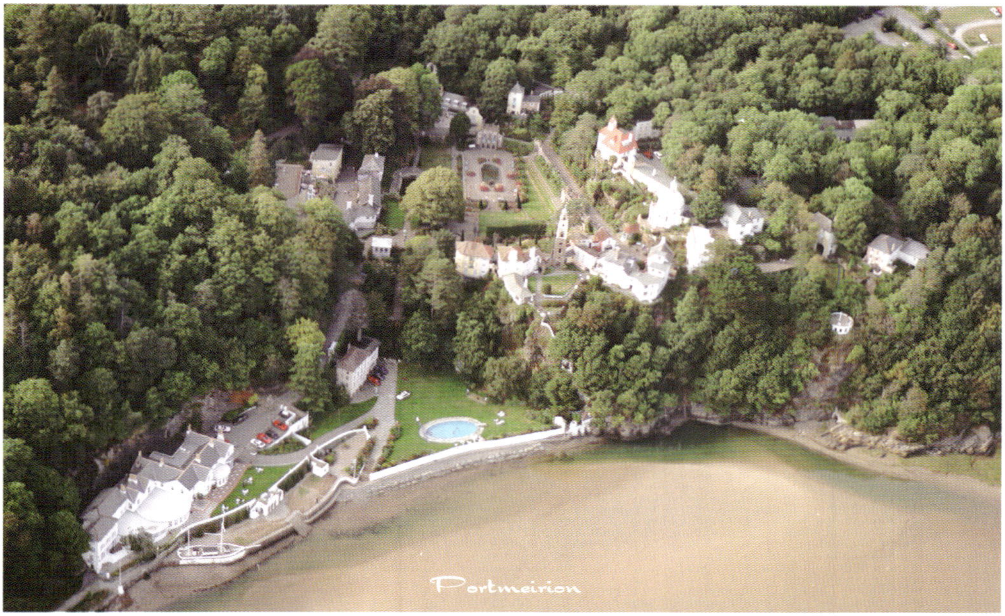

● At Portmeirion a pastel-shaded mock Italian village was build by eccentric Sir Clough Williams-Ellis, inspired by his love for the Mediterranean fishing village of Porto Fino. Amongst the scented woods one summer evening an old lady strolled through the romantic setting and remarked: If I had ever spent a honeymoon here I would have wanted at least two men. The "Prisoner" TV series was also made here. Sir Clough passed away in 1978, leaving behind his pastel creation.

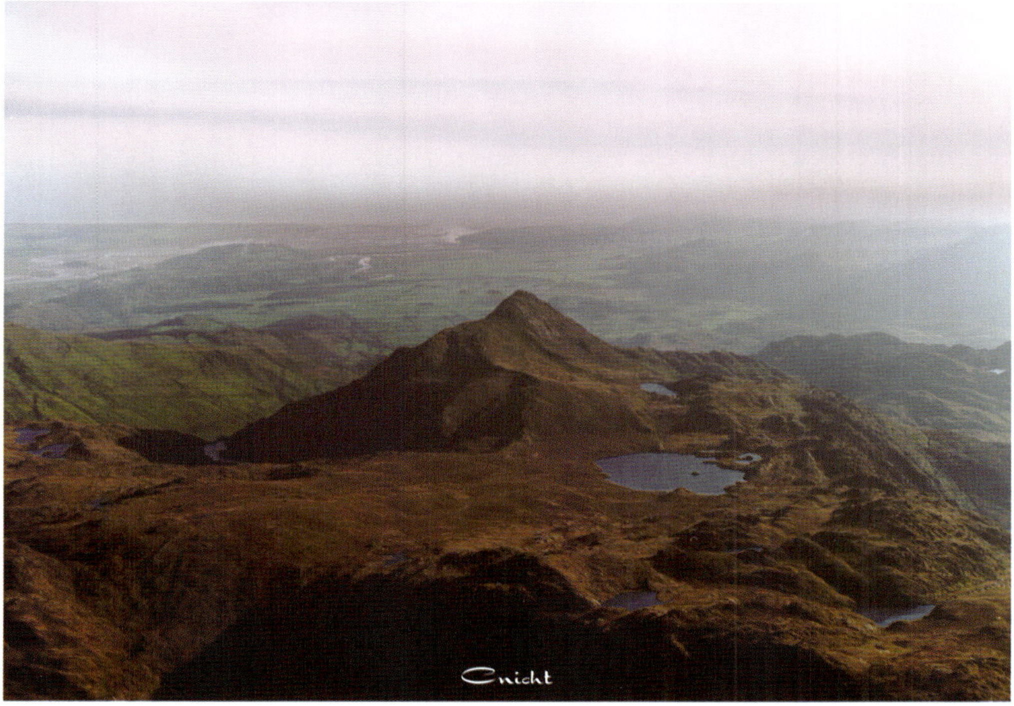

● Before the Cob was built, mariners could sail on a wind-stirred tide up the broad river towards Beddgelert. Writer Thomas Love Peacock mourned the loss of the Glaslyn Estuary because of the beauty of Cnicht and other mountains reflected in its wide waters.

Fairy Gold

The mountains of Snowdonia cradle a wealth of minerals. Two thousand years ago the Romans mined gold here, and it was re-found during the 19th century. Most of the gold in North Wales outcrops along the Dolgellau Gold-belt. This encircles the Rhinog Mountains from Barmouth along the Mawddach Estuary, curving through Coed y Brenin to Trawsfynydd, then down to Harlech before disappearing, presumably, beneath Cardigan Bay.

At Clogau, above the Mawddach, the discovery of a rich gold vein in 1859 started a yellow fever rush in buying shares in the mine. Everyone got excited, until three years later the golden vein dried up. Clogau's gold came and went, companies opened and closed, and 1911 was their last good year.

At Gwynfynydd, near two waterfalls, Pritchard Morgan took over the running of another mine. In 1887 he struck lucky after driving only 11' (3.5m) into quartz bedrock. Next year he mined more than his own weight in gold during one fortnight and earned his nickname, the Gold King. As with Clogau, some years were very productive, and some were bad. Later on, his mine made wedding rings for the Royal Family, including the Queen Mother, the Queen, and Princess Diana.

In the 13th century their royal ancestor, Edward I, didn't know about the gold outcropping near Harlech but he built a castle there 200' (60m) above the sea. It became Owain Glyndwr's Welsh court but it was besieged by the English. Glyndwr escaped with one son to the mountains. However, his son-in-law died here of starvation, and his wife and children were sent to the Tower of London, where they died four years later of despair.

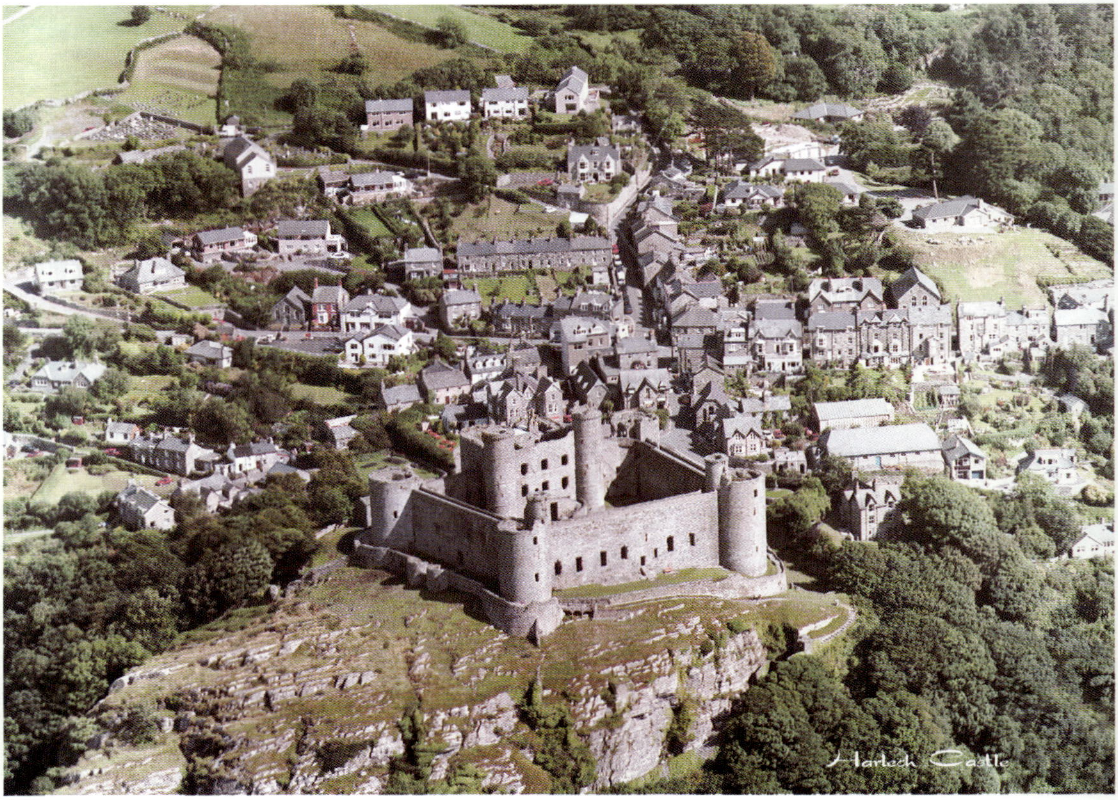
Harlech Castle

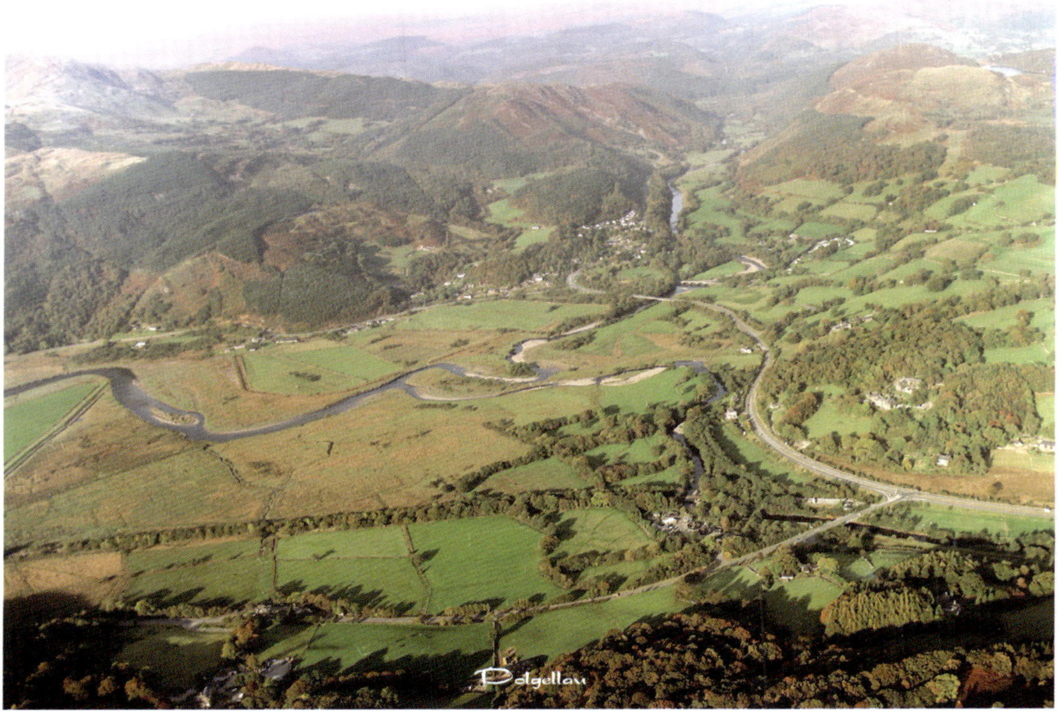

• At the head of the Mawddach Estuary, beneath towering Cader Idris, Dolgellau lies in the fork of two rivers. A seven-arched bridge spans the shallow River Wnion, and among the crooked streets the houses are slate-roofed and built of sturdy grey stone. Dolgellau was founded by Cadwgan, Prince of Powys, as a serf village. In the hills nearby the white monks of Cymer Abbey reared high quality horses for Llywelyn the Great. During the 18th century Dolgellau's many coaching inns catered for tourists, including some from the royal families of Europe, and provided ponies to take them up to the summit of Cader Idris.

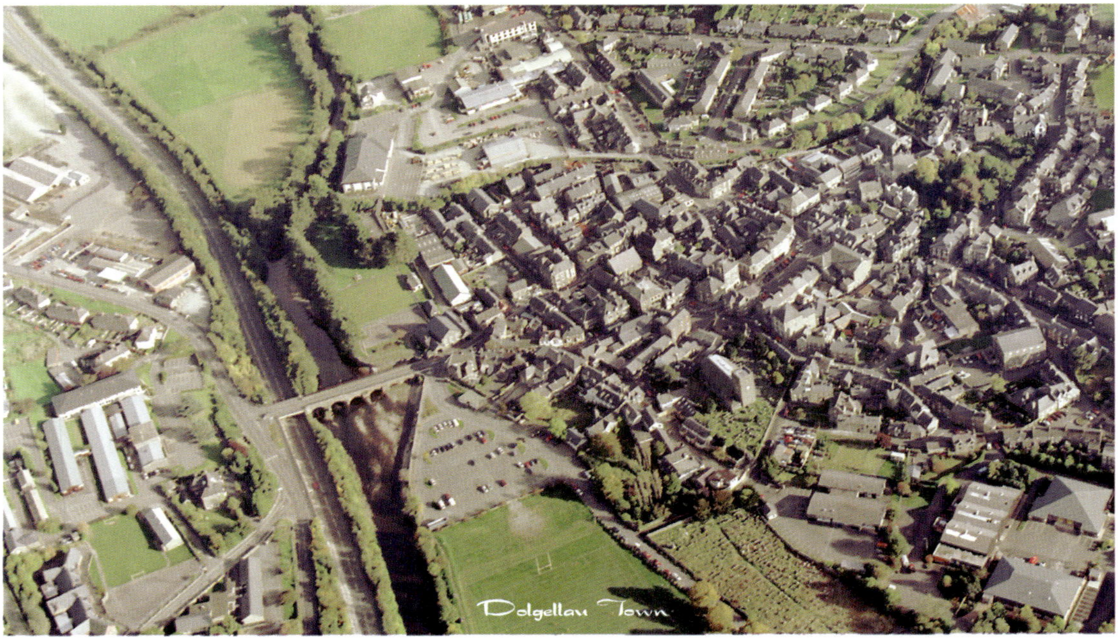

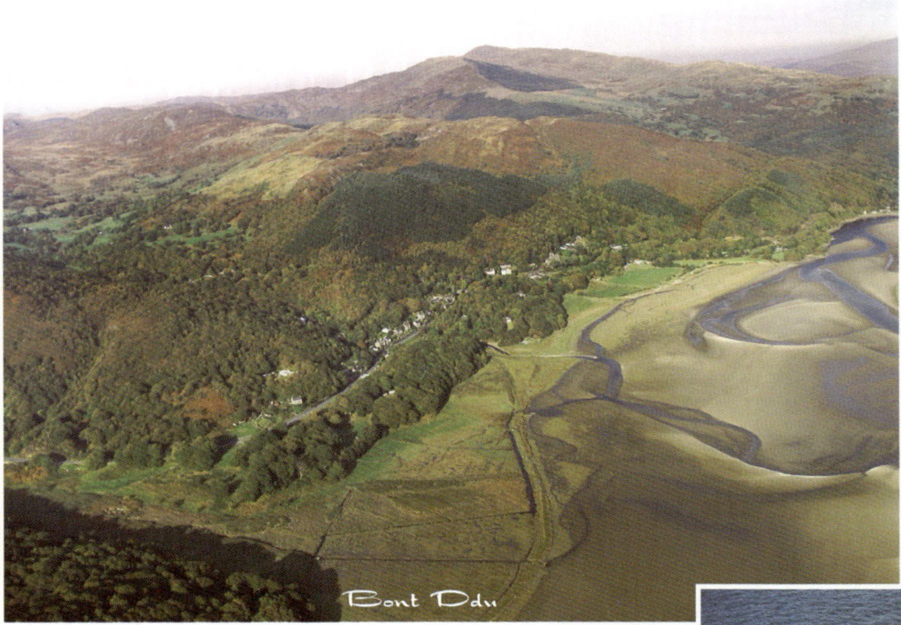

Bont Ddu

- Clogau was probably the most important of all the goldmines in this area, yielding 18,417 ounces between the years 1900-05. Output from all the mines in the region since 1850 came to 130,000 ounces of gold. It's been said that there's none left! The Romans said that too!

- Beneath Cader Idris the beautiful Mawddach Estuary ebbs and flows. John Ruskin, Victorian art critic, said the only walk to equal Barmouth to Dolgellau was the one from Dolgellau to Barmouth. They say there's gold deep down in the Mawddach sands after washing there over thousands of years from the hills. Welsh gold is called "Fairy Gold" because it's so elusive and hard to find. True, perhaps, for strangers but the locals know different and that's there secret.

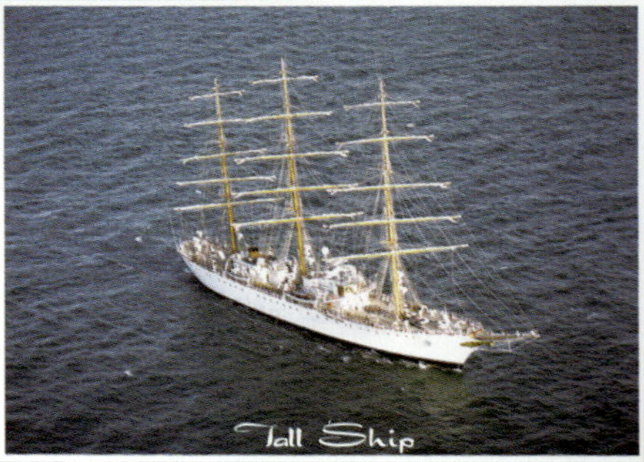

Tall Ship

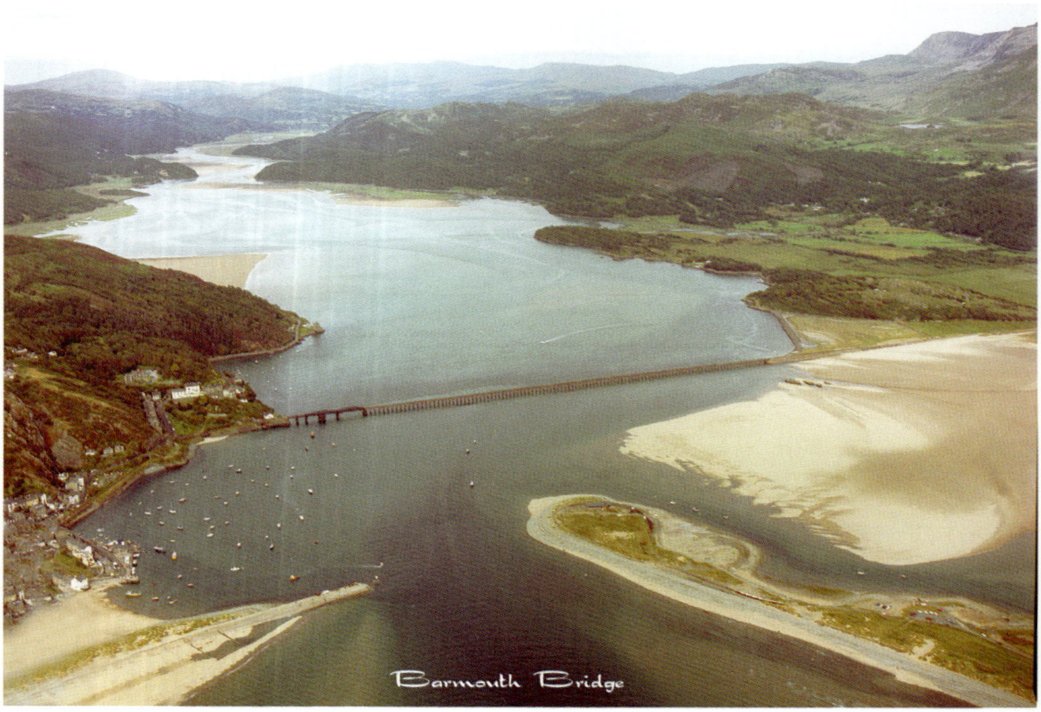

Barmouth Bridge

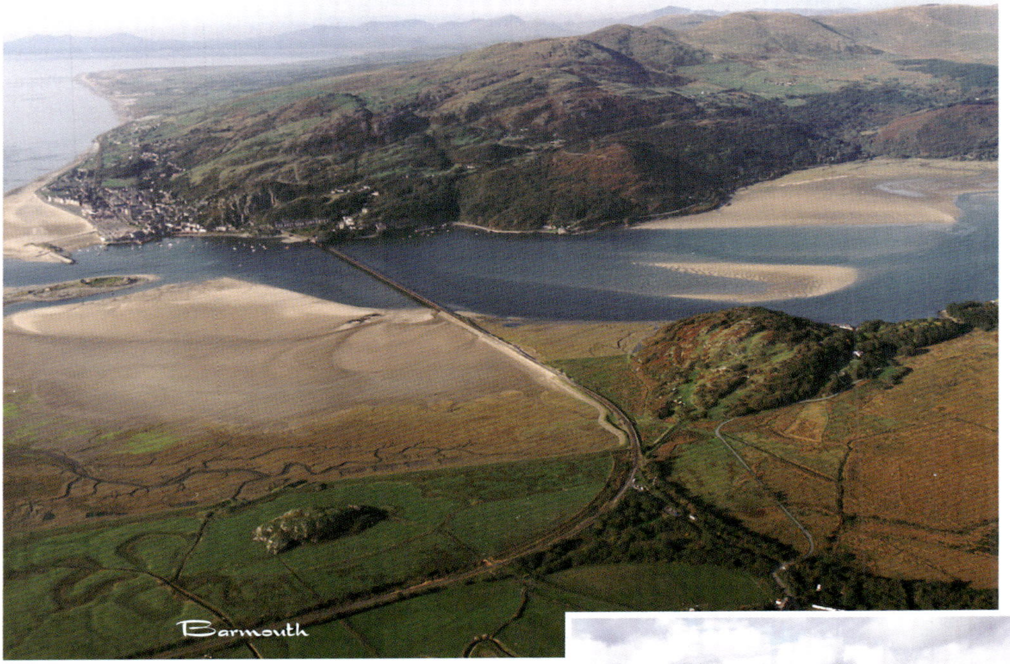

• The ruins of Castell y Bere rise from an isolated outcrop in a marine-green valley. The castle was built by Llywelyn the Last, and when he was killed his brother occupied it. Dafydd continued Llywelyn's role of fighting the English. The castle was besieged, but he escaped to Dolwyddelan, only to be beheaded.

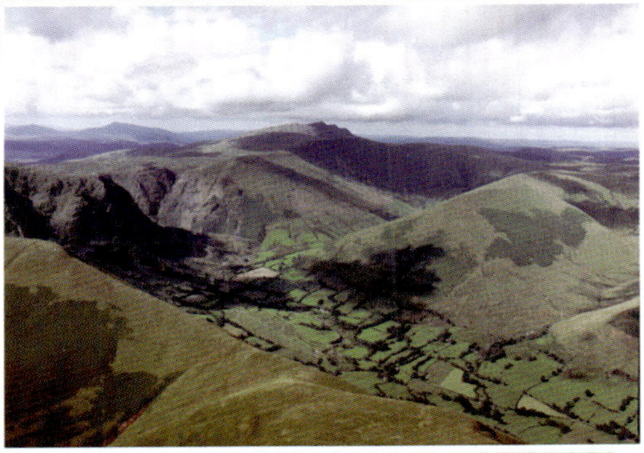

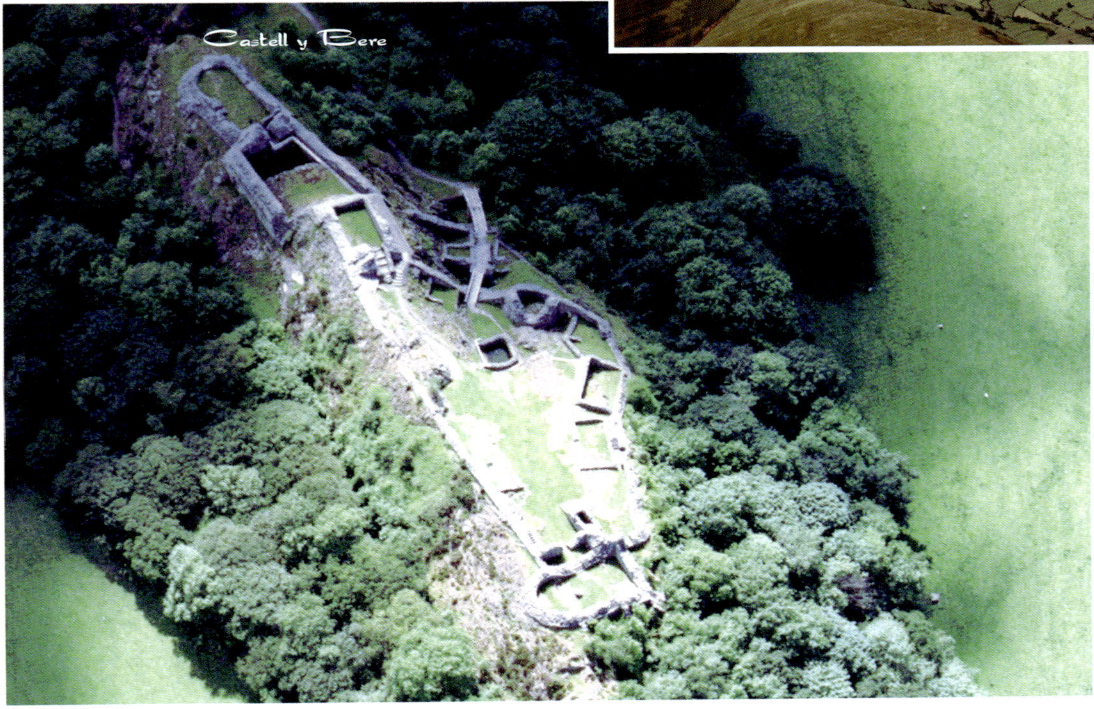

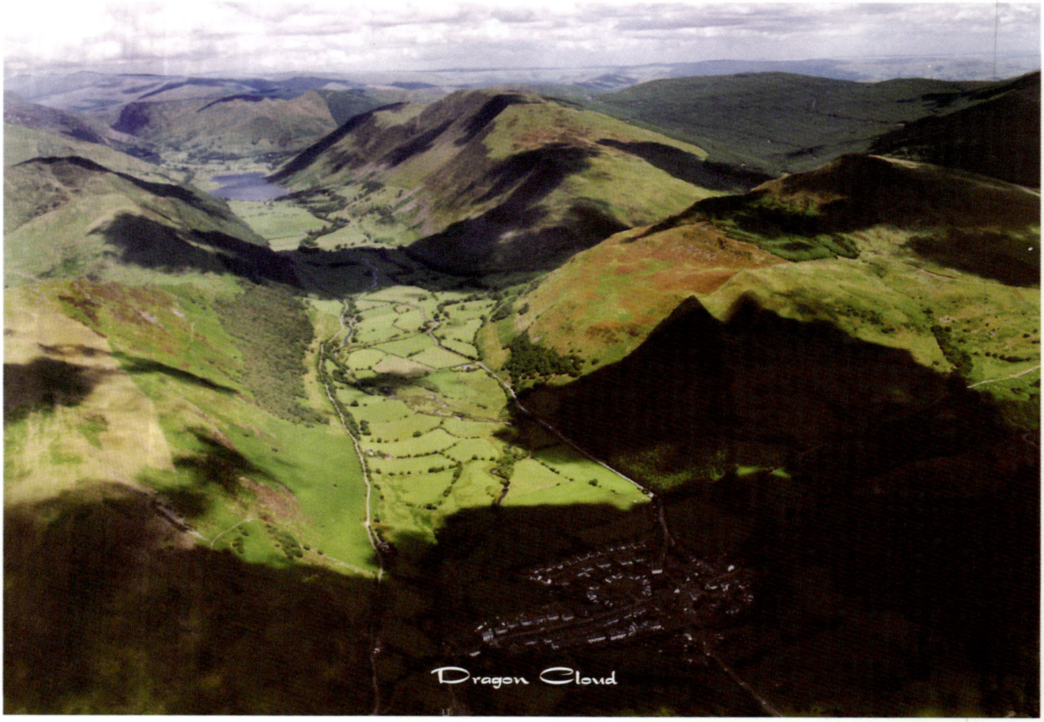

Dragon Cloud

- Gwilym took this stunning photograph of a green valley, but when he developed it he discovered a mysterious dragon, shaped by the clouds. The dragon lazily guards the valley, curled up in her lair. "Trade not Cymru," she breathes. "It's a priceless paradise, already rich since the dawns of time. I will always guard my motherland, my people and my lair. Respect my delicate breath for I've taken years to evolve into the pure creature I am!"
- Beneath the aquamarine sea at Aberdyfi bells can be heard ringing from a legendary drowned village. A song was written about the bells by Charles Dibdin for his opera 'Liberty Hall'. He was a successful composer of nautical songs, and many were sung by Nelson's navy on the high seas.

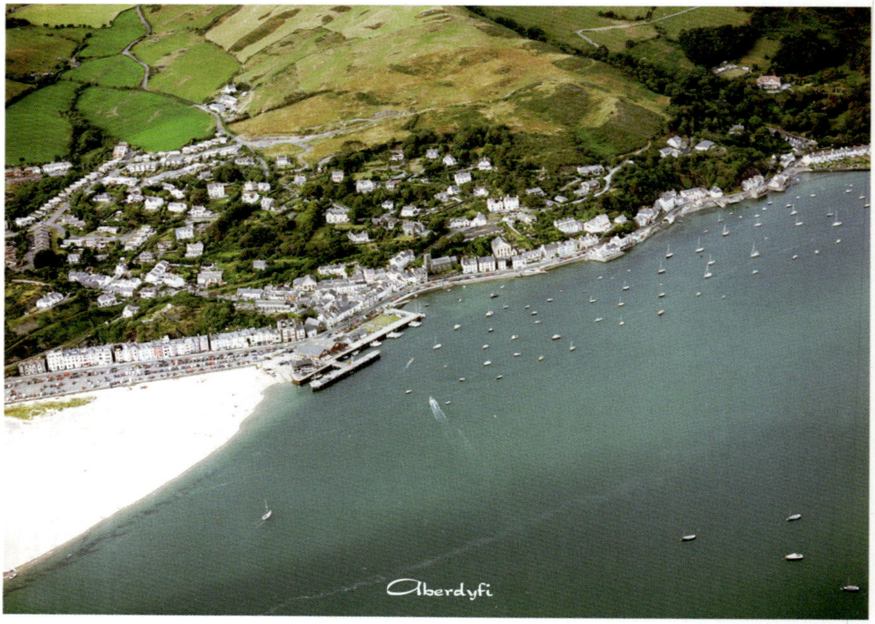

Aberdyfi

Hint of Stillness

For a little village, Trawsfynydd has an important place in the history of Wales. Two thousand years ago the Romans built a fort, Tomen y Mur, on top of the sweeping moors. It might be cold and windy outside at 1000' (300m) above sealevel but there were some comforts for the legionaries. These included a heated bath-house, guest-house for visitors, and an amphitheatre with grassy seats for applauding your comrades military skills.

At village-level the UK's first inland nuclear power station stands proudly beside the lake's green waters. It's now closed and standing down after 30 years commission.

Trawsfynydd lakeside was also the location for Camelot in the film "First Knight". Strangely, it starred Scottish Sean Connery as King Arthur and American Richard Gere as Lancelot. Other scenes were shot in Blaenau Ffestiniog and Llanfair Slate Caverns.

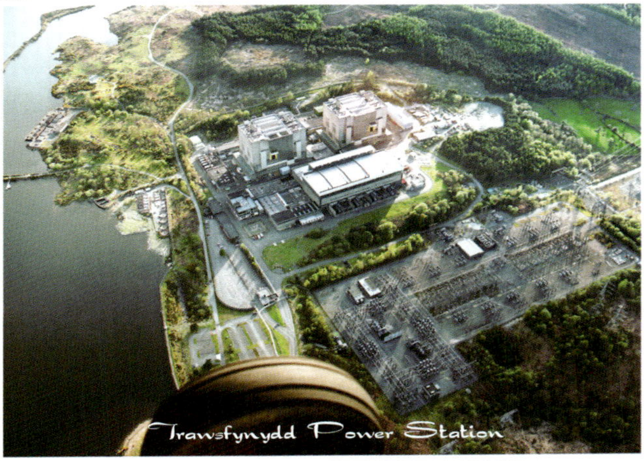
Trawsfynydd Power Station

A local hero is the shepherd, Hedd Wyn, whose name means "perfect peace". He won the Chair for poetry at the National Eisteddfod in 1917 but was killed fighting in Flanders before hearing the news.

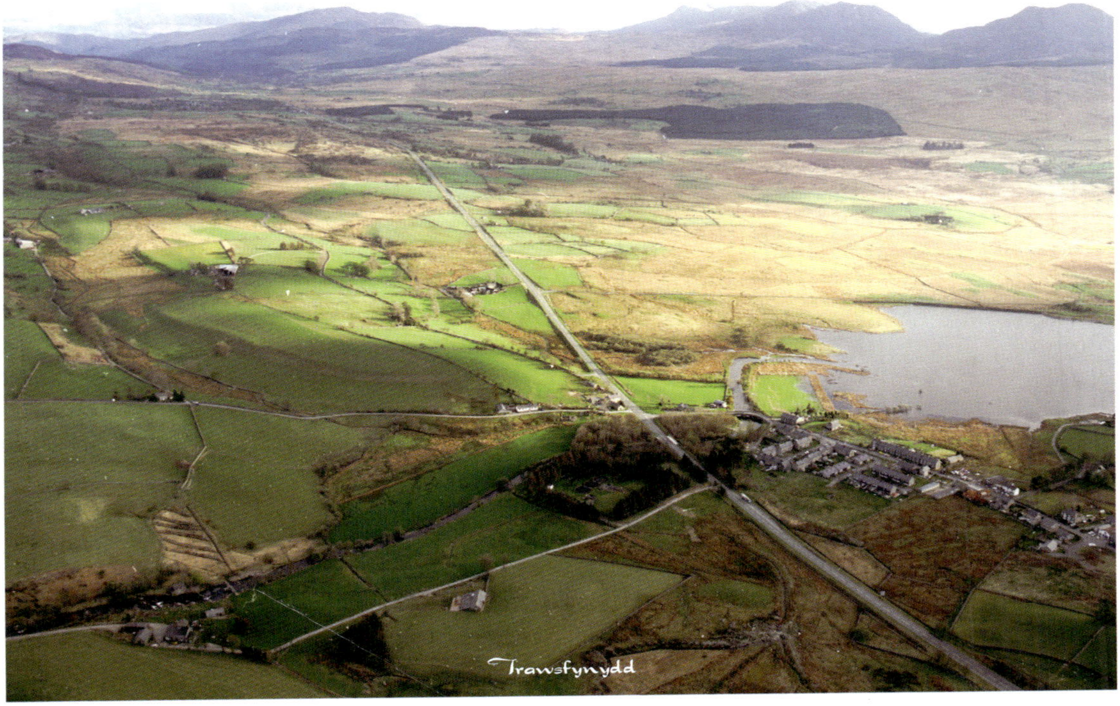
Trawsfynydd

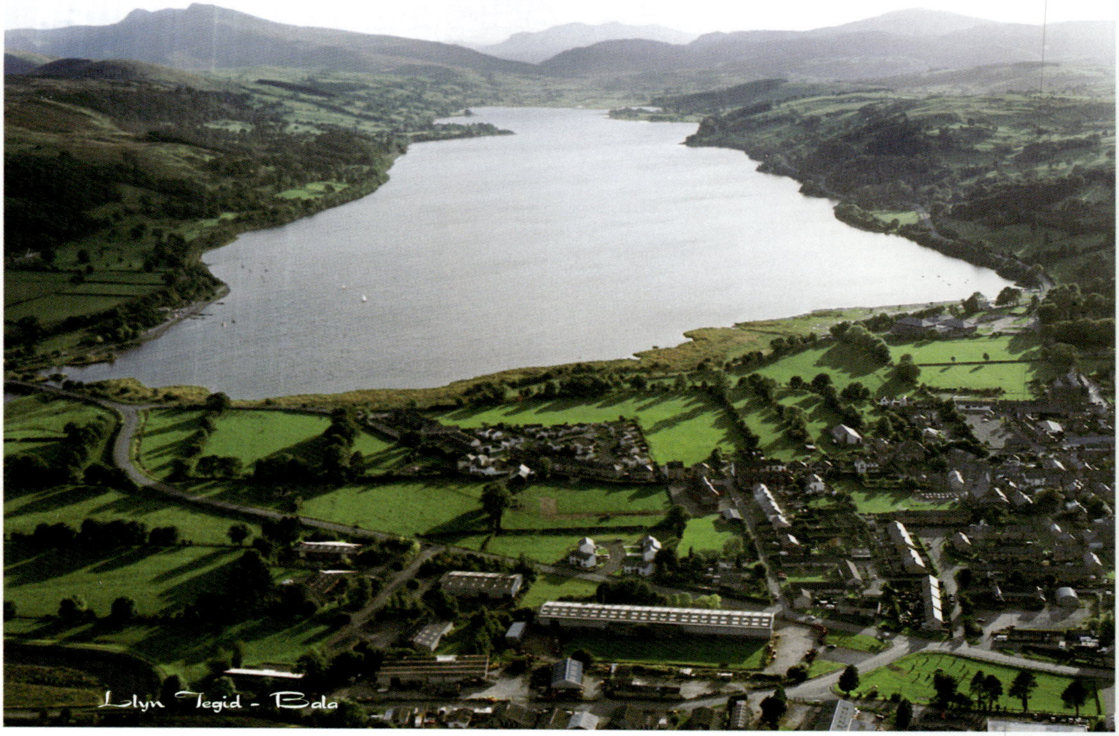

- Legend gives a strange birth to the mighty River Dee, saying that it enters Llyn Tegid (Bala Lake) as a small stream and passes through the waters completely unchanged before rushing towards the sea at Chester.
- The residents of Llandderfel had a busy night in January 1974. It was the scene for bright lights and bumps in the night when a UFO was seen crashing into the Berwyn mountains. People ran into the streets, and plates smashed to the floor. What really did happen on that cold and windy dark January night?

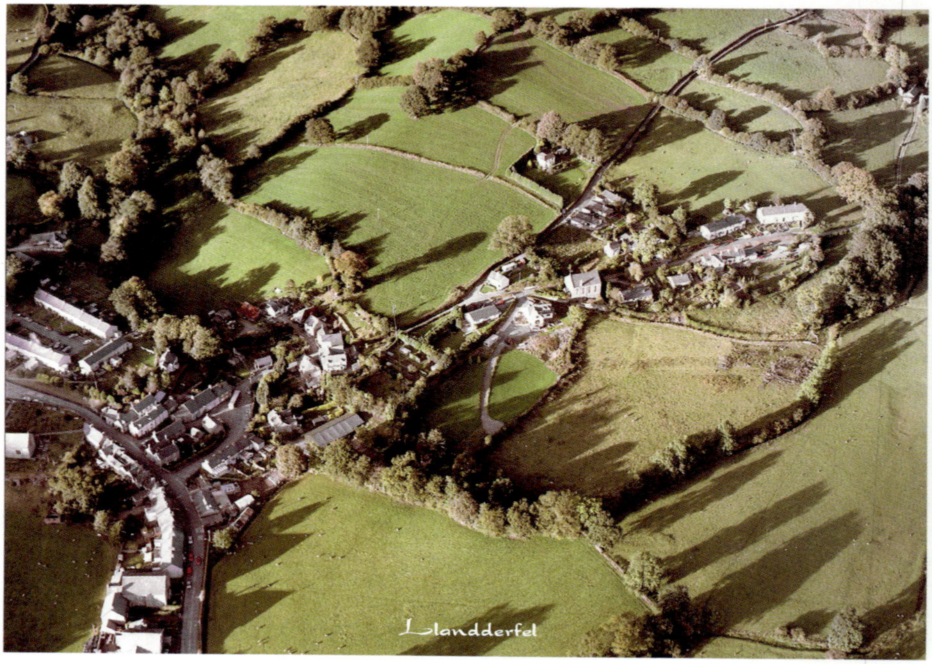

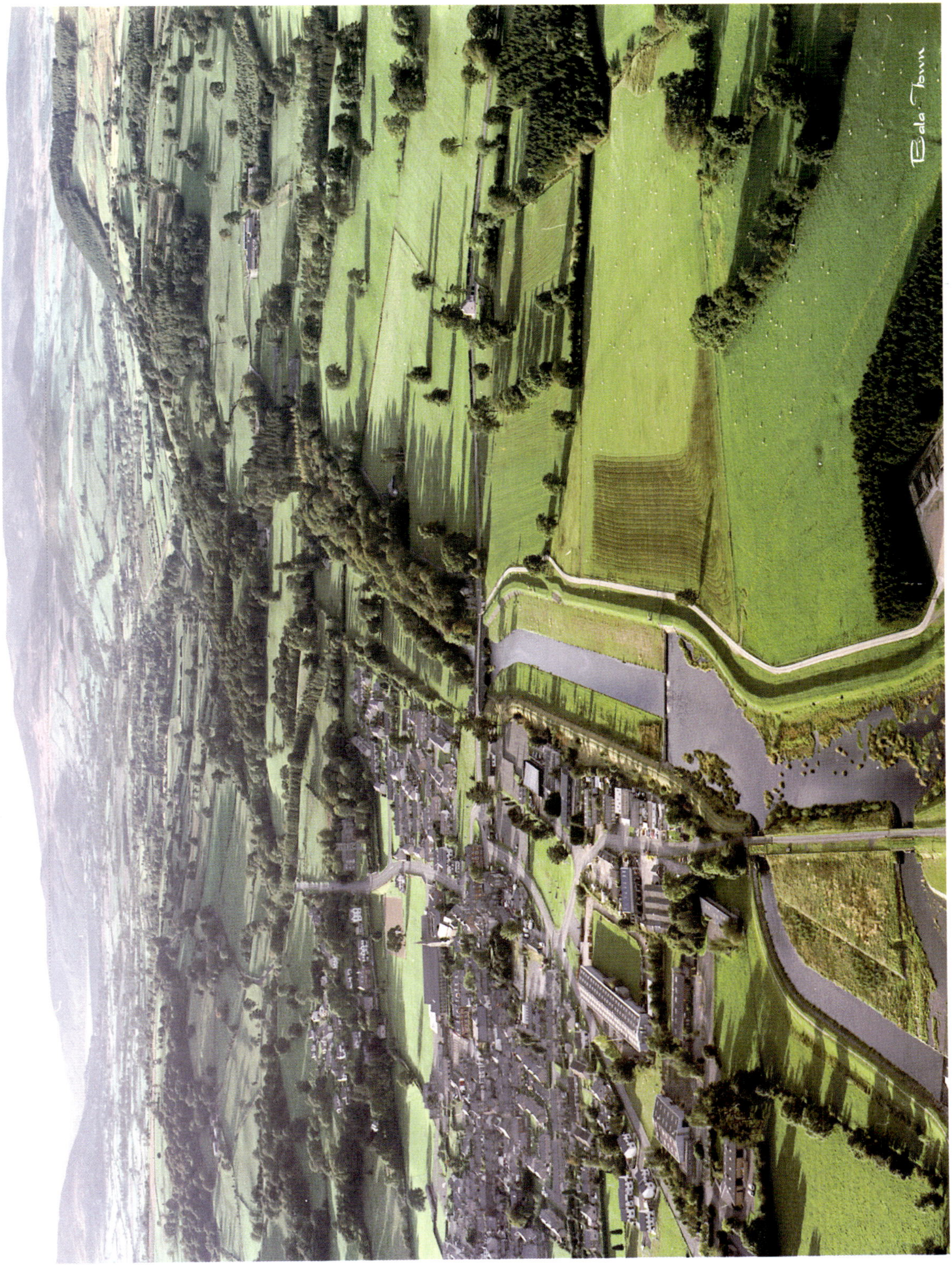
Bala Town

Textures of Time

On a dull day the grey waste of the slate quarries loom menacingly above the town of Blaenau Ffestiniog. It can never be a riot of bright Mediterranean colours, but in rain or sunshine the blue slate glistens, drips, winks and gleams. For the quarrymen it was a bitterly dark, cold and damp place to work. Those at Llechwedd worked underground in gangs of four.

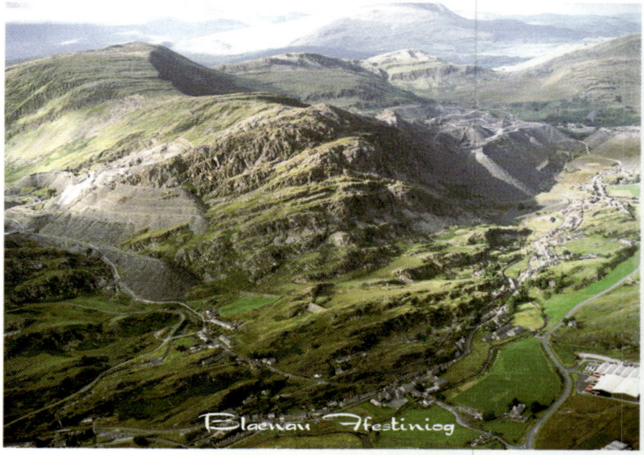

They spent up to 15 years working the same chamber, by candlelight, on a diet of tea and bread. Many of them died before they reached 50 of lung disease. Ironically, in World War Two six large underground chambers were dug out of Manod Quarry to house the National Gallery Collection, threatened by bombs in London. Of course, the paintings were allowed air-conditioning, constant temperatures and humidity.

West of Blaenau the hills rise towards the spongy moors of the Migneint. This is black grouse country, sailed over by Hen Harrier, and cropped by limping, coughing sheep. It's here that the Conwy River trickles from out of a still lake amongst purple heather. This moorland once belonged to the Knights of St John of Jerusalem. The village of Ysbyty Ifan retains its name, meaning hospital of John, from a hospice which the knights kept here for pilgrims on the way to Bardsey.

In time, problems arose. The King's law did not prevail over Ysbyty so it became a hideout for thieves and vagabonds, safe from the clutches of the King's soldiers. Soon they were out of control, rampaging about the hills and creating havoc in the valleys.

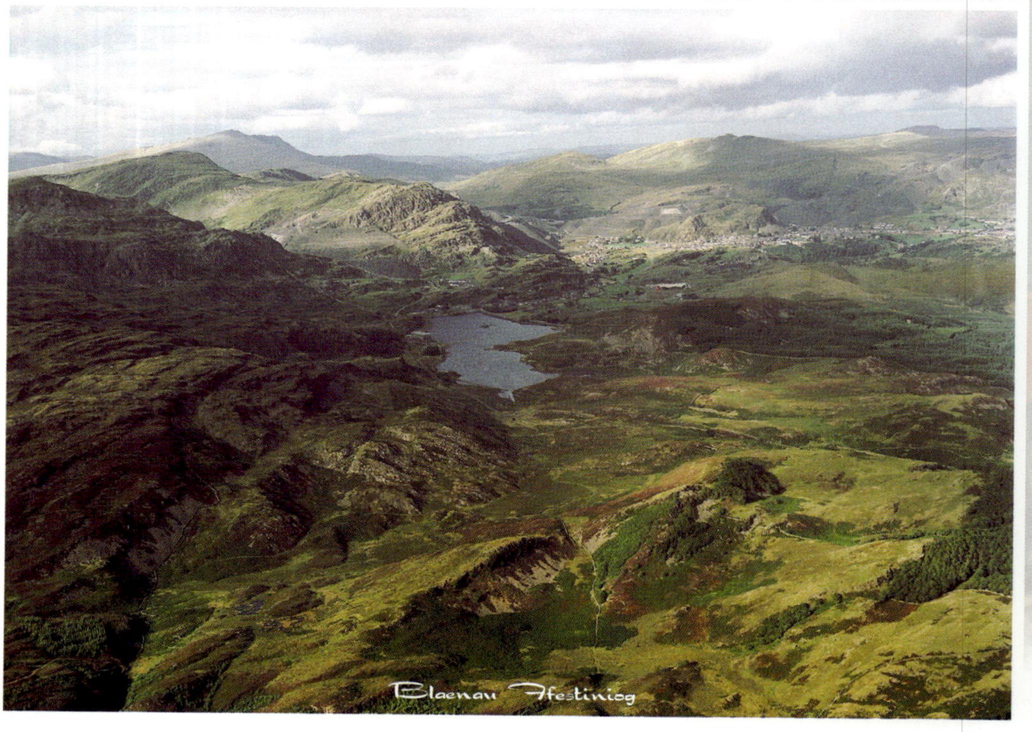

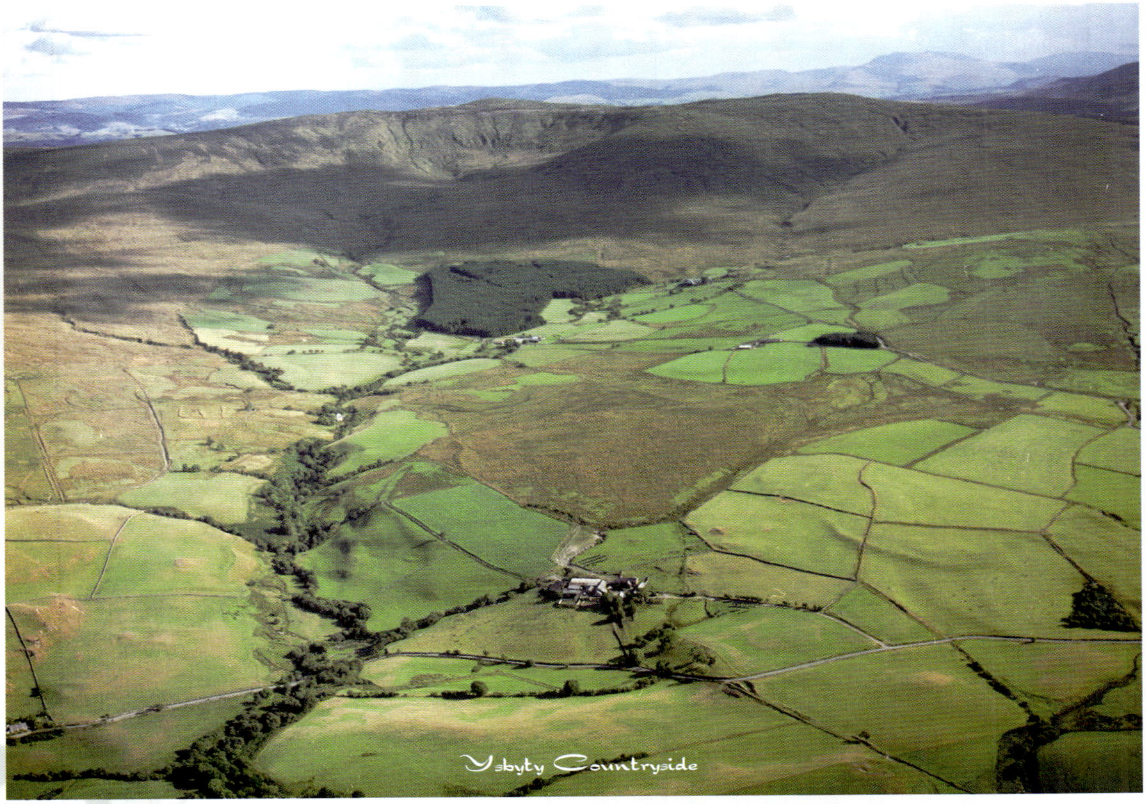

Ysbyty Countryside

- Eventually, some of the brigands of Ysbyty Ifan were captured and hanged. Others escaped over the hills and found their way to the rugged valley of Dinas Mawddwy near Dolgellau.

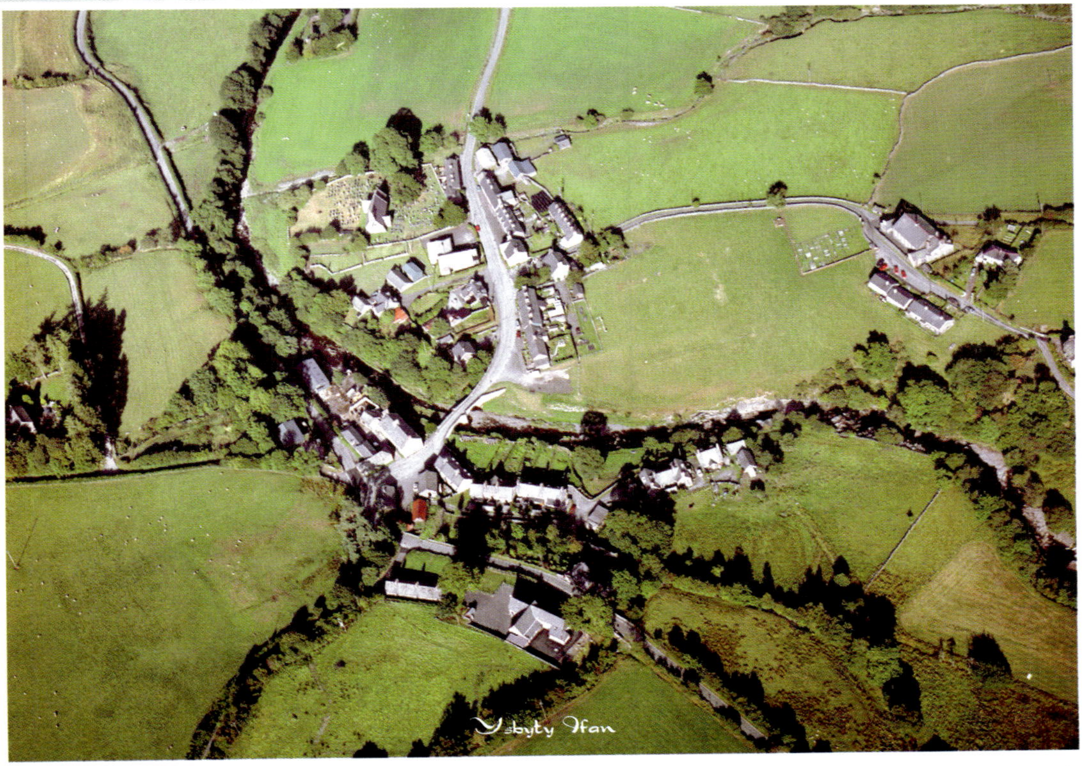

Ysbyty Ifan

Dragons Below

The dragon considers itself, quite rightly, a very important creature in Wales. The red dragon flicking its tail on the Welsh flag is probably a youthful descendant of the fiery dragon of Rome. Every cohort of the army had a dragon as its sign, and it became a symbol of power. After the Romans left these shores Welsh warriors adopted the idea, and the bards Aneirin and Taliesin spoke of them as "dragons" in their appreciative verses.

The Mabinogion tells a dragon's tale based on Vortigern's fight against the Saxons. He fled to Wales and tried to build a castle on the crags of Dinas Emrys but the stonework kept collapsing. Myrddin the Magician knew why. Beneath the stones was a hidden pool in which two dragons were fighting for control. Although the white dragon (a Saxon interloper) seemed to be winning, ultimately, the red British dragon would triumph!

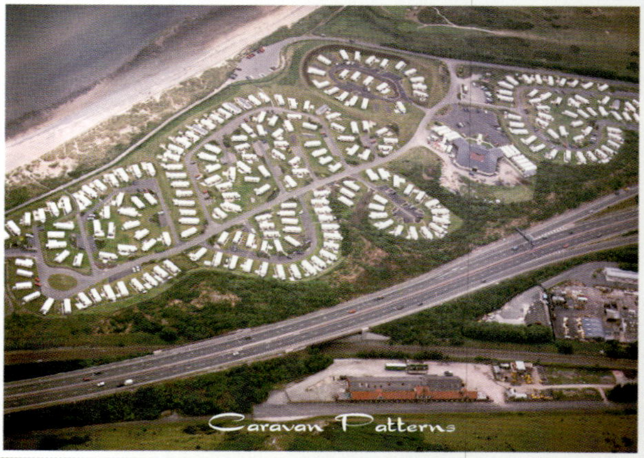
Caravan Patterns

The village of St George near Abergele is supposedly where the knight fought his dragon, and his horse's hooves could once be found on the churchyard's stone wall. However, the real St George was born in Turkey and became a Roman soldier. He was tortured and beheaded when he stood up against the slaughter of Christians.

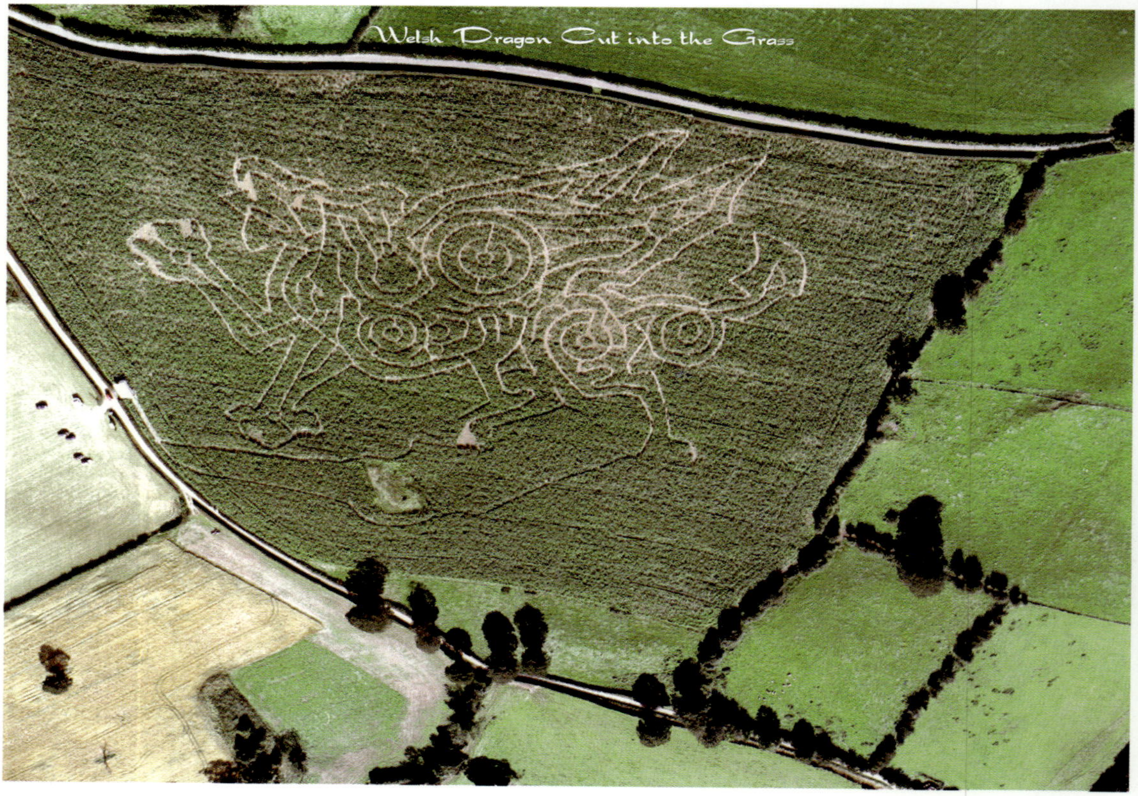
Welsh Dragon Cut into the Grass

• The oil and gas production platform on the Douglas gas complex based off Rhyl was holed in one by its support vessel, the Highland Pioneer. Three lifeboat crews stood ready for an operation, whilst a RAF Rescue helicopter from Valley hovered anxiously overhead: the diagnosis was that none of the rig's legs seemed to be broken. The Pioneer received three holes on her starboard side and limped sadly back to Liverpool.

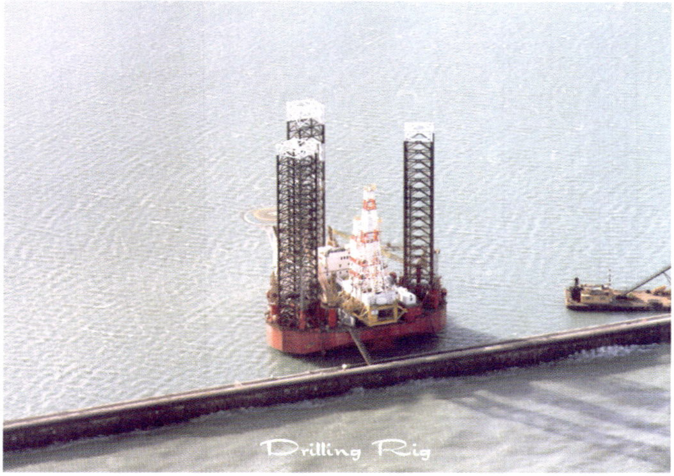
Drilling Rig

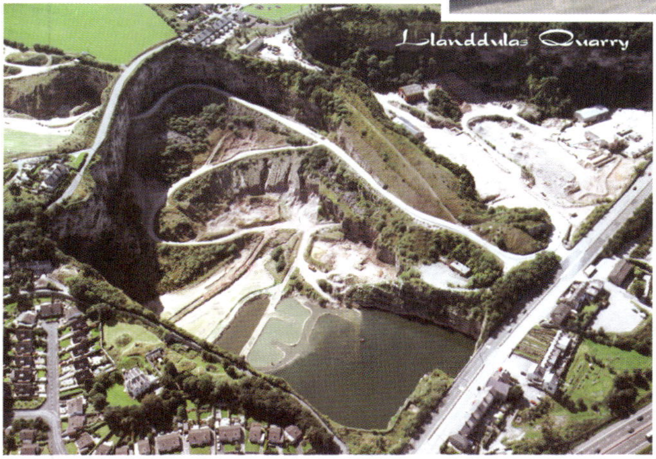
Llanddulas Quarry

• Creamy magenta limestone outcrops on the craggy cliffs of the Great Orme before curling inland along the sturdy Clwydian Range. Traditionally, limestone was used for ballast in sailing ships or burnt in kilns to make agricultural lime. Llanddulas Quarry ships high quality stone to Europe and is overlooked by fluorescent cyclists flashing by on the new Cycle Route.

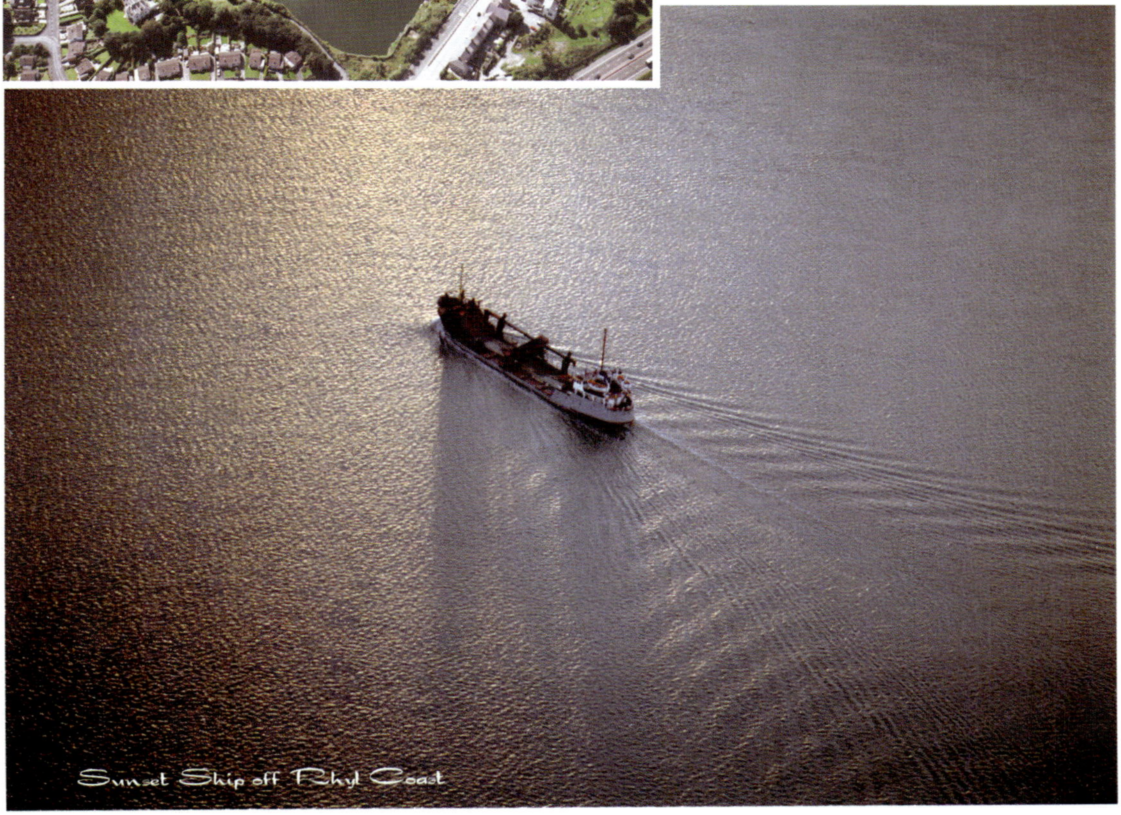
Sunset Ship off Rhyl Coast

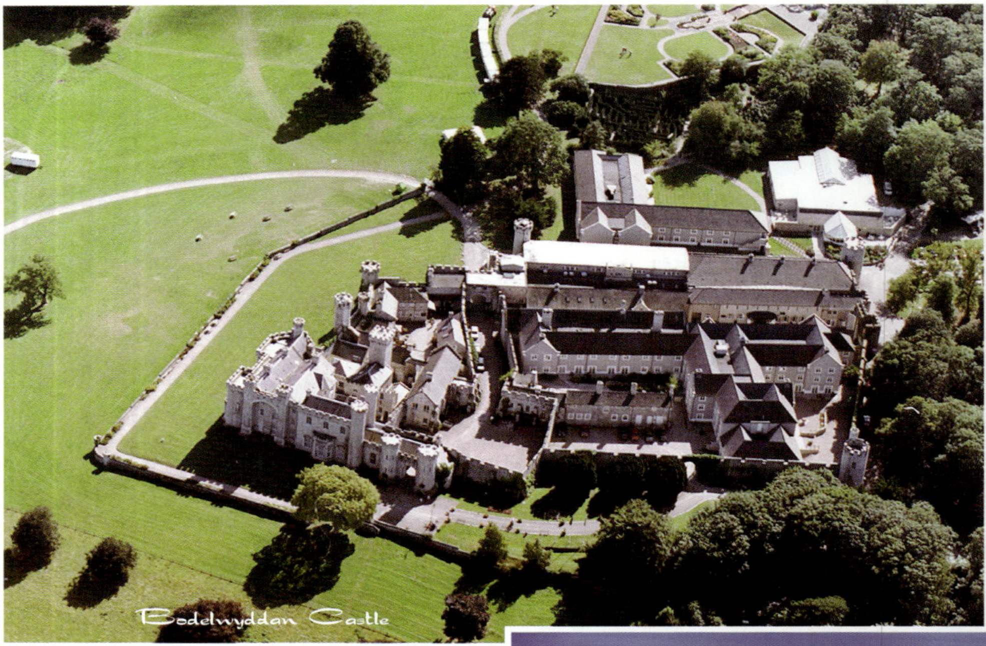

Bodelwyddan Castle

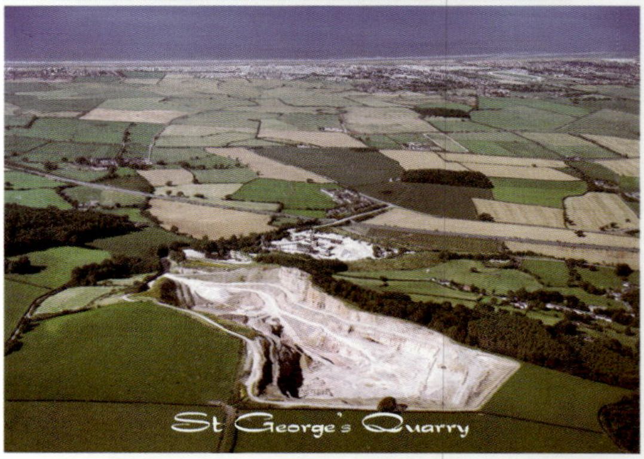

St George's Quarry

● The fairy-story grey castle of Bodelwyddan is a riot of turrets and battlements, with false arrow slits to fire at imaginary enemies. It was the fanciful home of the Williams family. Their coat of arms, depicting two cross foxes, still swings in the breeze on many pubsigns.

● Brilliant pearl white limestone gleams harshly amongst green patchwork fields but it's been used to build many graceful churches. St George's Quarry offered up much from the earth.

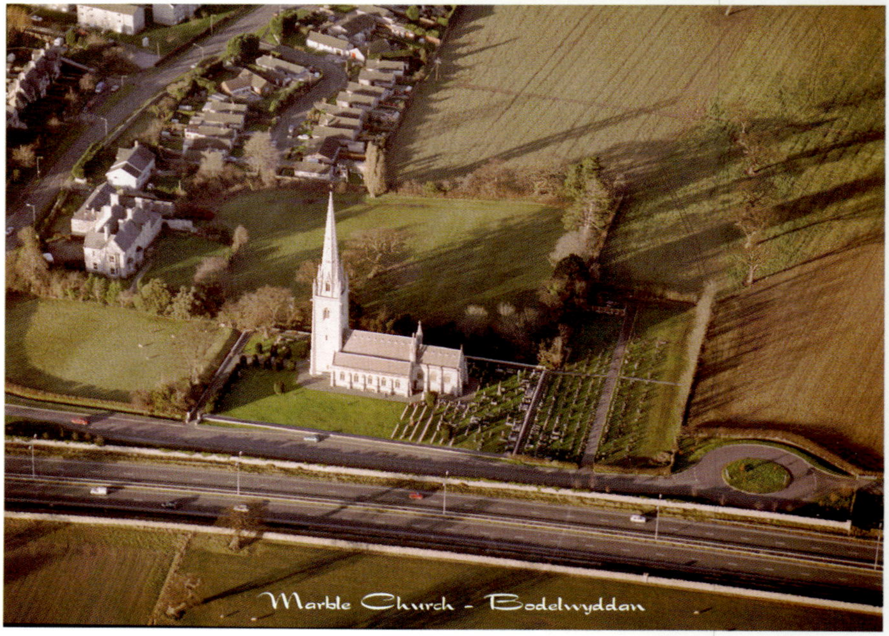

Marble Church - Bodelwyddan

● Marble Church aspires to heaven with the delicate grace of a wedding cake. Creamy limestone icing surrounding a crunchy marble interior. Sadly, some of its graves belong to Canadian soldiers who were waiting to return home after the Great War. Most died of flu but five were shot dead in a riot at Kinmel Park Military Camp.

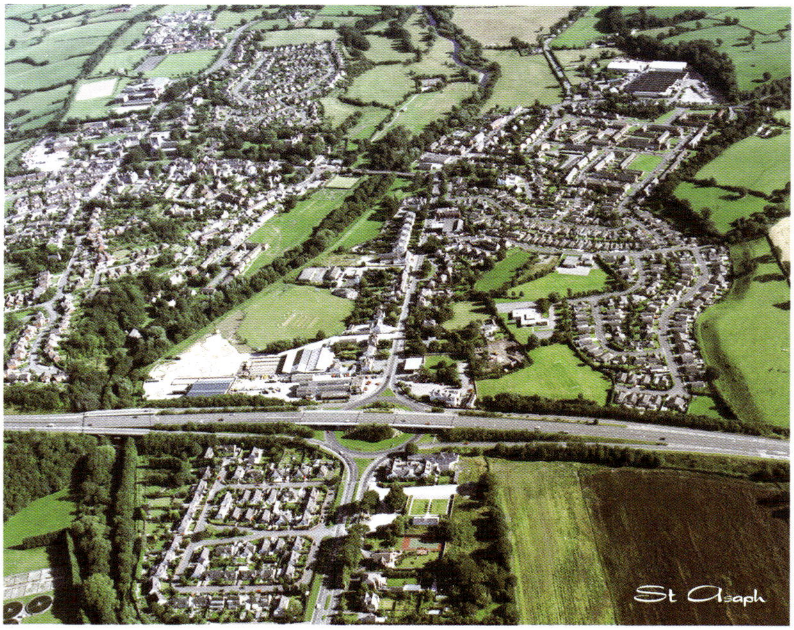

- H M Stanley, who discovered "Dr Livingstone, I presume" in darkest greenest Africa, lived in St Asaph Union Workhouse as a child. The Workhouse has been transformed into a hospital and named H M Stanley Hospital after him (although his real name was John Rowlands).
- "Old Blue Stockings" bravely defended Denbigh Castle in the name of King Charles I. He survived the sickness and starvation of a 6-month siege by the Roundheads, only giving up the castle when the King gave him permission to surrender.

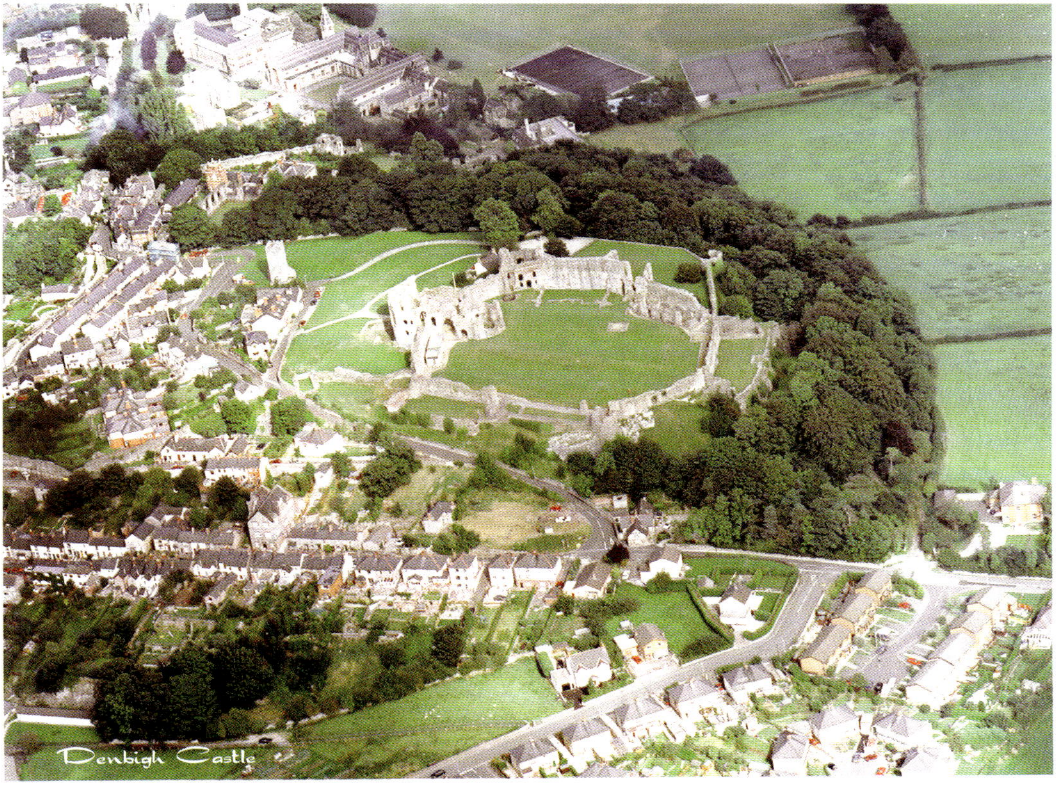

Rhythms of Clwyd

Along the north-east coast from Shotton to the Point of Ayr the Dee Estuary is a winter wonderland for birds. Thousands of waders and waterfowl feed on its rich salt marshes and mudflats. Overhead fly peregrine or skeins of pink-footed geese and whooper swan.

Inland the lush Vale of Clwyd is a quieter haven. When poet Gerard Manley Hopkins decided to become a Jesuit priest he stopped writing poetry. But the Clwydian hills inspired him to start writing again whilst studying theology (and learning Welsh) at St Beuno's in Tremeirchion.

In the past, admittedly, it could be as noisy as living on a reservation in the middle of the A55. Many battles were fought between the Princes of Wales and their English neighbours. The tide turned against the Princes when Edward I brought back his favourite architect, Master James of Savoy, from the Crusades.

The first castle to be built was at Flint, and Rhuddlan became the second. Rhuddlan was set up to guard the crucial river crossing. So that ships could sail up the River Clwyd to supply the Castle, it was straight-jacketed into a deep water channel two miles long. The digging took the tired workmen three long years to achieve. Denbigh and Ruthin Castles were also constructed under the watchful eye of Master James.

During the Civil War Welsh landowners were mostly Royalists and ended up besieged within the castles built originally for English Edward. The castles suffered badly. Walls were destroyed either by direct cannon-fire, mortar from overhead, or burrowing from below. There were surprise night attacks, threats, gentle appeals and bribery. Some castles, as at Rhuddlan, were starved into submission.

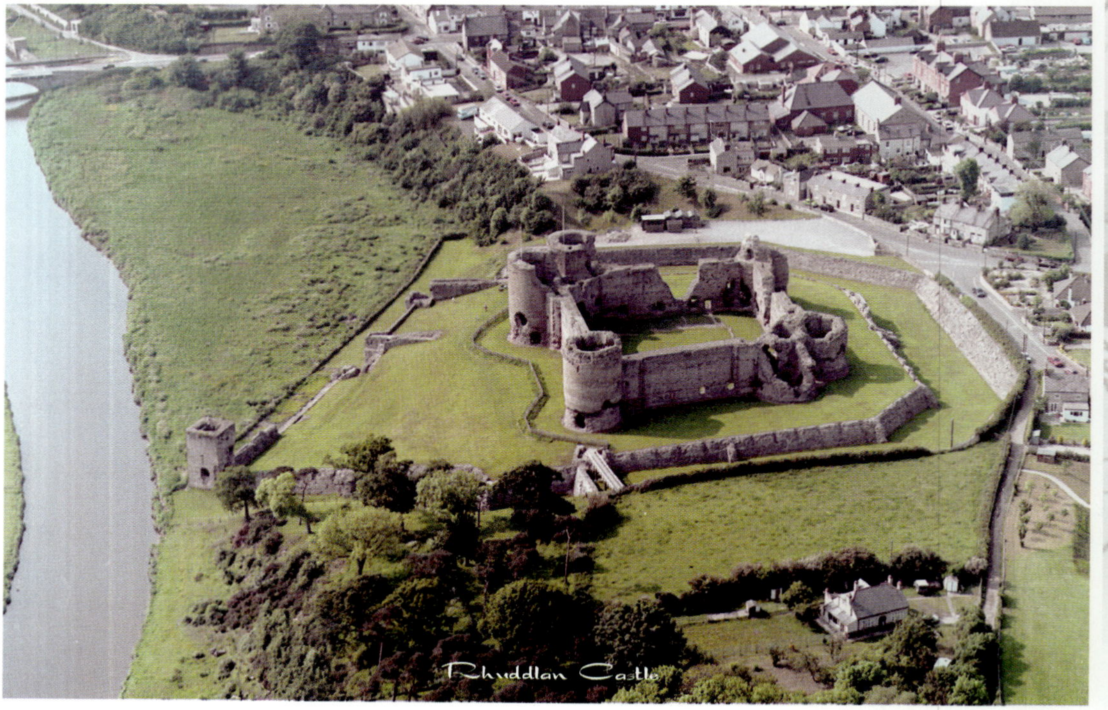

Rhuddlan Castle

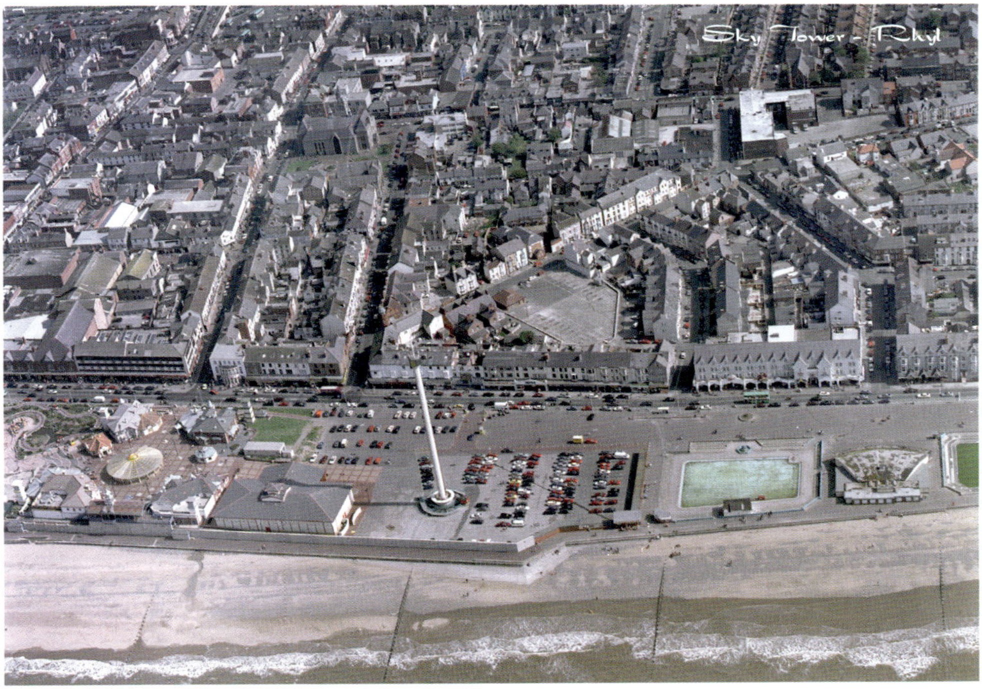

• Today's tourists in Rhyl can revolve dizzily above the surf at the top of the Sky Tower, which began life peering down on pleasure-seekers in Blackpool. Rhyl was a small port until it became a hotspot for holiday-makers in Victorian times, with steam packets bringing Liverpudlians for the good air and golden beaches.

• Off the blue-washed coast of Rhyl the Resurgam, the first mechanically propelled submarine, sank in 1879 during a test run. She was powered by steam and made of wood and iron. The Resurgam was caught over 100 years later, tangled up in the nets of a Colwyn Bay fisherman.

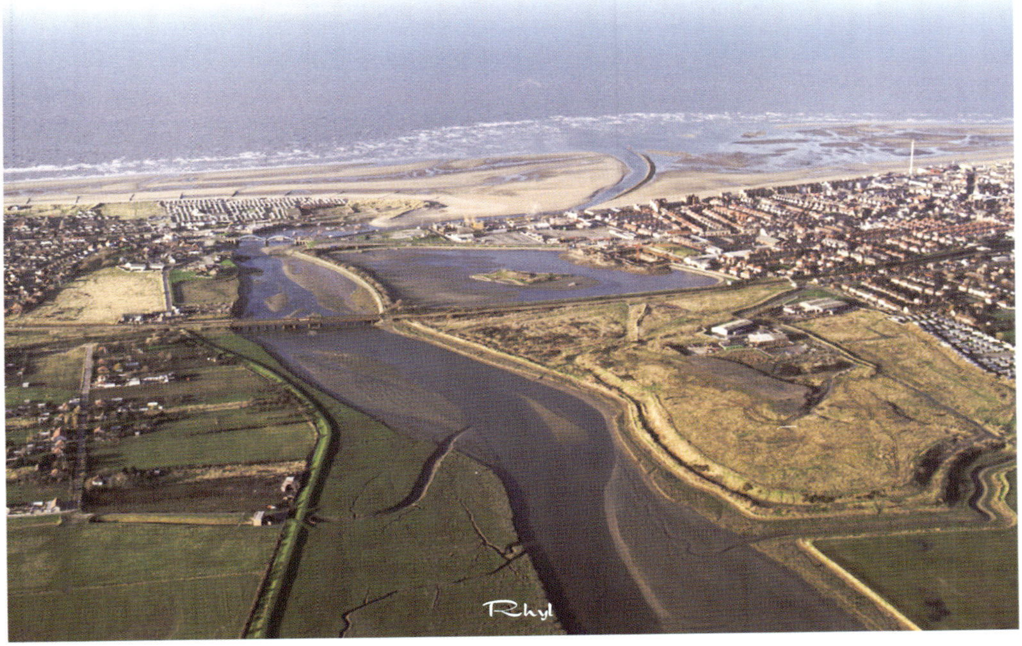

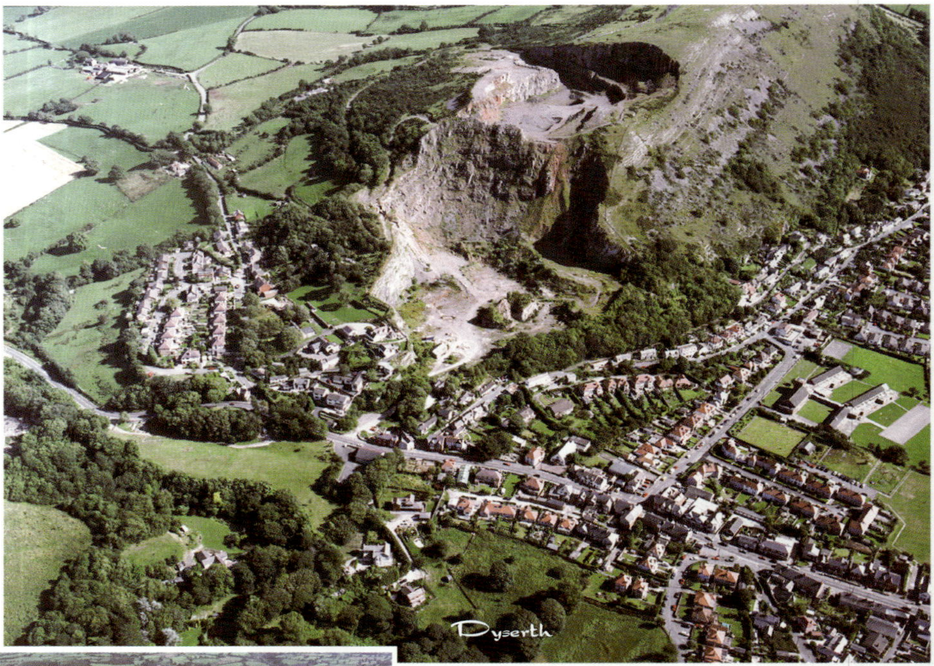

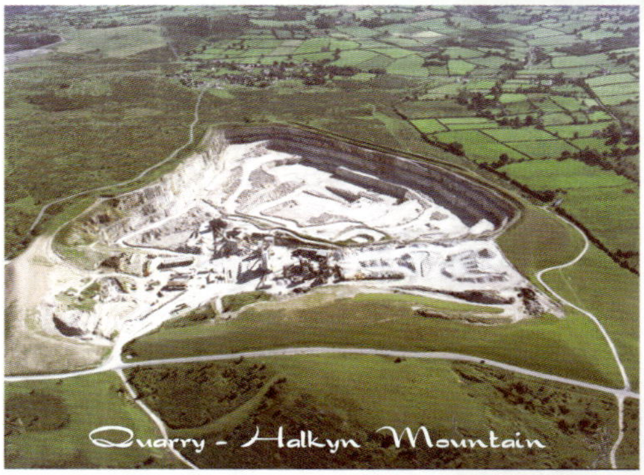

- In Dyserth highstreet a waterfall cascades down a rocky gorge. On the hill above are the remains of a castle of the Welsh princes, eaten away by the limestone quarry.
- Beached on the Dee Estuary a white ship sits forlorn. The Duke of Lancaster used to be a British Rail ferry and then a floating disco. For now, the fun is over.

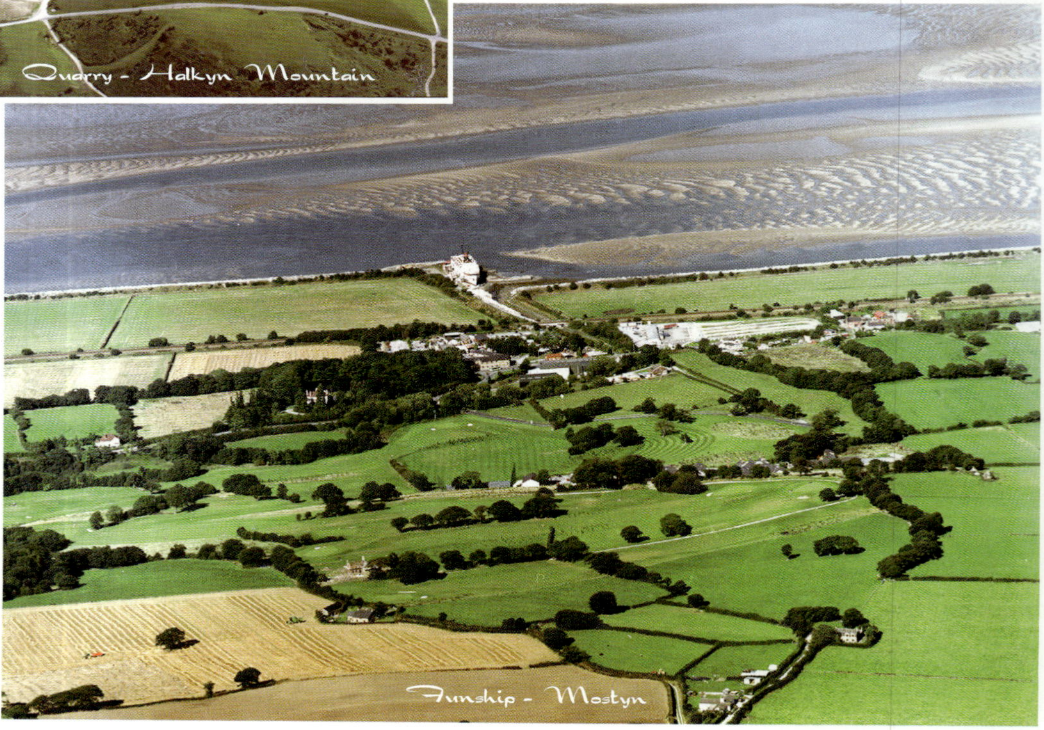

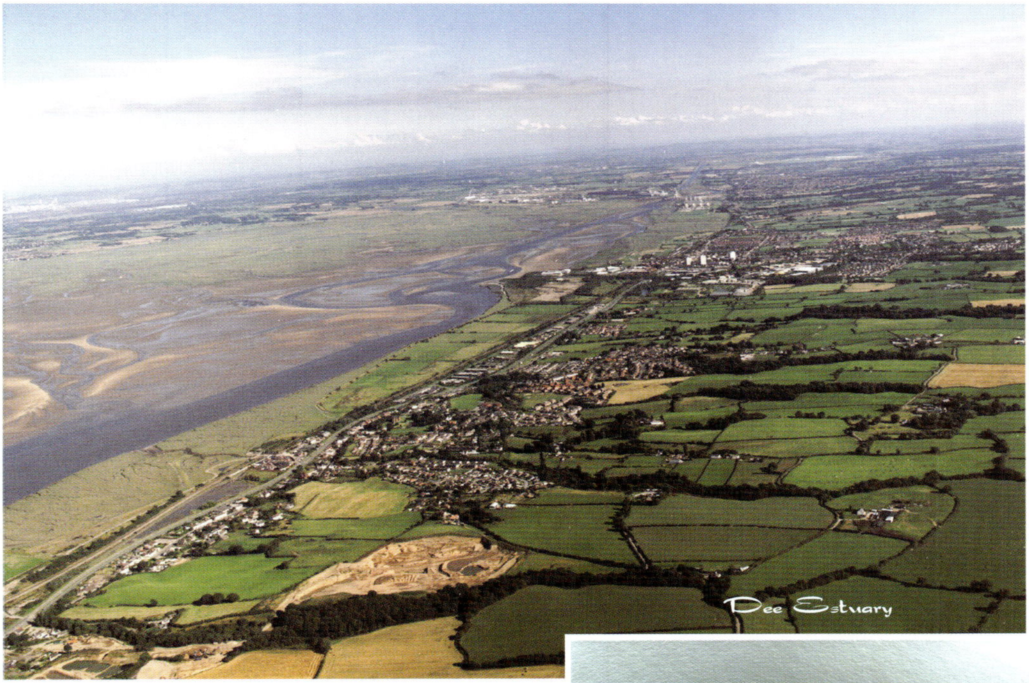

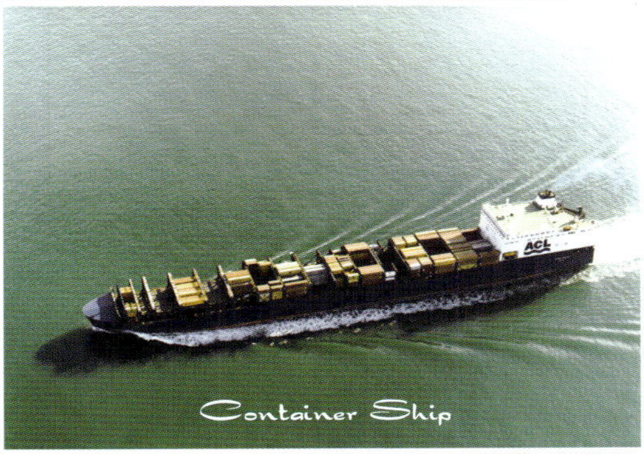

- Richard II lost his English throne to Henry at Flint Castle, and Richard's ghostly greyhound still howls at the moon in the quiet night of its ruins.

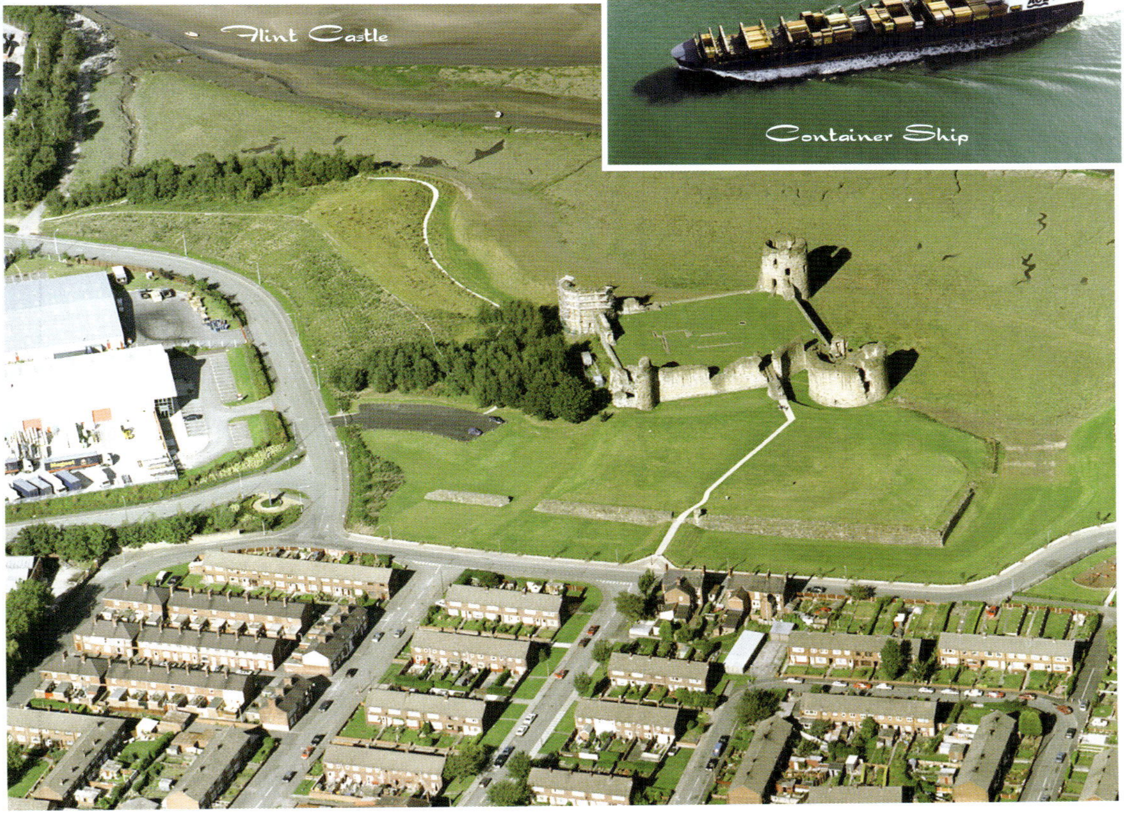

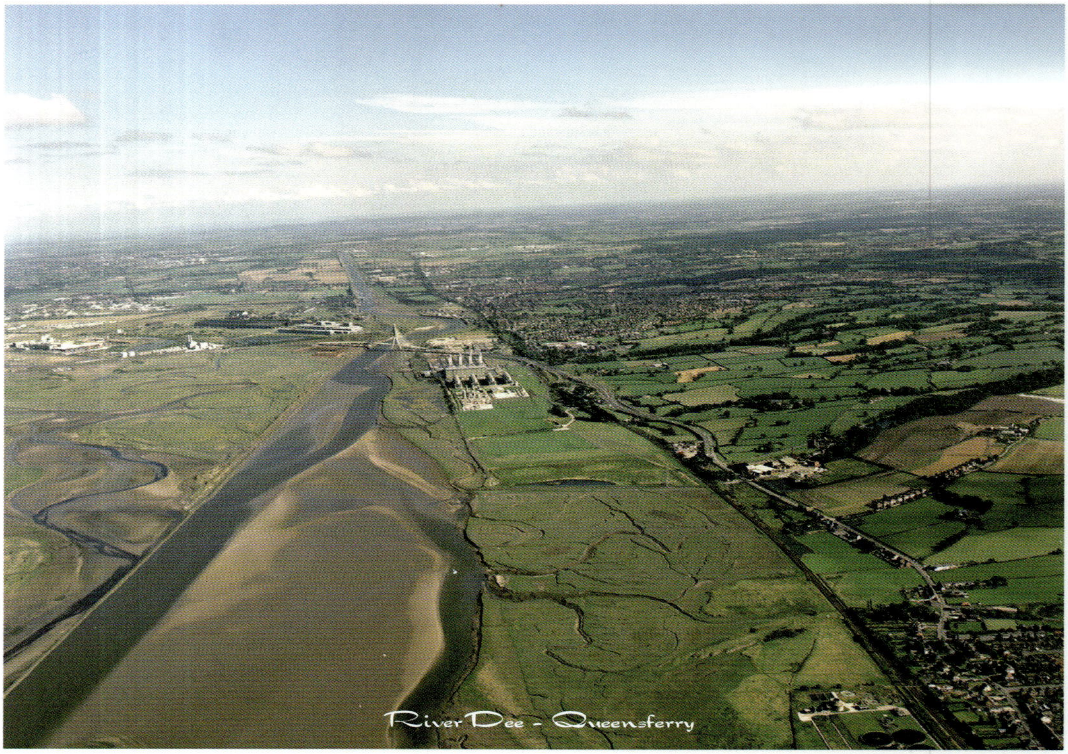

● The River Dee makes shifting sand patterns on its way to the Irish Sea. Man has tried to shackle the river with his bridges but he can never tame its wild beauty or disturb its calm soul.

In the Can!

Although Gwilym was still flying at the age of 83, sadly, he no longer does so. But he still has a passion for photography, gazing at his stunning photographs, and an enthusiasm for his cameras in their "cradles". But most of all these days one of his greatest pleasures will be sharing his images with you.

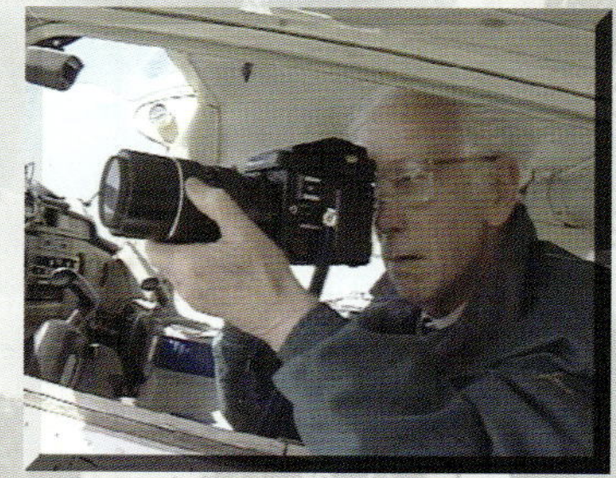

Gwilym Davies - "Eye of the Eagle"

If you would like a print of any of the photographs from this book, *Shades from the Sky*, please write to: ValleyStream, Plas y Graig, Iolyn Park, Conwy, North Wales, LL32 8UX or e-mail us at: pictureoffer@valleystream.co.uk. For current prices, visit our website at: www.valleystream.co.uk